Master ASL!

Fingerspelling, Numbers, & Glossing

By

Jason E. Zinza

Sign Illustrations by:
Xiaohong Fang
James Sbarra
Linda C. Tom
Svetlana Zinovieva

Non-sign art by:
James Sbarra

Sign Media, Inc.
4020 Blackburn Lane
Burtonsville, MD 20866-1167
www.signmedia.com

ISBN 978-1-881133-21-6

How to order:
Copies may be ordered from Sign Media, Inc., 4020 Blackburn Lane, Burtonsville, MD 20866-1167. For credit card orders, place your order on line at www.signmedia.com or phone 1-800-475-4756.

TABLE OF CONTENTS

Glossary

Index

WELCOME

Welcome to **Master ASL! Fingerspelling, Numbers, and Glossing.** Fingerspelling, Numbers, and Glossing are some of the hardest topics for beginning American Sign Language students to master. To help improve your skills, each topic includes 10 units of practice exercises and drills (over 400 in all). Special sections within each unit provide helpful hints for improving your skills along with answers to frequently asked questions.

The book also includes a glossary of important terms to help your understanding of American Sign Language and an index of vocabulary with the corresponding gloss for each item.

While this book is designed to accompany the **Master ASL!** curriculum, it can be used independently to develop and improve fingerspelling, numbers, and glossing skills.

Additional information about the **Master ASL!** curriculum is available from:

Sign Media, Inc.
4020 Blackburn Lane
Burtonsville, MD 20866-1167

www.signmedia.com
www.masterasl.com

The American Sign Language Manual Alphabet
as seen by the person reading the letters

The American Sign Language Manual Alphabet
as seen by the person signing the letters

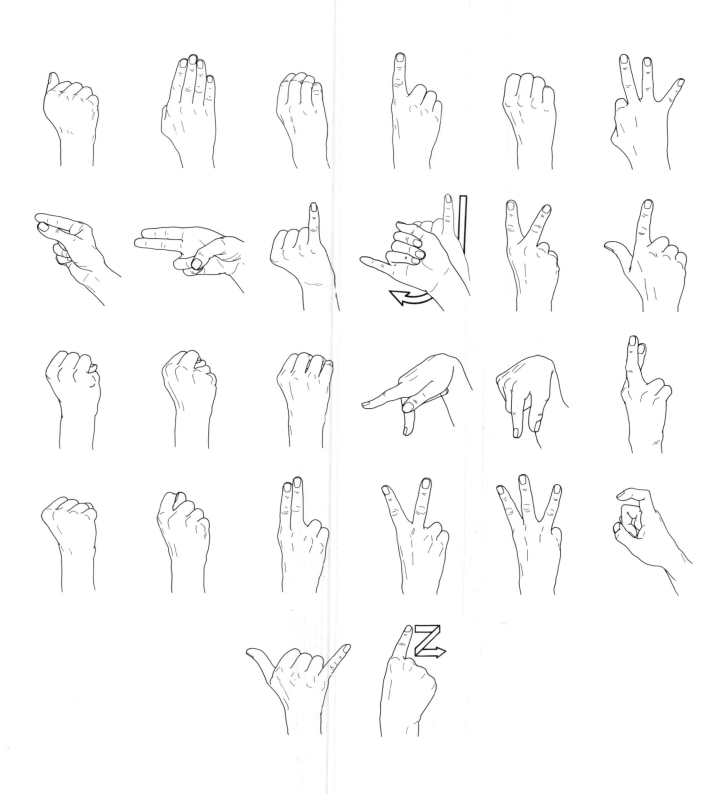

Fingerspelling

Each activity is designed to help you develop the skills needed to understand fingerspelling without decoding it letter by letter, and to form clear letters. By practicing fingerspelling alone or with a partner and participating in activities during your ASL class, you will learn to fingerspell clearly and confidently.

Note: The fingerspelling in illustrations has been created from left to right, for greater ease of use and comprehension when looking at the illustration. However, the hand moves <u>away</u> from the body when fingerspelling.

Fingerspelling: Do's and Don't's

- Don't jerk, bounce, or move your hand.
- Keep your elbow down, close to your side.
- Hold your hand to the side of your chest, not in front of your face.

Unit 1

1 *Three letter names.* Hold your hand in one place as you fingerspell short, three-letter names.

1	2	3	4	5	6	7	8	9	10
Pam	Ira	Ray	Uma	Meg	Amy	Tim	Ana	Ben	Rea
Joe	Gus	Bob	Val	Dan	Ina	Ram	Fae	Kia	Eve
Mia	Van	Ngi	Wes	Ken	Ned	Abe	Mel	Nan	Sue
Sue	Tad	Sal	Jan	Ron	Ted	Ace	Kay	Ari	Aga
Tom	Gil	Tia	Zoe	Kim	Sam	Ian	Rob	Ona	Don

2 *What are their names?* Complete each sentence by fingerspelling the name in bold. An example is provided.

Her name is Jan.

1. His name is **Hal**.
2. Her name is **Kim**.
3. Their names are **Jed** and **Gil**.
4. Her name is **Ana**.
5. His name is **Tom**.
6. We are named **Sue**, **Tia**, and **Ron**.
7. Her name is **Kay**.
8. Her name is **Eva**.
9. Her name is **Flo**.
10. My name is _____.

FYI Instead of signing *and*, simply point towards two (or more) different locations.

Accent Steps

Using the correct handshape while fingerspelling is as important as not swinging your hand outward for the letters O, H, D, C, and G. Look at the two versions of the letter *i*. Even a slight error like the thumb is noticeable. Make sure your handshapes are correct, and your fingerspelling skills will improve.

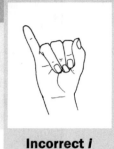

Incorrect *i*

Correct *i*

3   *Common errors.* Look at both handshapes and fingerspell each name or word using the correct form of the letter.

Handshape Error	Fingerspelling Handshape			Handshape Error	Fingerspelling Handshape		
		Ada	Ali			ghi	hat
		tax	ham			Huy	hah
		Abe	Ava			ohm	Hoy
		dye	dim			Kia	Lin
		Dan	doe			mix	Ian
		Ed	Dar			tie	ice
		Ida	bad			Kay	kid
		den	dab			kin	kite
		id	cod			Ken	kit
		Eve	Ben			Meg	mud
		vet	tea			amp	Sam
		sea	hem			gem	Mia
		Guy	sag			jog	Joe
		wag	hug			oat	Opi
		Aga	gas			Ron	ox

4   *The ABCs.* Complete the fingerspelling prompts below.

1. fingerspell the ASL alphabet
2. fingerspell the vowels: A, E, I, O, U
3. fingerspell your entire name
4. fingerspell the name of your hometown

5 *Trouble letters.* The following words and names contain one or more trouble letters. Fingerspell each column using the correct handshapes.

1	2	3	4	5	6	7	8	9	10
Deb	Eve	Fox	get	Hao	key	Mae	Ned	top	Paz
Del	eat	elf	Gap	hop	Kay	Max	Noe	oat	pet
Dex	Eva	fin	Gus	hen	Rik	map	Neo	toy	pop
Dom	Ely	if	Aga	ham	koi	emu	Nhu	opt	ape

6 *First & last names.* Complete the sentence by fingerspelling the first and last names shown in bold. Pause briefly before signing the last name.

1. My name is ... **(Rob Paz)**
2. My name is ... **(Mel Ash)**
3. My name is ... **(Ina Ris)**
4. My name is ... **(Jan Kol)**
5. My name is ... **(Ed Dio)**
6. My name is ... **(Bev Wan)**
7. My name is ... **(Ly Kur)**
8. My name is ... **(Sam Hyn)**
9. My name is ... **(Gil Och)**
10. My name is ... **(?)**

7 *Introductions.* Practice fingerspelling the complete names of the following people.

1. yourself
2. your ASL teacher
3. your boss / supervisor
4. a sibling

I Want to Know . . .

How important is fingerspelling?

Consider fingerspelling to be like your handwriting. Being clear is vital to being understood, be confident enough not to worry whether each letter is exactly right, and be able to spell words quickly instead of breaking them down letter by letter. Everybody has their own fingerspelling style, just as you have your own style of handwriting. It takes time and practice to become an excellent fingerspeller! Fortunately fingerspelling is **generally** used in specific instances:

1. first, last, and middle names;
2. names of places (cities, states, stores);
3. titles of movies and books;
4. certain foods;
5. for clarification when one sign has several meanings;
6. technical terms.

The first two instances are the most important parts of fingerspelling for a beginning student. You want to sign your name and where you're from without stumbling! Warning: Don't fingerspell words and sentences if you don't know a sign. Doing this is like saying A . . R . . E . . Y . . O . . U . . and is hard to understand.

8 *Four letter names.* Fingerspelling a four-letter name follows the same pattern as three-letter names. Hold your hand in one place and keep your elbow by your side. Spell each column of names.

1	2	3	4	5	6	7	8	9	10
Glen	Evan	Mike	Alex	Hala	Tara	Alma	Lita	Dana	Leif
Saul	Tura	Liza	Jose	Kyle	Jean	Brad	Joey	Greg	Iris
Huey	Ivan	Nora	Nick	Erin	Fran	Mira	Carl	Mary	Vika
Kara	John	Dave	Sara	Amos	Raul	Ajax	Roni	Neil	Sala

9 *Name exchange.* Fingerspell a name beginning with the first letter shown in each letter-pair to a partner, who will respond by spelling a different name using the second letter of the pair. Use the list of four-letter names below if needed. An example is provided.

Example

Student A		Student B
L	. . . . .	J

1. P . . . . . Y	6. J C	11. D . . . . N	16. L L
2. B . . . . E	7. R I	12. F . . . . Z	17. X . . . . H
3. V V	8. A . . . . . P	13. A . . . . A	18. S . . . . S
4. G . . . . M	9. O . . . . H	14. K . . . . F	19. J . . . . P
5. T . . . . S	10. U L	15. Q V	20. A . . . . R

10 *Making introductions.* Sign the introductions with a partner, who will respond using the information in bold.

1. Hi, my name is Lou Eads. What's your name?
   (My name is Adam Chen.)

2. Her name is Amy Kiva. What's his name?
   (His name is Doug Brin.)

3. His name is Paul Reys, and her name is Tara Reys.
   (What are their names?)

4. My name is _____ _____. What's your name?
   (My name is _____ _____.)

5. Her name is Vera Yan.
   (No, her name is Vera Yang.)

Four-letter Names

Alan	Ivan	Mary	Raul	Teri
Alec	Jack	Mike	Reba	Thad
Alex	Jake	Mina	Rick	Thom
Brad	Jana	Nick	Risa	Tina
Bret	John	Nora	Rolf	Tony
Cara	Kira	Olaf	Ryan	Troy
Dana	Kris	Olga	Sana	Uday
Dean	Kyle	Opal	Sara	Ulan
Eric	Lana	Paco	Sean	Vera
Erin	Lara	Paul	Sela	Vern
Fran	Lars	Pete	Seth	Ward
Gail	Leah	Phil	Shea	Xena
Gwen	Lisa	Prue	Skye	Xuan
Hank	Lori	Qira	Stan	Yael
Hedy	Marc	Quin	Tara	Yuri
Iris	Mark	Rain	Tate	Zach

11 *Double letters.* When fingerspelling double letters, do not "slide" your hand towards the right. There are three different guidelines to follow, depending where the double letters occur. But always remember to keep your hand in one place, unless you know why you shouldn't!

Double letters: Beginning or Middle

Don't move your hand but make a quick repetition of the letter. For the letter A, your thumb doesn't move but the rest of your fingers do. Words with the letters A, D, E, F, M, N, O, P, S, and T follow this pattern.

1. Isaac	4. Tess	7. Penny
2. Brittany	5. Minnie	8. Tissa
3. Jenna	6. Appia	9. Emma

Some Double letters: Beginning or Middle

Rather than making a letter repetition that doesn't move, some letters require a double movement, as if you were fingerspelling a letter "on top" of the previous one. The letters B, C, G, K, L, P, R, U, and X follow this pattern.

10. Molly	13. Bobby	16. Peggy
11. Abby	14. Kelly	17. Tuuva
12. Accra	15. Perry	18. Wakka

Double letters: Ending

When double letters come at the end of a word, move your hand slightly to the right. This is the only time you'll move your hand!

19. Jeff	22. Troll
20. Emilee	23. Tess
21. Kenaii	24. Glenn

▶ Accent Steps

Fingerspelling shouldn't look like a typewriter, moving with each new letter. There are exceptions, but the general rule is, don't move your hand! If a word uses double letters, moving the hand may be needed.

12 *Five letter names.* Just as three and four-letter names are fingerspelled as a whole, avoid breaking five-letter names into syllables. You don't need to pause or move your hand as you fingerspell five-letter words and names.

1	2	3	4	5	6	7	8	9	10
Keila	Amata	Quinn	Akira	Jonas	Pablo	Boris	Jared	Annie	Norma
Davey	Devin	Paula	Leyla	Clint	Mabel	Maher	Freda	Pavel	Alisa
Alexa	Scott	Sarah	Tomas	Merna	Amina	Ivana	Geena	Tasha	Chuck
Kerry	Jatin	Bryan	Kenny	Percy	Carla	Karen	Raven	Edgar	Logan

13 *More introductions.* Sign each sentence in ASL, choosing names from the list on the right.

1. His name is _____. He's Deaf.
2. Is your name _____?
3. Her name is _____. She is learning ASL.
4. Their names are _____ , _____. They're hearing.
5. I want you to meet my friend. His/her name is _____.
6. No, his name is not _____. It's _____.

Kelly	Nabil	Walt	Kevin
Mina	Anna	Tisha	Shane
Nikki	Lee	Chris	Blair
John	Ross	Bree	Jeff
Laura	Devon	Tala	Abdul

I Want to Know . . .

What if I make a mistake while fingerspelling?

First, do not wave your hands to "erase" what you spelled! Simply shake your head and begin spelling the entire word again. If you become confused when someone is fingerspelling to you, spell the letters that you did understand and ask for the remainder. This is better than asking a signer to spell the word several times until you understand it.

14 *First & Last.* Fingerspell each pair of names, including a brief pause between the first and last name.

1. David Singh	5. Jeff Marsh	9. Nikki Boren
2. Anna Stoll	6. Nabil Ahmed	10. Ryan King
3. Chris Velez	7. Lisa Biggs	11. Jose Perez
4. Larry Zhou	8. Trudy Wall	12. Scott Reed

15 *Mc-names.* There is no special system for fingerspelling names like McCoy, even though the second C is capitalized. Simply spell the whole name.

1. McKay	5. McMan
2. McCoy	6. McGee
3. McVee	7. McNab
4. McCul	8. McBay

16 *OH drill.* The letter combinations OH and HO are challenging for ASL students. Fingerspell each name or word making sure the O and H run together smoothly.

1. John	5. Duc Hoang	9. Ohare
2. Ohio	6. Carl Hoene	10. Lara Sohn
3. Hoh	7. Alex Hoig	11. Kyle Johra
4. Hoag	8. Noah Ahorn	12. Jose Bohn

17 *Double-letter drill.* Fingerspell each word quickly and clearly.

1. Sonny	6. Reed	11. Queen	16. Liann
2. Deonn	7. Deena	12. Larry	17. Aaron
3. Anne	8. Perry	13. Harry	18. Cliff
4. Jesse	9. Ziggy	14. Belle	19. Allen
5. Merry	10. Matt	15. Rocco	20. Holly

18 *Fingerspelled words.* These words are generally fingerspelled. Learn to spell them quickly and clearly.

1. cake	6. puppy
2. job	7. truck
3. TV	8. van
4. DVD	9. taco
5. OK	10. VCR

19 *Handshape drills.* Practice fingerspelling each letter combination until your hand becomes used to the shapes.

1	2	3	4	5	6	7	8	9	10
ea	oe	kp	nn	gh	qr	fe	ah	mn	tt
ea	oe	kp	ll	gh	qr	fee	oh	mn	hh
ea	oee	pk	mm	hg	rq	fell	ih	st	oo
ea	oeo	pkp	oo	hg	gq	feel	uh	st	nn
ea	oeee	kpkp	ee	ge	gq	fool	eh	stm	kk

20 *Fingerspelling challenge.* Can you spell these words quickly and clearly, and understand them when spelled to you?

1. ASL
2. oil
3. Ohio
4. oleo
5. London
6. Logan
7. Gallaudet
8. gall bladder

Unit 2

1 *Five letter names.* Hold your hand in one place unless fingerspelling a name ending with double letters. Improve your clarity and speed with each set.

1	2	3	4	5	6	7	8	9	10
Sal	Jonah	Levi	Judd	Allan	Daisy	Brian	Hasan	Danny	Shurr
Homer	Tom	Keith	Meira	Theo	Abdul	Carol	Brent	Lauri	Julie
Maria	Cindy	Duane	Hugo	Susan	Paul	Helen	Sonja	Romeo	Cecil
Tanya	Eric	Ginny	Elmer	Leon	Ralph	Reza	Alma	Luis	Terry

2 *Who?* Create a complete sentence using a name and vocabulary sign from each column.

Column A

1. Vicky Lopez
2. Bill Reiki
3. James Price
4. Siok Lam
5. Louie Cipri
6. Kari Moore

Column B

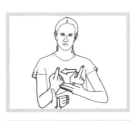  

3 *K, P drill.* The letters K and P are challenging for ASL students. Increase accuracy and speed with each set of letters.

<u>1</u>	<u>2</u>	<u>3</u>	<u>4</u>	<u>5</u>	<u>6</u>	<u>7</u>	<u>8</u>	<u>9</u>	<u>10</u>
ka	kf	kk	kp	ku	kz	ep	jp	op	tp
kb	kg	kl	kq	kv	ap	fp	kp	pp	up
kc	kh	km	kr	kw	bp	gp	lp	qp	vp
kd	ki	kn	ks	kx	cp	hp	mp	rp	wp
ke	kj	ko	kt	ky	dp	ip	np	sp	xp

4 *K, P words.* The letters K and P are challenging for ASL students. Fingerspell each name or word.

1. Kurik
2. Paula
3. apple
4. Kari
5. papa
6. kayak
7. Peony Wang
8. Kenya Harris
9. Kathy Kreis
10. Paolo King
11. Paddy Lin
12. Karl Apke

5 *Six letter names.* Avoid breaking six-letter names into syllables as you fingerspell. Hold your hand steady and fingerspell the whole name at once, rather than letter by letter with pauses.

1. Hannah
2. Freddy
3. Rachel
4. Glenda
5. Joshua
6. Amanda
7. Taylor
8. Brenda
9. Kelsey
10. Harold

6 *Six letter drill.* Don't pause between each letter or break the name into two parts.

<u>1</u>	<u>2</u>	<u>3</u>	<u>4</u>	<u>5</u>	<u>6</u>	<u>7</u>	<u>8</u>	<u>9</u>	<u>10</u>
Alysse	Steven	Daniel	Judith	George	Julian	Hector	Joseph	Arnold	Tamika
Robert	Bryant	Arlene	Stuart	Sheila	Sabine	Moesha	Dwayne	Trevor	Walter
Fatima	Mickey	Miguel	Darren	Arthur	Tamera	Travis	Lauren	Jackie	Hailey
Tyrell	Ingrid	Louise	Regina	Joanie	Carlos	Acacia	Tracey	Xavier	Reuben

I Want to Know . . .

Why aren't there signs for words like *truck*?

The quick answer is that for some words, it's faster to fingerspell! Using fingerspelling rather than a sign does not mean Deaf people haven't "gotten around" to a sign yet. It's just that fingerspelling certain words is quicker or more efficient. Unfortunately, many hearing people try to avoid fingerspelling and instead create signs. To become fluent in ASL, you must become a fluent fingerspeller!

Accent Steps

When reading fingerspelling, try to break down the letters into chunks of sound. Instead of thinking *S ... T ... A ... N*, pronounce it to yourself as *ST ... AN*. If you try to decode fingerspelling letter by letter, you will struggle to understand what is being spelled.

7 *Reservations.* You are responsible for taking reservation requests. To take the reservation you need the person's last name first. Ask a partner to fingerspell the last name to you. An example is provided.

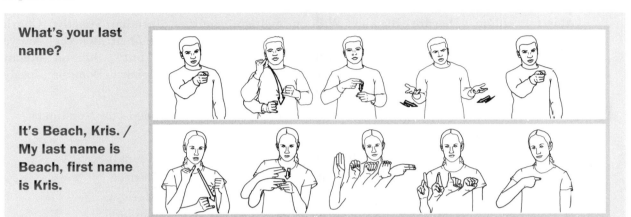

What's your last name?

It's Beach, Kris. / My last name is Beach, first name is Kris.

1. Marc Zamora	5. Kim McRae	9. Alec Silva
2. Carol Bourne	6. Gale Igano	10. Pat Okubo
3. Daryl Peters	7. Felix Chaney	11. Bart Robles
4. Lee Adams	8. Sharon Lewis	12. Omar Katara

8 *Handshape drills.* Practice fingerspelling each letter combination until your hand becomes used to the shapes.

1	2	3	4	5	6	7	8	9	10
aa	ef	jk	op	tu	yz	ye	yj	nz	ne
ab	eg	jl	oq	tv	ya	yf	yk	na	nf
ac	eh	jm	or	tw	yb	yg	yl	nb	ng
ad	ei	jn	os	tx	yc	yh	ym	nc	nh
ae	ej	jo	ot	ty	yd	yi	yn	nd	ni

9 *First & Last.* Fingerspell each pair of names, including a brief pause between the first and last name.

1. Calvin Eads	5. Darren Walsh	9. Masako Ito
2. Sarah Vance	6. Ebony Royce	10. Jamila Smith
3. Manuel Huerta	7. Vaughn Hogue	11. Maher Oskui
4. Callie Jones	8. Marcus White	12. Tracie Modine

10 *Party.* Over the weekend you attended a party. Use the Question-Maker to ask your partner if he or she knows each person. Your partner will respond following the information provided.

1. Deion Sandes **(Yes, I know Deion.)**
2. Tariq Jamal **(Yes, I work with Tariq.)**
3. Jill Brasos **(No, I don't know Jill.)**
4. Darnell James **(Yes, I know Darnell.)**
5. Eveyln Amos **(No, I don't know Evelyn.)**

Question-Maker

11 *Seven letter names.* Don't pause between each letter or break the name into two parts, and hold your hand steady in one place.

1	2	3	4	5	6	7	8	9	10
Albert	Lillian	Dierdre	Buckley	William	Belinda	Gabriel	Jasmine	Timothy	Charles
Antonio	Sahara	Beverly	Neville	Carissa	Anthony	Madison	Stephen	Rebecca	Aaliyah
Tanisha	Aileen	Houston	Michael	Matthew	Zachary	Nathan	Trinity	Juliana	Melanie
Latoya	Desmond	Vanessa	Abigail	Jessica	Kaitlyn	Destiny	Richard	Dominic	Jocelyn

12 *Double letter challenge.* Fingerspell each name clearly, using the double-letter techniques explained on page 5.

1. Hakeem
2. Matthew
3. Shannon
4. Derrick

5. Kenneth
6. Brianna
7. Jeffrey
8. Cassidy

9. Kendall
10. Desiree
11. Marissa
12. Johanna

13 *More introductions.* Sign each sentence in ASL.

1. His name is Miguel Arroyo. He's learning ASL.
2. My ASL teacher is named Debbie Marston.
3. Her last name is McFeely.
4. Their names are Shannon Wang, Denise Edwards, and Colin Davison.

> **FYI** Use deixis when fingerspelling several names instead of using *and*.

14 *Famous people.* Fingerspell the first name of a celebrity to your partner, who will spell the celebrity's last name to you. Use the list if needed. When done, switch roles and repeat the exercise. The answer key is at the bottom of the page.

1. Helen ...
2. Michael ...
3. Bill ...
4. Daniel ...
5. Meg ...

6. Maya ...
7. Walt ...
8. Keanu ...
9. Thomas ...
10. Edgar Allan ...

Celebrities

Disney	Angelou
Rosa	Cosby
Keller	Lauren
Ryan	Malcolm
Jordan	Jesse
Elvis	Bill
Babe	Crazy
Poe	John F.
Harriet	Boone
Edison	Reeves

15 *More famous people.* Fingerspell the last name of a celebrity to your partner, who will spell the first name to you. Use the list if needed. When done, switch roles and repeat the exercise.

1. ... Parks
2. ... Presley
3. ... Tubman
4. ... X
5. ... Kennedy

6. ... Hill
7. ... Gates
8. ... Ruth
9. ... Jackson
10. ... Horse

16 *MN drill.* The letter combinations MN and NM are challenging for ASL students. Fingerspell each name or word.

1.	lemon	5.	column	9.	number
2.	Norman	6.	autumn	10.	numb
3.	Raymond	7.	solemn	11.	nimble
4.	hymn	8.	minus	12.	Nampa

17 *Famous artists.* Fingerspell the name of each artist clearly and accurately.

1.	Henri Matisse	5.	Auguste Rodin	9.	Paul Cezanne
2.	Pablo Picasso	6.	Vaughn Hogue	10.	Vincent van Gogh
3.	Jackson Pollock	7.	Andy Warhol	11.	Mark Rothko
4.	Edgar Degas	8.	Cecilia Alvarez	12.	Judith Leyster

18 *Fingerspelled words.* These words are generally fingerspelled. Learn to spell them quickly and clearly.

1.	pizza	6.	sale
2.	latte	7.	bank
3.	bus	8.	tax
4.	grade	9.	berry
5.	haha	10.	mile

19 *Handshape drills.* Practice fingerspelling each letter combination until your hand becomes used to the shapes.

1	2	3	4	5	6	7	8	9	10
ntn	rt	ax	mp	gee	ha	fa	pa	oc	ks
nnt	tr	ex	pm	goo	aha	af	ape	ec	sk
tnn	ttr	ix	am	gum	haha	df	Pez	ce	sks
tnt	rrt	axe	map	mug	hero	fd	apex	ceo	skim
ttt	tar	Xerox	Pam	gulf	Hiro	ag	hyper	coo	silk

20 *Fingerspelling challenge.* Can you spell these words quickly and clearly, and understand them when spelled to you?

1.	spa	3.	chips	5.	brilliant	7.	cartoon
2.	spy	4.	Chris	6.	brilliance	8.	contract

Unit  3

1 *Different places.* Spell each location clearly.

1. Seattle	6. Ukiah	11. Oswego	16. Austin
2. Utah	7. Montana	12. Maine	17. Ontario
3. Calgary	8. Newark	13. Tucson	18. Trenton
4. Miami	9. Tulsa	14. Boise	19. Chicago
5. Arizona	10. Juneau	15. Spokane	20. Exeter

2 *Eight letter names.* Don't pause between each letter or break the name into parts, and hold your hand steady in one place.

1	2	3	4	5	6	7	8	9	10
Percival	Lokelani	Franklin	Michelle	Isabella	Kimberly	Rajneesh	Salvador	Jeremiah	Laquetta
Terrence	Mariposa	Leonardo	Giovanni	Alphonse	Tallulah	Marshall	Caroline	Santiago	Jonathan
Jennifer	Shantell	Mathilda	Khalidah	Geoffrey	Napoleon	Sapphire	Emmanuel	Macauley	Samantha
Michaela	Algernon	Courtney	Lakeesha	Danielle	Lorraine	Nicholas	Kathleen	Savannah	Fernando

3 *Fingerspelling subtleties.* ASL students are uncertain how to fingerspell these types of words. Read each explanation and practice fingerspelling the terms.

Terms using O' — Twist the O towards you, and then fingerspell the remaining letters.

1. O'Neal	4. O'Dugan
2. O'Malley	5. O'Neill
3. O'Brien	6. O'Corrain

Terms using St. — Ignore the period and fingerspell the ST, followed by the remaining letters.

1. St. Paul	4. St. Kitts
2. St. Andrews	5. St. James
3. St. Albans	6. St. Thomas

Several terms — When a name includes several words, don't pause between each.

1. Mark de la Cruz	4. Sault Ste. Marie
2. St. Charles Place	5. Tierra del Fuego
3. Upper Springfield	6. Ocracoke Island

I Want to Know . . .

I only understand parts of words. What can I do?

First, asking a signer to repeat the word several times doesn't make you any less frustrated. Learning to understand fingerspelling, especially when there's little context to help you, takes time and practice. Here are some tips to help:

- copy the word as it is being fingerspelled to you
- try to guess the word based on what you did understand
- if you ask someone to repeat again, spell the letters you understood

4 *Long names.* Fingerspelling a long name is no different than those with few letters. Set a steady speed and be consistent from start to finish. With practice you will develop a natural rhythm and style.

1. Mississippi
2. Wilmington
3. Sacramento
4. Charlottetown
5. Ponchatoula
6. Summersville
7. Laguna Beach
8. Minneapolis
9. Albuquerque
10. Oconomowoc
11. Brattleboro
12. St. Augustine

5 *The Fifty States and Canadian Provinces.* Most names of states and provinces are fingerspelled using abbreviations, though some have signs. The states and provinces that have signs are designated by * and illustrated below. Practice fingerspelling the abbreviation or sign for each location. Where do you live?

States

Alabama (ALA)
Alaska*
Arizona*
Arkansas (ARK)
California*
Colorado*
Connecticut (CONN)
Delaware (DEL)
Florida (FLA)
Georgia (GA)
Hawaii*
Idaho (IDAHO)
Illinois (ILL)
Indiana (IND)
Iowa (IOWA)
Kansas (KAN)
Kentucky (KY)
Louisiana (LA)
Maine (MAINE)
Maryland (MD)
Massachusetts (MASS)

Michigan (MICH)
Minnesota (MINN)
Mississippi (MISS)
Missouri (MO)
Montana*
Nebraska (NEB)
Nevada (NEV)
New Hampshire (NH)
New Jersey (NJ)
New Mexico (NM)
New York*
North Carolina (NC)
North Dakota (ND)
Ohio (OHIO)
Oklahoma (OKLA)
Oregon*
Pennsylvania (PA)
Rhode Island (RI)
South Carolina (SC)
South Dakota (SD)
Tennessee (TENN)
Texas*
Utah (UTAH)

Vermont (VT)
Virginia (VA)
Washington*
West Virginia (west +VA)
Wisconsin (WISC)
Wyoming (WY)
Washington, D.C. (state + DC)

Canadian Provinces

Alberta*
British Columbia (BC)
Manitoba*
New Brunswick (NB)
Newfoundland (NFLD)
Northwest Territories (NWT)
Nova Scotia (NS)
Nunavut (NVT)
Ontario*
Prince Edward Island (PEI)
Quebec*
Saskatchewan (SASK)
Yukon (YUKON)

| Alaska | Arizona | California | Colorado | Hawaii | Montana | Oregon |

| Texas | Washington | Alberta | Manitoba | Ontario | Quebec |

6 *Birthplaces.* Where were these celebrities born? Sign the information provided in a complete sentence.

1. Maya Angelou **(St. Louis, Missouri)**
2. James Dean **(Marion, Indiana)**
3. Jack London **(San Francisco, California)**
4. Martin Luther King, Jr. **(Atlanta, Georgia)**
5. Bill Gates **(Seattle, Washington)**
6. John F. Kennedy **(Brookline, Massachusetts)**
7. Amelia Earhardt **(Atchison, Kansas)**
8. Halle Berry **(Cleveland, Ohio)**
9. Jim Carrey **(Newmarket, Ontario)**
10. Carrie-Anne Moss **(Vancouver, B.C.)**

7 *Places near you.* Make a list of cities and towns in your area, and fingerspell each. Do any have name signs or well-known abbreviations? Use the following prompts as needed.

1. town / city with the shortest name
2. town / city with the longest name
3. your hometown name
4. town / city you enjoy visiting

8 *Places on the map.* Ask a partner where particular cities are found. Your partner will fingerspell the name of the state or province to you. The answer key is at the bottom of the page. Switch roles for 11-20.

1. Vancouver
2. Austin
3. Memphis
4. Buffalo
5. Nome
6. Tallahassee
7. Madison
8. Cheyenne
9. Toronto
10. Santa Fe
11. Seattle
12. Missoula
13. Lansing
14. Dallas
15. Mobile
16. Des Moines
17. Carson City
18. Myrtle Beach
19. Topeka
20. Sacramento

Answer Key to Exercise 8:

Exercise 8: 1. British Columbia; 2. Texas; 3. Tennessee; 4. New York; 5. Alaska; 6. Florida; 7. Wisconsin; 8. Wyoming; 9. Ontario; 10. New Mexico; 11. Washington; 12. Montana; 13. Michigan; 14. Texas; 15. Alabama; 16. Iowa; 17. Nevada; 18. South Carolina; 19. Kansas; 20. California.

9 *LP drill.* The letter combinations LP and PL are challenging for ASL students. Fingerspell each item shown.

1. lplplp	5. lump	9. Ralph
2. pllp	6. Paul	10. Alphonso
3. lamp	7. pulp	11. apples
4. palm	8. Lupe	12. Playa del Sol

10 *Names & Places.* Fingerspell each group of names quickly and clearly.

<u>1</u>	<u>2</u>	<u>3</u>	<u>4</u>	<u>5</u>
DaShawn	Katherine	Manchester	Spartanburg	Ocean Shores
Honolulu	Manassas	Travis	Columbus	Minneapolis
Sylvia	Puerto Rico	Olathe	Olivia	Stephanie
Redondo Beach	Kallispell	Santa Cruz	Four Corners	Kevin Salman
Bismark	Detroit	Hala	Champaign	Baton Rouge

11 *Abbreviations.* Fingerspell the name of the town or city, and use the correct abbreviation or sign of its location.

1. Fargo, North Dakota
2. Bangor, Maine
3. Bowling Green, Ohio
4. Washburn, Wisconsin
5. Amarillo, Texas
6. Baltimore, Maryland
7. Klamath Falls, Oregon
8. Shreveport, Louisiana
9. Naalehu, Hawaii
10. Pascagoula, Mississippi
11. Louisville, Kentucky
12. Saskatoon, Saskatchewan

Accent Steps

If you fingerspell the name of a town followed by a state abbreviation, pause the same way you do when spelling a first and last name.

12 *Hometowns.* Explain in a complete sentence where each person is from.

1. Kevin Newport **(Bellingham, WA)**
2. Cassandra O'Riley **(Pittsburgh, PA)**
3. Ayisha Reza **(Detroit, MI)**
4. Enrique Lopez **(El Paso, TX)**
5. Luc Nguyen **(Fresno, CA)**
6. Sam Guthrie **(Portland, OR)**
7. Angelique Maurier **(Montreal, Quebec)**
8. Kumiko Hatori **(Washington, D.C.)**
9. Bianca Albertini **(Princeton, NJ)**
10. Kong Li **(New York City, NY)**

13 *Strange place names.* Fingerspell each name quickly and clearly.

1. Dead Horse, Alaska
2. Last Chance, Colorado
3. Two Egg, Florida
4. Santa Claus, Indiana
5. What Cheer, Iowa
6. Smileyburg, Kansas
7. Krypton, Kentucky
8. Shoulderblade, Kentucky
9. Hot Coffee, Mississippi
10. Truth or Consequences, New Mexico
11. Walla Walla, Washington
12. Aces of Diamonds, Florida
13. Bald Head, Maine
14. Plain City, Utah
15. Toad Suck, Arkansas
16. Cold Foot, Alaska
17. Lawyersville, New York
18. No Name, Colorado
19. Looneyville, Texas
20. Double Trouble, New Jersey

14 *Famous names.* Fingerspell each famous name clearly and accurately.

1. Frankenstein
2. Queen Victoria
3. Cesar Chavez
4. Pocahontas

5. Marie Curie
6. Mother Theresa
7. Cleopatra
8. Mark Twain

9. Frederick Douglass
10. Beethoven
11. Elizabeth Cady Stanton
12. Harry Houdini

15 *Capital cities.* Ask a partner to identify and fingerspell the capital city of each location. Switch roles for 9-16.

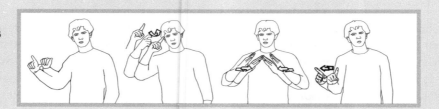

Where is Louisiana's capital?

1. Maryland
2. Nebraska
3. Utah
4. British Columbia
5. Florida
6. South Dakota
7. Tennessee
8. New Hampshire
9. Colorado
10. Minnesota
11. Indiana
12. Alabama
13. Rhode Island
14. Alaska
15. Illinois
16. New Mexico

Select Capital Cities

Lincoln, Nebraska	Providence, Rhode Island
Edmonton, Alberta	Denver, Colorado
Olympia, Washington	Tallahassee, Florida
Nashville, Tennessee	Indianapolis, Indiana
Pierre, South Dakota	Santa Fe, New Mexico
Columbia, South Carolina	Frankfort, Kentucky
Victoria, British Columbia	St. Paul, Minnesota
Concord, New Hampshire	Annapolis, Maryland
Salt Lake City, Utah	Montgomery, Alabama
Austin, Texas	Springfield, Illinois
Dover, Delaware	Juneau, Alaska

16 *Famous places.* Fingerspell the name of each famous place and in a complete sentence explain where it is located.

1. Kitty Hawk **(North Carolina)**
2. The Alamo **(San Antonio)**
3. Grand Canyon **(Arizona)**
4. Pentagon **(Virginia)**
5. Gettysburg **(Pennsylvania)**
6. Ellis Island **(New York)**

7. Liberty Bell **(Philadelphia)**
8. Niagara Falls **(New York)**
9. Plymouth Rock **(Massachusetts)**
10. Sears Tower **(Chicago)**
11. Gateway Arch **(St. Louis)**
12. Fort Sumter **(Charleston)**

Capital Cities in the United States, Canada, and Puerto Rico

United States	Capital	United States	Capital
Alabama	Montgomery	Ohio	Columbus
Alaska	Juneau	Oklahoma	Oklahoma City
Arizona	Phoenix	Oregon	Salem
Arkansas	Little Rock	Pennsylvania	Harrisburg
California	Sacramento	Rhode Island	Providence
Colorado	Denver	South Carolina	Columbia
Connecticut	Hartford	South Dakota	Pierre
Delaware	Dover	Tennessee	Nashville
Florida	Tallahassee	Texas	Austin
Georgia	Atlanta	Utah	Salt Lake City
Hawaii	Honolulu	Vermont	Montpelier
Idaho	Boise	Virginia	Richmond
Illinois	Springfield	Washington	Olympia
Indiana	Indianapolis	West Virginia	Charleston
Iowa	Des Moines	Wisconsin	Madison
Kansas	Topeka	Wyoming	Cheyenne
Kentucky	Frankfort		
Louisiana	Baton Rouge	Puerto Rico	San Juan
Maine	Augusta		
Maryland	Annapolis		
Massachusetts	Boston	**Canada**	**Capital**
Michigan	Lansing	Alberta	Edmonton
Minnesota	St. Paul	British Columbia	Victoria
Mississippi	Jackson	Manitoba	Winnipeg
Missouri	Jefferson City	New Brunswick	Fredericton
Montana	Helena	Newfoundland	St. John's
Nebraska	Lincoln	Northwest Territories	Yellowknife
Nevada	Carson City	Nova Scotia	Halifax
New Hampshire	Concord	Nunavut	Iqaluit
New Jersey	Trenton	Ontario	Toronto
New Mexico	Santa Fe	Prince Edward Island	Charlottetown
New York	Albany	Quebec	Quebec City
North Carolina	Raleigh	Saskatchewan	Regina
North Dakota	Bismark	Yukon	Yukon

17 *More long names.* Fingerspell each name clearly and accurately.

1. Madeline
2. Siobhan
3. Francisco
4. Alessandra
5. Sebastian
6. Kimimela
7. Esperanza
8. Constantine
9. Nathaniel
10. Gwendolyn
11. Guadalupe
12. Heathcliff
13. Josephina
14. Suleiman
15. Ferdinand
16. Christina

18 *Fingerspelled words.* These words are generally fingerspelled. Learn to spell them quickly and clearly.

1. oak
2. pine
3. iron
4. xray
5. truffle
6. Atlantic
7. Pacific
8. cafe
9. cabin
10. burn

19 *Handshape drills.* Practice fingerspelling each letter combination until your hand becomes used to the shapes.

1	2	3	4	5	6	7	8	9	10
fd	ed	ps	eh	ir	Joe	Bea	TV	uh	ea
df	Dee	psy	ih	ri	eon	Ben	VT	ugh	eo
deft	Eddie	phys	ah	air	ion	Benjy	vet	uhn	oven
fade	Dean	Epsy	hah	rial	Jeep	Beau	vat	urn	even
fudge	Aden	ESPN	hay	Risa	jelly	beach	veg	Utah	never

20 *Fingerspelling challenge.* Can you spell these words quickly and clearly, and understand them when spelled to you?

1. boa
2. bee
3. dolphin
4. Daphne
5. prom
6. plum
7. blueberry
8. bluebonnet

Unit 4

1 *Last names.* Hold your hand in one place unless fingerspelling a name with double letters. Improve your clarity and speed with each set.

1	2	3	4	5
Smith	Taylor	Kazanstakis	Peterson	Nguyen
Greenman	Fernandez	Zeigler	Vasquez	Pickering
Heaney	Collins	Murphy	Browne	Ghiselli
Cheng	Richardson	Lopez	Cooper	King
Miles	Young	Groves	Barnes	Morris

2 *Your family.* What are the names of your family members? Individuals you may wish to mention include:

1. parents
2. siblings
3. cousins
4. aunts / uncles
5. friends
6. pets
7. coworkers
8. neighbors

3 *The Hernandez Family Tree.* You are working on a family tree. Fingerspell each name and explain who each person is and their relationship to each other.

The Hernandez Family

Hector   Ana

Pedro   Sylvia   Carlos   Inez

Julio   Victor   Elizabeth   Christopher

4 *C, E, O words.* The letters C, E, and O are challenging for ASL students. Fingerspell each name or word.

1. croon
2. Creon
3. creed
4. code
5. cede
6. corde
7. epoch
8. ocelot
9. ocean
10. porcelain
11. Horace
12. creosote
13. Rolls Royce
14. solace
15. economics

I Want to Know . . .

How can I improve my understanding of fingerspelling?

Watching, or reading, fingerspelling is called a **receptive** skill. Some ASL teachers suggest fingerspelling into a mirror to practice receptive skills, and that may help. Because Deaf people fingerspell quickly, you may miss letters and become confused or need to ask for repetition several times. Try to guess the missing letters or think of words you know that use the letters you understood. Struggles with receptive fingerspelling is most often caused by decoding letter by letter and trying to see the word. Try sounding out the letters to yourself as they are being fingerspelled instead of focusing on what each letter is. The best practice is real-life signed conversations with Deaf people.

5 *Titles.* Titles of books, movies, songs, poetry, and artwork are fingerspelled, even if a title includes words that have signs. Ask a partner if he or she has read certain books, following the example shown below. Switch roles for 11-20.

Have you read the book, *Beach Season*?

1. The Iliad
2. Great Expectations
3. Deaf Like Me
4 A Separate Peace
5. Ragtime
6. A Loss for Words
7. The Hobbitt
8. The Great Gatsby
9. Dune
10. The House on Mango Street

11. The Scarlet Letter
12. Beowulf
13. Frankenstein
14. The Good Earth
15. Diary of Anne Frank
16. The Odyssey
17. In This Sign
18. Green Eggs and Ham
19. Middle Passage
20. James and the Giant Peach

6 *TV Shows.* Match the name of a character with his or her television program. Fingerspell the character's name to a partner, who will spell the name of the show.

1. Gilligan
2. Phoebe
3. MacGuyver
4. Darlene Connor
5. Elmo

6. Homer
7. Lucy
8. Fox Mulder
9. Captain Kirk
10. Rose Nylund

TV Shows

The Lucille Ball Show
Star Trek
The X-Files
MacGuyver
Sesame Street
The Golden Girls
Gilligan's Island
Roseanne
The Simpsons
Friends

7 *EO drill.* The letter combinations EO and OE are challenging for ASL students. Fingerspell each name or word.

1. George
2. Joey
3. toes
4. peony
5. Zoe
6. freon

7. Oedipus
8. Noelle
9. reorder
10. Yeoman
11. poetry
12. geodesic

8   *The Brooks Family Tree.* You are working on a family tree. Fingerspell each name and answer the questions to explain how they are related.

1. Mel and Elaine are _____.
2. _____ is Mike and Sarah's uncle.
3. Alta is a ____, and an _____.
4. Kendra and Carin are _____ and _____.
5. _____ is Alan's sister.
6. Mike and Sarah's father is named _____.
7. _____ and _____ are Edward's _____ and _____.
8. Elaine has four _____ named _____ _____ _____ _____.
9. _____ _____ are parents.
10. _____ _____ are married.

The Brooks Family

Mel — Grandfather
Elaine — Grandmother

Alan — Uncle
Alta — Aunt
Carole — Mother
Edward — Father

Parents

children

Kendra — Cousin
Carin — Cousin
Mike — Son
Sarah — Daughter

Accent Steps

Don't worry for now about signing the *'s* when fingerspelling. Simply sign the information needed. While ASL does have an *'s* sign, it is rarely used and only for specific reasons. See page 56.

9   *Common family names.* Don't pause between each letter or break the name into parts. Hold your hand steady in one place.

1	2	3	4	5	6	7	8	9	10
Thomas	Hines	Findley	Jones	McKinley	Harris	Taylor	Patel	Hughes	Murphy
Nguyen	Guevara	Sayers	Sutton	Truong	Strong	Shah	Chen	Simon	Knutson
Michaels	Peabody	Brown	Haroun	Parsons	Guthrie	Rodriguez	Pimentel	Valdez	Daniels
Chung	Severson	Li	Reynolds	Flores	Kerry	Smith	Graham	Olson	Park

10   *EA drill.* The letter combinations EA and AE are challenging for ASL students. Fingerspell each name or word.

1. health
2. teamwork
3. aesthetic
4. Raphael
5. Meadow
6. Yael
7. Aegean Sea
8. Rhea
9. peaceful
10. measles
11. Aesop
12. alumnae

11 *Keeping track.* Use the Listing & Ordering Technique to arrange multiple names in the sentences below. An example of listing names is provided.

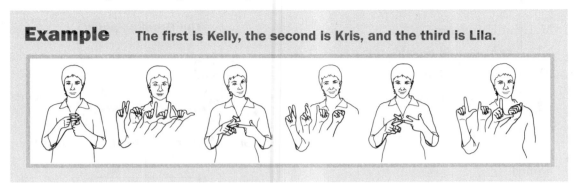

Example The first is Kelly, the second is Kris, and the third is Lila.

1. Lisa, Jeff, Michael
2. Troy, Sarah
3. Lionel, Vivian, Craig, Ed
4. Russel, Georgia, Isabel
5. Jody, Pete, Amy
6. Jonathan, David, Louise

7. Cathy, Frank, Steven, Shauna, Perry
8. Elizabeth, Ryan, Nina, Tara, John
9. Jenny, Keisha, Naomi
10. Patricia, Kevin, Neil
11. Cyrus, Nicole, Helen
12. Juan, Anna, Barbara, Sonya, Michelle

12 *More lists.* Sign the following sentences in ASL, using the Listing & Ordering Technique as needed.

1. My younger brother loves to read *Spiderman*, *X-Men*, and *Batman*.
2. Michelle, Kerry, Tom, and I are learning ASL.
3. On the weekend we watch TV. We like *Friends*, *Seinfeld*, and *Jeopardy*.
4. Have you read *The Odyssey*, *Beowulf*, and *Dracula*?
5. Joan, Melissa, and David work at a restaurant.

13 *Fingerspelling initials.* To include an initial while fingerspelling a name, shake the letter very slightly for a moment before continuing on. You don't need to include a period after the initialized letter.

1. Michael P. Udall
2. A.K. Reyes
3 John F. Kennedy

4. Lisa A. Boggs
5. Victor S. Salcedo
6. P.T. Barnum

14 *Famous authors.* Fingerspell each author's name clearly and quickly.

1. John Updike
2. Amy Tan
3. Toni Morrison
4. Umberto Eco
5. Tom Clancy
6. J.K. Rowling
7. Leo Tolstoy
8. Graham Greene

9. Jane Austen
10. Pearl S. Buck
11. Ken Kesey
12. Mary Shelley
13. Danielle Steele
14. Nathaniel Hawthorne
15. Barbara Kingsolver
16. Marian Zimmer Bradley

15 *Television.* Ask a partner about his or her favorite television program. Your partner will respond using the information given in a complete sentence. Switch roles for 9–16.

Example **What's your favorite TV show?**

1. Picket Fences	7. News	13. Hollywood Squares
2. Will and Grace	8. Antiques Roadshow	14. Jeopardy
3. McNeil News Hour	9. Monday Night Football	15. M.A.S.H.
4. Road Rules	10. Friends	16. Family Feud
5. Oprah	11. Wheel of Fortune	
6. The Simpsons	12. Frasier	

16 *Interview.* Do you and a partner share similar tastes? Interview each other to learn about the things you enjoy. Ask and respond using complete sentences. Use the Listing & Ordering Technique if needed.

1. favorite actor	3. favorite game	5. 2 or 3 favorite songs
2. 2 favorite books	4. 3 favorite TV shows	6. 3 or 4 favorite movies

17 *Various names.* Fingerspell each name clearly and accurately.

1. John F. Kennedy	5. Patrick Stewart	9. Vanna White
2. Kelsey Grammer	6. Tom Hanks	10. Jude Law
3. Angelina Jolie	7. Peter Jennings	11. Elisabeth Shue
4. Gwynneth Paltrow	8. Julia Roberts	12. Sean Astin

18 *Fingerspelled words.* These words are generally fingerspelled. Learn to spell them quickly and clearly

1. tan	5. lasagna	9. beige
2. trout	6. carpool	10. Dr. (non-medical)
3. plum	7. Antarctica	
4. Ph.D.	8. Sahara	

19 *Handshape drills.* Practice fingerspelling each letter combination until your hand becomes used to the shapes.

1	2	3	4	5	6	7	8	9	10
ika	ape	Ira	efi	amna	enmi	ash	elm	Lam	Joe
aki	ipa	ure	afe	emne	anme	esh	alm	Lau	toe
uki	epa	Ari	ufi	imna	onma	osh	ulm	lai	Moe
iku	upe	eru	ife	omni	unmi	ush	ilm	lae	doe
oke	opi	era	ofo	umna	inma	ish	olm	Lao	foe

20 *Fingerspelling challenge.* Can you spell these words quickly and clearly, and understand them when spelled to you?

1. coral	3. retainer	5. cereal	7. tease
2. couple	4. trainer	6. corporal	8. treason

Unit 5

1 *School towns.* Sign a complete sentence using the name of the school and the information provided.

1. Langley High School (**McLean, Virginia**)
2. Yale University (**New Haven, Connecticut**)
3. Kent State University (**Kent, Ohio**)
4. Cordova High School (**Memphis, Tennessee**)
5. Hilo High School (**Hilo, Hawaii**)
6. Gallaudet University (**Washington, D.C.**)
7. Del Norte High School (**Albuquerque, New Mexico**)
8. Columbia University (**New York, New York**)
9. Brown University (**Providence, Rhode Island**)
10. Mankato East High School (**Mankato, Minnesota**)

2 *Colleges & universities.* Fingerspell each name clearly and quickly, holding your hand in one position.

1. Biola	8. Hawaii Pacific	15. Mount Holyoke
2. San Jose State	9. Ball State	16. Vassar
3. Quinnipiac	10. Cornell	17. Old Dominion
4. Loma Linda	11. St. Ambrose	18. Marquette
5. Howard	12. Tulane	19. Boston Conservatory
6. Wheaton	13. Bowdoin	20. Colorado School of Mines
7. Florida State	14. Johns Hopkins	

3 *Background.* Interview a classmate to learn about his or her background. Prepare to share the information to your class.

1. Where did you go to kindergarten?
2. Did you go to a middle school or junior high school? What was it named?
3. Where do you go to school now?
4. Is it a high school or college?
5. Where do you live?
6. Where do you want to live?

4 *Trouble letters.* The following words and names contain one or more trouble letters. Fingerspell each column using the correct handshapes.

1	2	3	4	5	6	7	8	9	10
ease	loon	fix	Rex	Eyre	mane	snap	Ghana	Hahn	deft
easy	loony	fax	reel	tyre	many	snack	Ghandi	half	defy
East	roomy	fox	reek	fyre	Manx	snare	Gough	halve	defeat
feast	gloomy	fex	greet	syre	Maori	sniff	trough	Hamlet	defend

5 *Youth conference.* A group of hearing and Deaf students are discussing where they go to school. Use the information provided to create a dialogue with a partner. Switch roles when finished. An example is provided.

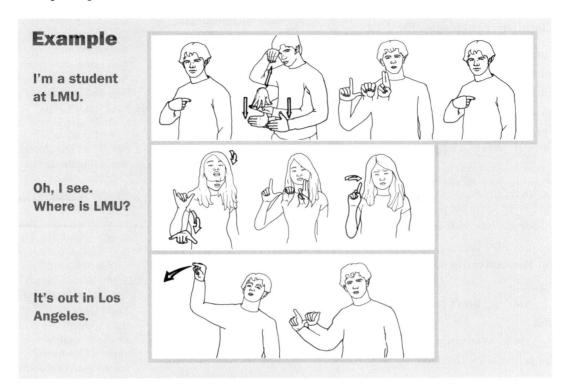

Example

I'm a student at LMU.

Oh, I see. Where is LMU?

It's out in Los Angeles.

1.
name: Megan
hearing
college student, sophomore
name of school: SLCC
from: Salt Lake City

2.
name: Brenda
hearing
high school student, junior
name of school: Acalanes High (Lafayette)
from: Lafayette, California

3.
name: Charles
Deaf
university student, freshman
name of school: Gallaudet (Washington, D.C.)
from: Huntsville, Alabama

4.
name: Scott
hearing
high school student, senior
name of school: Eureka High School
from: Eureka, California

5.
name: Juan
Deaf
university student, senior
name of school: Spellman (Atlanta)
from: Jackson, Mississippi

6 *Schools for the Deaf.* Do you know where the School for the Deaf is in your state? Sign or fingerspell the name of a state to a partner, who will tell you where the School for the Deaf is located. Switch roles for 7-12.

1.	Minnesota	7.	Arizona
2.	Kentucky	8.	Mississippi
3.	California	9.	South Dakota
4.	Texas	10.	Oregon
5.	Wyoming	11.	Rhode Island
6.	?	12.	?

7 *Schools.* Sign each of the following sentences in ASL.

1. California has two schools for the Deaf, in _____ and _____.
2. The Pennsylvania school for the Deaf is in _____.
3. ____ and ___ don't have a school for the Deaf.
4. _____ is in Washington, D.C.
5. The schools for the Deaf in New York are in _____, _____, _____, _____.

8 *College days.* Fingerspell the acronym of a college to a partner, who will select the correct school from the list provided. Switch roles for numbers 11-20.

1.	UW	11.	UVA
2.	UCLA	12.	UBC
3.	CCSN	13.	SPU
4.	MSU	14.	UCONN
5.	LMU	15.	WSU
6.	CSUN	16.	BU
7.	GT	17.	ASU
8.	NTID	18.	CUNY
9.	UNDF	19.	GWU
10.	SMU	20.	USAFA

FYI Some schools have name signs, like Notre Dame. Most shorter names are fingerspelled completely, with the rest known by their acronyms.

Schools for the Deaf in the United States

Alabama (Talladega)	Montana (Great Falls)
Alaska (Anchorage)	Nebraska (none)
Arizona (Phoenix)	Nevada (none)
Arkansas (Little Rock)	New Hampshire (none)
California (Fremont & Riverside)	New Jersey (West Trenton)
Colorado (Colorado Springs)	New Mexico (Santa Fe)
Connecticut (West Hartford)	New York (Buffalo, Rochester, Rome, & White Plains)
Delaware (Newark)	
Florida (St. Augustine)	North Carolina (Morganton)
Georgia (Cave Spring)	North Dakota (Devil's Lake)
Hawaii (Honolulu)	Ohio (Columbus)
Idaho (Gooding)	Oklahoma (Sulphur)
Illinois (Jacksonville)	Oregon (Salem)
Indiana (Indianapolis)	Pennsylvania (Pittsburgh)
Iowa (Council Bluffs)	Rhode Island (Providence)
Kansas (Olathe)	South Carolina (Spartanburg)
Kentucky (Danville)	
Louisiana (Baton Rouge)	South Dakota (Sioux Falls)
Maine (Falmouth)	Tennessee (Knoxville)
Maryland (Frederick)	Texas (Austin)
Massachusetts (Allston)	Utah (Odgen)
Michigan (Flint)	Vermont (Brattleboro)
Minnesota (Faribault)	Virginia (Staunton)
Mississippi (Jackson)	Washington (Vancouver)
Missouri (Fulton)	West Virginia (Romney)
Model Secondary (Washington, D.C.)	Wisconsin (Delavan)
	Wyoming (none)

Colleges & Universities

Gardner-Webb University
Arizona State University
University of British Columbia
Washington State University
University of California, Los Angeles
Georgetown
City University of New York
University of Washington
Boston University
United States Air Force Academy
Michigan State University
University of Virginia
Seattle Pacific University
Community College of Southern Nevada
Loyola Marymount University
National Technical Institute for the Deaf
University of Connecticut
Southern Methodist University
University of North Dakota, Fargo
California State University, Northridge

9 *Famous artists.* Fingerspell each name clearly and accurately.

1. Leonardo da Vinci
2. Salvador Dali
3. Mary Cassatt
4. Willem de Kooning

5. Katsushika Hokusai
6. Auguste Rodin
7. El Greco
8. Piet Mondrian

9. Helen Frankenthaler
10. Dale Chihuly
11. Andrew Wyeth
12. Diego Rivera

10 *Using the Agent Marker.* Fingerspell each term to a partner, who will sign its meaning using the vocabulary shown and the Agent Marker. Switch roles for 8–14.

The Agent Marker

1. Physicist
2. Canadian
3. Entrepreneur
4. American
5. Engineer
6. Musician
7. Presenter
8. Mathematician
9. Employee
10. Singer
11. Journalist
12. Drafter
13. Educator
14. Sociologist

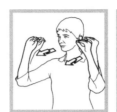   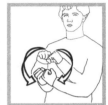

11 *Students.* In a complete sentence, explain where each student attends school. You can use the signs *college* and *university* as needed, and don't need to spell *of*.

1. Michelle Davis (University of Oregon)
2. Sharon Young (Mills College)
3. Davonte Simpson (Carnegie Mellon)

4. Joel Fletcher (Union County College)
5. Ariel Langley (University of Texas, Austin)
6. Tracey Helmutt (University of Cincinnati)

I Want to Know . . .

If one sign has several meanings, how do I make sure I'm clear?

Did you notice that *singer* and *musician* have the same sign, even though they have different meanings? While *singing* and *music* can be grouped together in a general sense, there may be times when the difference must be clear. In those instances, use the sign and then immediately afterward fingerspell the exact term you need.

12 *Mascots.* What is your school mascot? Explain in a complete sentence the name of the school's mascot. You may use the sign *university* if needed. The word *mascot* is fingerspelled.

1. U.C. Santa Cruz **(Banana Slug)**
2. Arizona State University **(Sun Devil)**
3. University of North Carolina **(Tar Heel)**
4. Georgetown University **(Hoya)**
5. University of Maryland **(Terrapin)**
6. Stanford University **(Cardinal)**
7. University of Miami **(Hurricane)**
8. University of Arkansas **(Razorback)**
9. Indiana University **(Hoosier)**
10. University of Nebraska **(Cornhusker)**

13 *College towns.* Spell each name quickly and clearly, holding your hand steady and in one place. Use a state sign if available.

1. Bozeman, Montana
2. Cortland, New York
3. Boulder, Colorado
4. Athens, Georgia
5. Princeton, New Jersey
6. Chico, California
7. Provo, Utah
8. Hays, Kansas
9. Rolla, Missouri
10. Eugene, Oregon
11. Madison, Wisconsin
12. Richmond, Kentucky
13. Bemidji, Minnesota
14. Ann Arbor, Michigan
15. Durango, Colorado
16. Keene, New Hampshire
17. Tahlequah, Oklahoma
18. Plattsburgh, New York
19. Tempe, Arizona

14 *Majors.* Ask a partner what he or she is studying, or wants to study, in college. Your partner will respond in a complete sentence using the information provided, fingerspelling the word in bold. An example is provided.

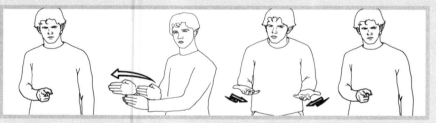

What are you majoring in?

1. **archaeology**
2. **zoology**
3. **early childhood** education
4. **botany**
5. business **administration**
6. **classics**
7. **fine arts**
8. **medieval** studies
9. **theology**
10. **microbiology**
11. Deaf **studies**
12. **neurology**
13. **Slavic** studies
14. **oncology**
15. **molecular** chemistry

FYI

Abbreviate administration with ADMIN.

15 *PP drill.* The letter combination PP is challenging for ASL students. Fingerspell each name or word.

1. scrapple
2. Eppie
3. opposite
4. appreciate
5. pepper
6. zipper
7. copper
8. apply
9. poppie
10. Trappist
11. supple
12. Appalachia

16 *Notable people.* Why are the following people famous? Use the information provided in a complete sentence.

1. Ansel Adams **(photographer)**
2. Mikhail Baryshnikov **(dancer)**
3. Joe DiMaggio **(athlete)**
4. Florence Nightingale **(nurse)**
5. Barbra Streisand **(actor, singer)**
6. Julia Child **(chef)**
7. Donald Trump **(business)**
8. Yo Yo Ma **(musician)**
9. Sigmund Freud **(psychologist)**
10. Isaac Newton **(scientist)**

17 *Nobel prizewinners.* Fingerspell the names of past winners of the Nobel Prize, and mention the field for which he / she was recognized in a complete sentence.

1. Roderick MacKinnon **(chemistry)**
2. Marie Curie **(chemistry)**
3. Sydney Brenner **(physiology)**
4. John Maxwell Coetzee **(literature)**
4. Carl E. Wieman **(physics)**
5. Toni Morrison **(literature)**

18 *Fingerspelled words.* These words are generally fingerspelled. Learn to spell them quickly and clearly.

1. pool
2. salmon
3. casserole
4. tip
5. apricot
6. ink
7. taffy
8. boardwalk
9. academy
10. fern

19 *Handshape drills.* Practice fingerspelling each letter combination until your hand becomes used to the shapes.

1	2	3	4	5	6	7	8	9	10
ic	fg	eoa	pear	cd	NBC	ghn	qb	sey	erv
ice	fgh	eoe	poor	CDC	CBS	ghm	qf	say	err
icy	ghf	eae	peer	cac	ABC	ghi	qd	siy	erb
ico	hgf	eue	pair	cic	Fox	gha	ql	soy	erk
ica	gfh	Oreo	Pierre	cec	UPN	ghy	qr	suy	erj

20 *Fingerspelling challenge.* Can you spell these words quickly and clearly, and understand them when spelled to you?

1. double
2. couple
3. map
4. imp
5. cell
6. cello
7. platinum
8. aquarium

Unit 6

---

1   *Famous athletes.* Fingerspell each name clearly and quickly.

1. Babe Ruth	**6.** Jesse Owens	**11.** Nadia Comenici
2. Muhammad Ali	**7.** Sugar Ray Leonard	**12.** Bret Favre
3. Sasha Cohen	**8.** Jackie Joyner-Kersee	**13.** Larry Bird
4. Wayne Gretzky	**9.** Mickey Mantle	**14.** Cobi Jones
5. Greg Louganis	**10.** Bob Bondurant	**15.** Shaquille O'Neal

2   *Personal calendars.* Follow the example and sign each sentence using the information provided. Remember that dates are *when* signs and come first in ASL sentences.

I'm going to New Orleans on April 2nd. / On April 2nd I'm going to New Orleans.

1. My sister was born on June 14.
2. Halloween is in October.
3. On August 22 we're going to Hawaii.
4. Class begins September 4th.
5. In February I'm going to a wedding.
6. Trevor arrives November 8th.
7. In January Spring semester starts.
8. My birthday is in December.
9. We have an ASL test on February 10th.
10. Is our vacation in March or April?

Accent Steps

When signing most dates, you don't need to include a *th* or *st* after numbers. October 10th would be signed *October 10.*

3   *Trouble letters.* The following words and names contain one or more trouble letters. Fingerspell each column using the correct handshapes.

1	2	3	4	5	6	7	8	9	10
flask	Cleo	please	Hilde	mesh	REI	clasp	Hosea	Ted	adjust
husky	Keoni	tense	Edison	sheep	heist	space	easel	Veda	adjourn
Haskell	Theodore	Dempsey	misdeed	fresh	Leitner	aspect	Korean	medal	adjunct
skylight	someone	season	grandeur	knish	neither	spectator	greenbean	sedate	adjacent

4 *Sports & Athletes.* Match the name of an athlete and the sport he or she is associated with. Fingerspell the name to your partner, who will select the correct sport. Switch roles for 9–16. Answers are at the bottom of the page.

1. Jesse Owens	**9.** Kristi Yamaguchi
2. Oscar de la Hoya	**10.** Mia Hamm
3. Tiger Woods	**11.** Bret Favre
4. Bo Jackson	**12.** Joe DiMaggio
5. Jet Li	**13.** Babe Ruth
6. Jonny Moseley	**14.** Lance Armstrong
7. Kareem Abdul Jabbar	**15.** Wayne Gretzky
8. Pele	**16.** Larry Bird

Sports

cycling	karate
track	soccer
baseball	ice skating
boxing	skiing
hockey	gymnastics
tennis	driving
swimming	golf
basketball	football

5 *Names & Ages.* Sign a complete sentence using the information provided. Remember that age signs originate at the Age Spot.

2 years old

1. Eli Stein (14)	**9.** Edith Carr (29)
2. Sara Green (22)	**10.** Robert Burns (40)
3. Melody Truvar (16)	**11.** Ryoko Kanagaki (25)
4. Anand Gupta (31)	**12.** Ivan Horvath (28)
5. Frank Alvarez (19)	**13.** Laura Dewey (8)
6. Tyrone Davis (11)	**14.** Ann & Abe Gray (9)
7. Adrian Grissom (3)	**15.** Stella (11)
8. Wayne Hynds (36)	**16.** Michael (13)

6 *Unique names.* Fingerspell each name clearly, holding your hand steady and in one place.

1. Laquetta Gibson	**6.** Ehawee Sioux	**11.** Nathan Ruualcaba
2. Zebediah Ericson	**7.** Tanesha McGrath	**12.** Lisa Saffarian
3. Alsoomse Bryant	**8.** Rahamim Urdaz	**13.** Cheketina Russell
4. Desdemona Cooper	**9.** Octavius Wallace	**14.** Tokuyama Tairo
5. Hortensio De Marco	**10.** Deehaven Brickner	**15.** Myrtice McGlothlin

7 *Olympic cities.* Fingerspell the names of past and future sites of the Olympic Games.

1. Athens, 1896	**6.** Lillehammer, 1994	**11.** Helsinki, 1952
2. Tokyo, 1964	**7.** Paris, 1924	**12.** St. Louis, 1904
3. Los Angeles, 1984	**8.** Melbourne, 1956	**13.** Vancouver, 2010
4. Turin, 2006	**9.** Seoul, 1988	**14.** Barcelona, 1992
5. London, 1908	**10.** Salt Lake City, 2002	**15.** Beijing, 2008

Answer Key:
Exercise 4: 1. track; 2. boxing; 3. golf; 4. football; 5. karate; 6. skiing; 7. basketball; 8. soccer; 9. ice skating; 10. soccer; 11. football; 12. baseball; 13. baseball; 14. cycling; 15. hockey; 16. basketball

8   *Q & A.* Ask a partner whether particular places have professional sports teams. Your partner will respond using the information provided in bold. An example is shown. Switch roles for 6-10.

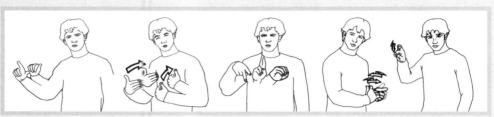

Example

Does Los Angeles have pro sports?

1. Florida **(yes, baseball, football, basketball)**
2. New Hampshire **(don't know)**
3. Houston **(yes, football team named Oilers)**
4. Las Vegas **(none)**
5. Pittsburgh **(yes, hockey team named Penguins)**

6. Alabama **(no pro team)**
7. Minnesota **(yes, Vikings)**
8. Dallas **(yes, football team named Cowboys)**
9. Anaheim **(yes, hockey team named Ducks)**
10. Baltimore **(yes, baseball team named Orioles)**

9   *Hyphenated names.* When fingerspelling a hyphenated name, use the same handshape for *period* to draw a small hyphen where necessary.

1. Tura-Klein
2. Simpson-Baxter
3. Lowell-Nye

4. Sharon Olson-Blake
5. Melanie Williams-Cole
6. Adrian Gomez-Braun

Period

I Want to Know . . .

Why is fingerspelling easy for Deaf people but not hearing people?

First, using fingerspelling as part of your language gives you the fluency needed to understand fingerspelling quickly. Second, recognizing the shapes and patterns of fingerspelling help the brain predict and decode groups of letters. As you improve your fingerspelling skills you will begin to see fingerspelled words as groups of shapes rather than a combination of letters. When you read a book, your eyes do not look at each letter forming a word. Instead, your eyes rely on the first and last letters to identify and understand the word. The same process applies to fingerspelling. Learning to identify the shape of a fingerspelled word takes time and practice but you can begin by analyzing the shape of particular letters:

☐ letters that don't extend up or to the side: A, C, E, M, N, O, S, T
☐ letters that extend up: B, D, F, I, K, L, R, U, V, W, X
☐ letters open sideways: G, H, Y, Z
☐ letters that open down: J, P, Q

10 *Shapes*. Look at each set of shapes. Based on the letters and shapes you see, what word is being fingerspelled? The answers are at the bottom of the page.

1. A ☐ L E

2. B ☐ A R

3. P ☐ ☐ R

4. H ☐ ☐ E

5. W ☐ ☐ G

6. S C ☐ ☐ ☐ L

7. G L ☐ R ☐ ☐

8. M ☐ ☐

9. J ☐ H ☐

11 *Hometown teams*. In a complete ASL sentence, explain where each team is from.

1. Raiders **(Oakland)**
2. Packers **(Green Bay)**
3. Earthquakes **(San Jose)**
4. Spurs **(San Antonio)**
5. Redskins **(Washington, D.C.)**
6. Sharks **(San Jose)**
7. Seahawks **(Seattle)**
8. Twins **(Minneapolis)**
9. Lakers **(Los Angeles)**
10. Patriots **(Boston)**
11. Bulls **(Chicago)**
12. 49ers **(San Francisco)**

12 *Famous poems*. Explain who wrote each poem in a complete sentence. Don't forget to use the *title* sign.

1. *Birches* (Robert Frost)
2. *How Do I Love Thee?* (Elizabeth Barrett Browning)
3. *Seven Ages of Man* (William Shakespeare)
4. *Goblin Market* (Christina Rossetti)
5. *Death Be Not Proud* (John Donne)
6. *The Raven* (Edgar Allan Poe)
7. *Jabberwocky* (Lewis Carroll)
8. *Balloons* (Sylvia Plath)
9. *I Held a Jewel* (Emily Dickinson)
10. *Birds of Passage* (Henry Longfellow)

13 *HE drill*. The letter combination HE and EH is challenging for ASL students. Fingerspell each name or word.

1. Heidi
2. chess
3. theme
4. Theo
5. dishevel
6. Chenelle
7. John Heide
8. Cheryl Yeh
9. morpheme
10. heartburn
11. Heidelberg
12. Khenany

14 *Sport terms*. Many of these words have regular signs. Fingerspell each word clearly and quickly, holding your hand steady and in one place.

1. discus
2. pole vault
3. fullback
4. mitt
5. frisbee
6. puck
7. red shirt
8. intramurals
9. foul
10. rebound
11. heavyweight
12. play-action pass
13. offense
14. match-up
15. league

Answer Key:
Exercise 10: 1. apple; 2. bear / boar; 3. pear / poor / peer; 4. hope; 5. wing / Wong; 6. school; 7. Gloria; 8. map; 9. John

15 *Using fingerspelling.* Sign each sentence in ASL and fingerspell the underlined words. Remember that time is a *when* sign and comes first in a sentence.

1. I will meet David at 6:00.
2. We will eat dinner at El Patio tonight.
3. Her new last name is McKinley-Eads.
4. The movie *Ghost* begins at 7:45.
5. My favorite basketball team is the Sacramento Kings.
6. Is Oscar de la Hoya a heavyweight?
7. My school has an intramural league.
8. We don't have a pro team.
9. The book is called "*Mother Father Deaf.*"
10. A long time ago my favorite movie was *The Wizard of Oz.*

16 *More famous athletes.* Fingerspell each name clearly and quickly, holding your hand steady and in one place.

1. Picabo Street
2. Hank Aaron
3. Brandi Chastain
4. Jean-Luc Brassard
5. Sugar Ray Leonard
6. Kerri Strug
7. Billie Jean King
8. Dave Dravecky
9. Michael Jordan
10. Serena Williams
11. Derek Jeter
12. Martina Navratilova

17 *Sports Halls of Fame.* Explain where each Hall of Fame is found in a complete sentence. You must fingerspell *Hall of Fame.*

1. baseball **(Cooperstown, New York)**
2. hockey **(Eveleth, Minnesota)**
3. football **(Canton, Ohio)**
4. basketball **(Springfield, Massachusetts)**
5. bowling **(St. Louis, Missouri)**
6. skating **(Gloucester, Ontario)**
7. skiing **(Ishpeming, Michigan)**
8. golf **(St. Augustine, Florida)**
9. driving **(Indianapolis, Indiana)**
10. soccer **(Oneonta, New York)**

18 *Fingerspelled words.* These words are generally fingerspelled. Learn to spell them quickly and clearly.

1. digital
2. NBA
3. eggplant
4. liver
5. NFL
6. NHL
7. off
8. WNBA
9. attorney general
10. speaker (stereo)

19 *Handshape drills.* Practice fingerspelling each letter combination until your hand becomes used to the shapes.

1	2	3	4	5	6	7	8	9	10
les	los	das	Bev	aug	pe	tre	ska	Brad	Chet
fes	SOS	dis	Eve	tug	peg	Trey	ski	Bree	Chan
zes	eos	dip	rev	bug	pen	Tran	Skip	Brie	Cheng
qes	nos	dos	Eva	hug	pep	trip	skim	Brea	Chase
ses	ros	des	evo	mug	pea	trap	skit	Brook	Chuck

20 *Fingerspelling challenge.* Can you spell these words quickly and clearly, and understand them when spelled to you?

1. equipment
2. equipped
3. popsicle
4. pickle
5. marigold
6. maricopa
7. festival
8. festive

1 *Brand names.* Fingerspell each name clearly and quickly.

1. Polo	**5.** Rossignol	**9.** North Face
2. Gucci	**6.** DKNY	**10.** Ralph Lauren
3. Adidas	**7.** Prada	**11.** Levi Strauss
4. Nike	**8.** Timberland	**12.** FUBU

2 *Where are you going?* You and a friend are comparing errands that need to be done. Ask your partner why he or she is going to different places. Your partner will respond using the information provided. Fingerspell the underlined items. Switch roles and repeat the exercise.

1. Why are you going to <u>Best Buy</u>? **(want a <u>DVD</u>)**
2. Why are you going to <u>Office Max</u>? **(need paper)**
3. Why are you going to <u>Target</u>? **(look for new shoes)**
4. Why are you going to <u>Barnes and Noble</u>? **(need a <u>thesaurus</u>)**
5. Why are you going to <u>Wash and Dry</u>? **(need to do laundry)**

3 *Trouble letters.* The following words and names contain one or more trouble letters. Fingerspell each column using the correct handshapes.

<u>1</u>	<u>2</u>	<u>3</u>	<u>4</u>	<u>5</u>	<u>6</u>	<u>7</u>	<u>8</u>	<u>9</u>	<u>10</u>
coda	gaffe	kelp	Dudley	Tobias	juice	finch	Kim	squid	Outre
soda	fealty	alpha	daddy	obey	Joyce	final	crimp	queen	mitre
Odathe	ferret	pulpit	Dodge	knob	celery	Sarafina	imply	quilt	attract
odalisk	Santa Fe	helpful	deduct	object	percent	infinity	dim sum	squeal	Katrina

I Want to Know . . .

Do any stores have name signs, or do I fingerspell everything?

Most store names should be fingerspelled, though there are some name signs used in local areas. Only a few name signs for stores are known nationwide. When a name sign is used, it tends to be followed with the fingerspelled name so everyone in the conversation knows the context. Remember that fingerspelling is used for names, including grocery stores, clothing stores, and brand names.

4 *Activities*. Select vocabulary from Columns A and B to create a complete sentence. Fingerspelled terms are underlined. An example is provided.

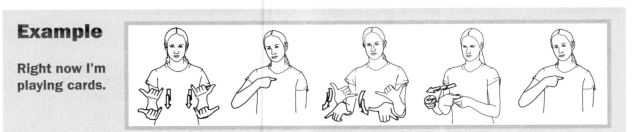

Example

Right now I'm playing cards.

Column A

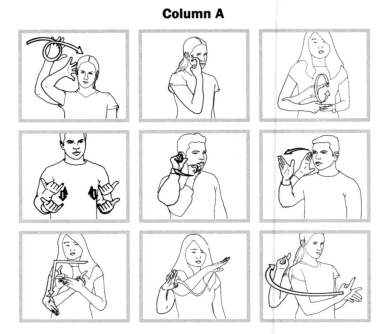

Column B

1. ... I play ...
2. ... my family ...
3. ... I love ...
4. ... I want ...
5. ... I play ...
6. ... I don't like ...

<u>Scrabble</u>
<u>tag</u>
football
<u>hide and seek</u>
<u>Risk</u>
cards
baseball
<u>Monopoly</u>
<u>charades</u>
<u>poker</u>
game
sports
<u>Balderdash</u>
<u>Pictionary</u>
checkers
<u>Go Fish</u>
<u>dominoes</u>
<u>Taboo</u>
<u>Solitaire</u>

5 *At the mall*. You and a friend are looking at the mall directory. Which stores are located at the mall? Fingerspell each name quickly and clearly, and don't move your hand.

1. Sears
2. Brookstone
3. Haagen-Dazs
4. Bombay Company
5. J. Crew
6. Urban Outfitters
7. J.C. Penney
8. Lenscrafters
9. Pottery Barn
10. Sephora
11. Foot Locker
12. Gap Kids
13. Nordstroms
14. All Cellular Phones
15. Brooks Brothers

6 *Famous shopping*. Match the name of a shopping area with its location. Fingerspell the name to your partner, who will tell you where it is found. Switch roles for 6-10.

1. Rodeo Drive
2. Champs-Elysee
3. Union Square
4. Fifth Avenue
5. Oxford Street
6. Tyson's Corner
7. Magnificent Mile
8. French Quarter
9. Back Bay
10. Uptown/Galleria

London	Beverly Hills
New York City	New Orleans
Boston	San Francisco
Houston	Chicago
Paris	Virginia

7 *Colors.* Often the particular name of a color is important. Generally, use signs to describe the color, such as *light blue* and then fingerspell the exact shade: *cyan.* Practice this format for each color, using the signs provided to help.

**Bright
(blue, in this case)**

Dark

Kind of, so-so

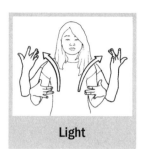

Light

Medium

1. magenta
2. mint green
3. sunflower yellow
4. wine red
5. beige

6. navy blue
7. chocolate
8. forest green
9. turquoise
10. lavender

11. hot pink
12. lime green
13. reddish orange
14. slate gray
15. olive

8 *More colors.* Use the clues shown to fingerspell the name of the color.

1
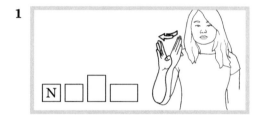

2

3

4

5

9 *What do people go there for?* Follow the example to ask a partner why people go to particular stores. Switch roles and repeat when done.

Example

Why do people
go to REI?

Maybe they need
new boots.

1. Staples **(pen/pencil, paper, scissors)**
2. Wal-Mart **(bicycle)**
3. Circuit City **(computer)**
4. Taco Bell **(want to eat)**
5. Abercrombie and Fitch **(?)**
6. Longs **(soap, earrings)**
7. J.C. Penney **(shirt, jeans, socks)**
8. Old Navy **(?)**
9. Florsheim Shoes **(?)**
10. The Men's Wearhouse **(suit)**

10 *Famous designers.* Practice fingerspelling each name clearly and quickly.

1. Vera Wang
2. Thomas Burberry
3. Coco Chanel
4. Giorgio Armani
5. Louis Vuitton
6. Christian Dior
7. Katherine Hamnett
8. Tommy Hilfiger
9. Alice Roi
10. Helmut Lang
11. Oscar de la Renta
12. Vivienne Westwood
13. Dolce & Gabbana
14. Fred Perry
15. Donna Karan

11 *Types of pets.* Few animal breeds have signs, with most being fingerspelled. Sign a complete sentence using the information provided, spelling the underlined terms.

1. Fido (dog, yellow Lab)
2. Wallace (bird, parrot)
3. Magda (fish, Beta)
4. Tivoli (cat, Siamese)
5. Snickers (dog, mutt)
6. T.J. (cat, calico)
7. Corbin (cat, tabby)
8. Bellingham (dog, boxer)
9. Checkers (bird, canary)
10. Trouble (dog, Rott)
11. Polly (dog, terrier)
12. Bubbles (cat, Burmese)

12 *Best pictures.* Use the information provided to explain whether each film is an Oscar winner. Words to be fingerspelled are underlined.

Title

To win

1. The Matrix (no Oscar)
2. Rain Man (won 4 Oscars)
3. Forrest Gump (won 6 Oscars)
4. Superman (no Oscar)
5. Silence of the Lambs (won 5 Oscars)
6. Harry Potter (no Oscar)
7. Mrs. Doubtfire (no Oscar)
8. Titanic (won 11 Oscars)
9. Robin Hood (no Oscar)
10. Return of the King (won 11 Oscars)

13   *When and who?* Explain the activities each person does on a given day. Remember that *when* signs come first in ASL sentences. An example is provided.

Example

I work with April on Mondays.

1. On the weekends I work at a restaurant named The Chowder House.
2. I eat lunch every day with my friends Neil, Ann, and Takaki.
3. Tonight my family will eat at the Olive Garden with my aunt and uncle.
4. I'm going to the mall after class to buy new shoes at Shoes For Less.
5. Every Monday and Wednesday I have an ASL class at Moffet College.

14   *Pets?* Practice fingerspelling each term clearly and quickly.

1. Chihuahua	6. Russian Blue	11. German Shepherd
2. parakeet	7. cockatiel	12. Persian
3. calico	8. St. Bernard	13. Basset hound
4. Beagle	9. Egyptian Mau	14. Greyhound
5. Dobermann	10. Rottweiler	15. pigeon

15   *Trouble letters.* The following words and names contain one or more trouble letters. Fingerspell each column using the correct handshapes.

1	2	3	4	5	6	7	8	9	10
Remea	arc	hare	Rhea	wish	chef	Neba	Bette	axle	Iwa
theme	Marc	area	rhyme	wicker	Jeff	nebula	better	lemur	kiwi
creme	arches	Marian	Rhine	twist	effort	Zayneb	Colette	pulley	kiwis
Yemen	parched	Arnold	rhubarb	Swiss	referee	Nebraska	brunette	Lestat	Saiwa

I Want to Know . . .

It takes me a long time to fingerspell. Can I just abbreviate?

Hearing signers often seek ways to avoid fingerspelling, usually by inventing signs or abbreviations. It is understandable since fingerspelling well takes a lot of time and practice. Modifying the language so it is easier for you disrepects ASL and the people who use the language. Using fingerspelling at the appropriate times and doing it well shows you take ASL seriously.

16 *Grocery stores.* Sign a complete sentence using each store name.

1. Safeway
2. Piggly Wiggly
3. QFC
4. Kroger
5. Dominick's
6. Albertson's
7. Whole Foods
8. Trader Joe's
9. Giant
10. Publix
11. Hickory Farms
12. Winn-Dixie
13. Spartan Stores
14. J. Sainsbury
15. Cracker Barrel

FYI See Page 56 to learn how to fingerspell words that include an 's.

17 *Long names.* Fingerspell each name quickly and clearly, keeping your hand in one location.

1. Gwendolyn Hofstetter
2. Suleiman Amin
3. Kathleen Davenport
4. Maximillian Sanderson
5. Alejandro Oliviera
6. Vyvyane Leung Nguyen
7. Tina Letulitas
8. Franklin Winchester
9. Phyllis Jefferson-Immiker
10. Surya Maheshwari

18 *Fingerspelled words.* These words are generally fingerspelled. Learn to spell them quickly and clearly.

1. gerbil
2. hamster
3. cockroach
4. wild
5. triplets
6. spice
7. native
8. Mr.
9. Miss
10. Mrs.

19 *Handshape drills.* Practice fingerspelling each letter combination until your hand becomes used to the shapes.

1	2	3	4	5	6	7	8	9	10
xp	Jin	og	kin	ust	bic	ahi	qui	cede	osh
xe	Jan	fog	Ken	rust	bac	mahi	quip	Cade	nosh
xk	June	bog	kan	roast	bec	kahi	quid	code	posh
xb	Jeff	cog	kiy	Rusty	boc	pahi	quos	cude	Josh
xh	John	dog	koy	rupee	Buck	dahi	squid	cider	Osh-Kosh

20 *Fingerspelling challenge.* Can you spell these words quickly and clearly, and understand them when spelled to you?

1. tarantula
2. terrarium
3. script
4. scraps
5. manifold
6. marigold
7. heartbeat
8. homesick

Unit 8

1 *The planets.* Practice fingerspelling each name clearly and quickly.

1. Uranus
2. Neptune
3. Jupiter
4. Saturn
5. Mercury
6. Venus
7. Pluto
8. Mars
9. Earth

2 *Bodies of water.* Fingerspell the name of a body of water to a partner, who will explain where each is located. Switch roles for 7–12.

1. San Francisco Bay **(California)**
2. Mississippi River **(begins in Minnesota, finishes near New Orleans)**
3. Hudson River **(New York)**
4. Puget Sound **(Washington)**
5. Chesapeake Bay **(Maryland)**
6. Gulf of Mexico **(near Florida, Texas, Alabama, Mississippi, Louisiana)**
7. Lake Michigan **(near Michigan, Wisconsin, Canada)**
8. Pamlico Sound **(North Carolina)**
9. Great Salt Lake **(Utah)**
10. Okeefenokee Swamp **(Florida)**
11. Lake Mead **(Nevada)**
12. Prince William Sound **(Alaska)**

3 *Flowers.* Match the illustration to each flower's name. Fingerspell the flower and then describe what it looks like.

1. daisy
2. rose
3. ivy
4. fern
5. dandelion
6. sunflower
7. carnation
8. tulip
9. daffodil
10. poinsettia

a.
b.
c.
d.
e.
f.
g.
h.
i.
j.

4 *Trouble letters.* The following words and names contain one or more trouble letters. Fingerspell each column using the correct handshapes.

1	2	3	4	5	6	7	8	9	10
Jane	Agra	rule	hunt	urge	Sr.	large	dyes	Traci	vacancy
Adjar	groan	prune	hurry	surge	Sri	Pilar	Hedy	circus	vaccine
Jacob	Grace	rubric	hustle	manure	Sree	Larry	dynamic	cicada	vacuous
Jason	grapple	grumpy	Hungary	urchin	Srivak	Skylar	Arkady	Valencia	vacuum

5   *Famous lakes.* Fingerspell each name clearly and quickly. Remember to pause briefly between words.

1. Great Bear Lake
2. Lake Powell
3. Lake Victoria
4. Lake Havasu
5. Blue Mesa Lake
6. Lake Pontchartrain
7. Lake Erie
8. Navarro Mills Lake
9. Lake Berryessa
10. Lake Chelan
11. Cave Run Lake
12. Lake Superior
13. Lake Champlain
14. Surry Mountain Lake
15. Lake Waccamaw

6   *Tactile fingerspelling.* Do you think you can understand tactile fingerspelling? Try to decode your partner's fingerspelling by placing your hand around the letters. No peeking!

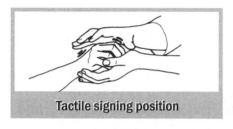

Tactile signing position

bank	Joey	atom
clam	flower	wow
name	Aaron	haha
hope	pencil	panda

1. Fingerspell:

   a. the name of a day of the week

   b. a name (but not your own, or your partner's)

   c. a word from the suggested list

2. When done, discuss the following with your partner:

   a. what was the most difficult part of tactile fingerspelling?

   b. are some letters easier to read than others? Why? Which are they?

   c. what could be done to make it easier to understand tactile fingerspelling?

7   *Oceans & Seas.* When signing about the name of a specific ocean or sea, fingerspell the entire name even though there is a sign for *ocean*. Fingerspell the name of each ocean or sea, holding your hand in one position.

1. Mediterranean Sea
2. Pacific Ocean
3. Black Sea
4. Indian Ocean
5. Bering Sea
6. Sea of Japan
7. Atlantic Ocean
8. Red Sea
9. Andaman Sea
10. South China Sea
11. Yellow Sea
12. Arabian Sea
13. Arctic Ocean
14. Sea of Okhotsk
15. Gulf of Mexico

I Want to Know . . .

How do Deaf-Blind people understand fingerspelling?

As you learned in exercise 6, tactile fingerspelling is challenging. Deaf-Blind individuals learn to read fingerspelling the same way hearing students of ASL do — with practice and exposure. The conversation's context helps to decode tactile fingerspelling. When using tactile signing or fingerspelling, remember that clarity is more important than speed.

8 *Notable mountains.* Explain in a complete sentence where each mountain is found, using the information provided. Instead of fingerspelling *Mount* or *Mt.*, use the *mountain* sign.

Mountain

1. Mt. Rainier **(Washington)**
2. Mt. Everest **(Nepal)**
3. Mt. Logan **(Canada)**
4. Ozark Mountains **(Arkansas)**
5. Bighorn Mountains **(Wyoming)**
6. Allegheny Mountains **(Pennsylvania)**
7. Blue Mountains **(Oregon)**
8. Mt. McKinley **(Alaska)**
9. Mt. Elbert **(Colorado)**
10. Catskills **(New York)**
11. Green Mountains **(Vermont)**
12. Sierra Nevada **(California)**

9 *Anatomy.* Match the functions of the brain with their locations. Fingerspell or sign a function to your partner, who will identify the region of the brain where it is controlled. Switch roles for 9-16.

1. math
2. sight
3. memory
4. walking
5. writing
6. taste
7. sadness
8. speech
9. riding a bike
10. sign language
11. facial expressions
12. happiness
13. hearing
14. breathing
15. smell
16. attention

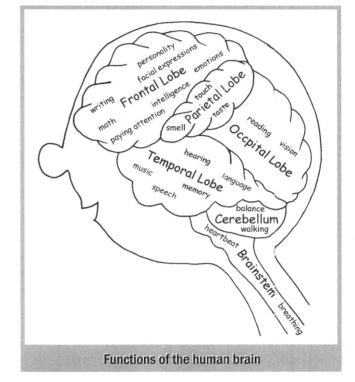
Functions of the human brain

10 *Anatomy II.* Use the Listing and Ordering Technique or the Spatial Organization Technique to identify the functions of the brain. To review — see page 5 for the Listing and Ordering Technique; the Spatial Organization Technique uses shoulder-shifting and the *group* sign to separate details into related groups.

1. Frontal lobe
2. Parietal lobe
3. Temporal lobe
4. Occipital lobe
5. Cerebellum
6. Brainstem

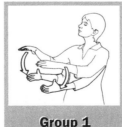
Group 1

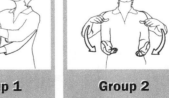
Group 2

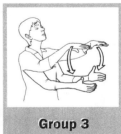
Group 3

11 *Famous deserts.* Fingerspell each name clearly and quickly.

1. Mojave
2. Sahara
3. Namib
4. Painted Desert
5. Gobi
6. Arabian
7. Kalahari
8. Great Sandy Desert
9. Sonora
10. Chihuahua
11. Thar
12. Atacama

12 **A.** *The skeletal system.* What are the names of the major bones in each part of the body? Use the Listing and Ordering Technique.

1. arm
2. foot
3. chest
4. head
5. leg
6. hand

B. *Making connections.* For each pair of bones, state in a complete sentence whether they are connected, nearby, or far from each other.

1. humerus / fibula
2. patella / tibia
3. clavicle / scapula
4. zygomatic bone / mandible
5. phylanges / carpals
6. metatarsals / tarsals
7. spinal column / pelvis
8. ulna / radius
9. ribs / femur
10. sternum / scapula

C. *Where?* Fingerspell the name of a bone to a partner, who will explain where the bone is located.

1. phalanges
2. mandible
3. sternum
4. fibula
5. humerus
6. radius

Accent Steps

Technical terms such as bones are always fingerspelled. When first introducing the term in a conversation, fingerspell the word slightly slower than usual, unless you and your friend are familiar with the context or the technical terminology.

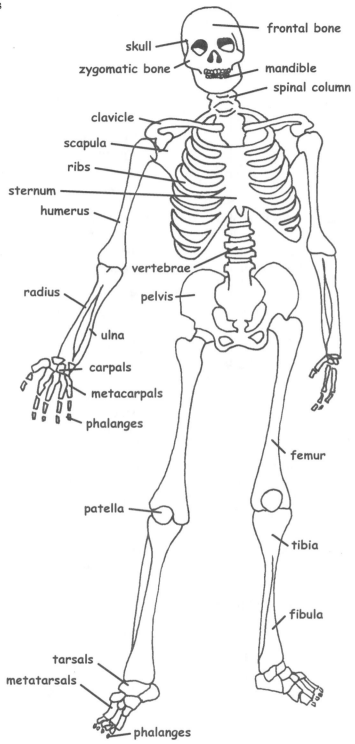

13 *Famous national parks.* Explain in a complete sentence where each park is found.

1. Grand Canyon **(Arizona)**
2. John Muir Woods **(California)**
3. Denali National Park **(Alaska)**
4. Banff **(Canada)**
5. Mesa Verde **(Colorado)**
6. Everglades **(Florida)**
7. Yellowstone **(Wyoming)**
8. Olympic **(Washington)**
9. Mammoth Cave **(Kentucky)**
10. Volcanoes National Park **(Hawaii)**
11. Cahokia Mounds **(Illinois)**
12. Great Smoky Mountains
   (North Carolina, Tennessee)

14 *Native American nations.* Fingerspell each name quickly and clearly. Remember to hold your hand in one place.

1. Mohave
2. Dakota
3. Innupiac
4. Lummi
5. Pima-Maricopa
6. Cherokee
7. Makah
8. Saskatchewan
9. Narragansett
10. Tlingit
11. Wampanoag
12. Crow
13. Kashaya Pomo
14. Mohawk
15. Seminole
16. Penobscot
17. Ohlone
18. Taos Pueblo
19. Chicasaw
20. Keetoowah

15 *Common illnesses.* Ask a partner if he or she has ever had these sicknesses. When done, switch roles and repeat. Follow the example shown below.

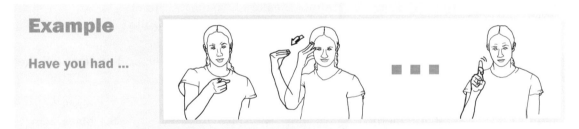

Example

Have you had ...

1. bronchitis
2. influenza
3. cancer
4. mumps
5. chicken pox
6. pneumonia
7. asthma
8. migraine
9. pinworms
10. tonsillitis
11. lice
12. pink eye
13. mono
14. skin rash
15. shingles

16 *Famous naturalists & explorers.* Fingerspell each name clearly and quickly.

1. Lewis and Clark
2. Thor Heyerdahl
3. Sally Ride
4. John Muir
5. Amelia Earhardt
6. Roald Amundsen
7. Ibn Batuta
8. Louise Arner Boyd
9. Marco Polo

17 *At the pharmacy.* Fingerspell the names of these common health-related items quickly and clearly. Remember to hold your hand in one place.

1. Tylenol
2. Nyquil
3. aspirin
4. Colgate
5. Benadryl

6. Dimetapp
7. Advil
8. Listerine
9. Robitussen
10. Alka-Seltzer

11. echinacea
12. Vicks VapoRub
13. Aqua Fresh
14. Neosporin
15. ibuprofen

18 *Fingerspelled words.* These words are generally fingerspelled. Learn to spell them quickly and clearly.

1. conditioner
2. sinus
3. syrup
4. galaxy

5. planet
6. iceberg
7. swamp
8. oak

9. DA (disabled)
10. bay

19 *Handshape drills.* Practice fingerspelling each letter combination until your hand becomes used to the shapes.

1	2	3	4	5	6	7	8	9	10
toe	Ben	iph	King	Noah	lake	pawn	quiz	Jake	sage
Coe	den	oph	Kang	ahoy	bake	pang	quip	Jane	wage
foes	Eng	zph	Kung	Ahna	sake	pats	quilt	jade	page
Joel	Ang	tph	Keng	Hahn	cake	pans	quiet	jail	stage
Coen	Inge	sph	Kong	John	fake	past	Quito	Java	Agean

20 *Fingerspelling challenge.* Can you spell these words quickly and clearly, and understand them when spelled to you?

1. asteroid
2. asterisk

3. meteor
4. method

5. space
6. spice

7. black hole
8. black bear

Unit 9

1 *At the car lot.* You and a Deaf friend are looking for a new vehicle. Fingerspell each name clearly and quickly.

1. Dodge Durango
2. Honda Civic
3. Volkswagen Beetle
4. Toyota Camry
5. Lexus
6. Saturn coupe
7. Mercedes

8. Jeep Cherokee
9. Nissan Sentra
10. Toyota Tundra
11. Mazda Miata
12. Mini Cooper
13. Ford Escape
14. Nissan Xterra

15. Ford Windstar
16. Pontiac convertible
17. Cadillac Seville
18. Chevrolet Tahoe
19. VW Jetta
20. Hyundai Santa Fe

2 *Road trip.* You and several friends are planning a summer road trip and want to visit monuments along the way. Ask a partner where each monument is located. Switch roles for 6–10.

1. Mt. Rushmore **(South Dakota)**
2. Alcatraz **(San Francisco)**
3. Vietnam Memorial **(Washington, D.C.)**
4. Space Needle **(Seattle)**
5. Daytona Speedway **(Florida)**
6. Devil's Tower **(Wyoming)**
7. Independence Hall **(Philadelphia)**
8. Gateway Arch **(St. Louis)**
9. Statue of Liberty **(New York)**
10. The Alamo **(Texas)**

3 *Doing errands.* A friend has a lot of errands to do and wants to know where he or she should go. Answer your partner's questions using the illustrations. Switch roles for 5–8.

1. My camera is broken.
2. I need to buy clothes.
3. I want to buy flowers.
4. I need to go to the bank.
5. I want to eat.
6. I need to exercise.
7. I need to do laundry.
8. Where can I buy a new DVD?

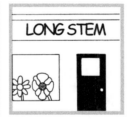

4 *Deaf population centers.* Where have large numbers of Deaf people settled over the years? Fingerspell the name of each location clearly and quickly.

1. Rochester, New York
2. Seattle, Washington
3. Gaithersburg, Maryland
4. Fremont, California
5. Sioux Falls, South Dakota
6. Austin, Texas
7. Washington, D.C.
8. Tucson, Arizona
9. St. Augustine, Florida
10. Los Angeles, California
11. Riverside, California
12. Indianapolis, Indiana
13. Toronto, Ontario
14. Frederick, Maryland
15. Martha's Vineyard, Massachusetts

5 *Trouble letters.* The following words and names contain one or more trouble letters. Fingerspell each column using the correct handshapes.

1	2	3	4	5	6	7	8	9	10
Howe	back	sure	afro	Noelle	basks	Diana	Mawa	slate	niece
Hector	lackey	Ursus	Frank	Noah	skate	zodiac	Sawyer	sleigh	Nievers
halogen	stuck	Turkey	fresh	noisy	Alaskan	codicil	rawhide	slogan	Joanie
Hughes	sickly	Uruguay	afraid	nuisance	skillet	diamond	mawkish	slides	Nietzsche

6   *City parks.* Explain in a complete sentence where each park is located.

1. Boston Common **(Boston)**
2. Rose Garden **(Portland)**
3. Central Park **(New York City)**
4. Millennium Park **(Chicago)**
5. Arboretum **(Seattle)**

6. Golden Gate Park **(San Francisco)**
7. Waterfront Park **(Charleston)**
8. Riverwalk **(San Antonio)**
9. Butchart Gardens **(Victoria)**
10. Rock Creek Park **(Washington, D.C.)**

7   *Hometown locations.* Use CL: Claw Mass to explain where each object is located based on the information provided. Fingerspelled terms are underlined.

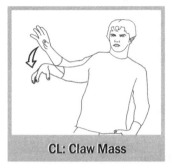

CL: Claw Mass

1. Starbucks is next to Tennis World.
2. The zoo isn't far fom the Grand Hotel.
3. My house is around the corner from the Starry Cafe.
4. Safeway, The Pizza Parlor, and Petsmart are next to each other.
5. Is the Asian restaurant across from or next to Taco Bell?

8   *The Yellow Pages.* Does your hometown have the following stores? Fingerspell each name clearly and quickly.

1. House of Bread
2. Baskin-Robbins
3. Worldwide Travel
4. Barnes and Noble

5. Neiman Marcus
6. Big 5 Sports
7. Perfect Auto
8. IKEA

9. Thrift Ally
10. Rescue Rooter
11. Williams-Sonoma
12. Walgreens

9   *Prices.* Explain the cost of each item in a complete sentence. Fingerspell the underlined terms.

1. Sprite (.65)
2. jeans ($34.00)
3. pizza ($6.50)
4. used car ($500.00)

5. gas ($2.00)
6. tuition ($1,200.00)
7. DVD ($10.00)
8. iced tea (.95)

9. aspirin ($4.33)
10. Dr. Pepper ($1.25)
11. bus ($1.00)
12. mocha ($3.10)

I Want to Know . . .

Why fingerspell a word when a sign exists?

Fingerspell the proper name of a business even when there is a sign that could be used for the entire, or part of, the business' name. This is especially important when giving directions or explaining locations. For example, you would fingerspell *hotel* when signing *My friend is staying at the Grand Hotel*, but not if you signed *The hotel is on the corner of Pine and Lark*. Once the context is established, you can refer to those locations using signs, if desired.

10 *Presidential birthplaces.* Explain in a complete sentence where each president was born. Remember to keep your hand in one place.

1. Harry S. Truman **(Lamar, Missouri)**
2. Bill Clinton **(Hope, Arkansas)**
3. Calvin Coolidge **(Plymouth, Vermont)**
4. John Adams **(Quincy, Massachusetts)**
5. Abraham Lincoln **(Sinking Spring, Kentucky)**
6. George W. Bush **(New Haven, Connecticut)**
7. Ronald Reagan **(Tampico, Illinois)**
8. John F. Kennedy **(Brookline, Massachusetts)**
9. Richard Nixon **(Yorba Linda, California)**
10. Jimmy Carter **(Plains, Georgia)**

11 *At the movie theater.* A local movie theater is hosting film trivia. Match the name of a film with the starring actor. The answer key is at the bottom of the page.

Actors

1. Dustin Hoffman
2. Harrison Ford
3. Marlee Matlin
4. Whoopi Goldberg
5. Tom Hanks
6. Russell Crowe
7. Julia Roberts
8. Denzel Washington
9. Kathy Bates
10. Geena Davis

Movies

a. Gladiator
b. Misery
c. Erin Brockovich
d. Witness
e. Training Day
f. Rain Man
g. Forrest Gump
h. The Color Purple
i. Children of a Lesser God
j. Thelma and Louise

12 *Travel plans.* Ask a partner if he or she wants to travel to each destination, who will respond with the information in parentheses. Use the example shown. Switch roles for 5–8.

Do you want to travel to … ?

1. Peru **(yes, I want to visit Machu Picchu)**
2. Alaska **(yes, but not during the winter)**
3. Paris **(yes, I want to walk up the Eiffel Tower)**
4. New Orleans **(Yes, I want to visit the National D-Day museum)**
5. Antarctica **(no, too cold)**
6. Colorado **(yes, I love to ski)**
7. Chicago **(no, too windy)**
8. Florida **(want to see the Everglades, not Disney World)**

Answer Key:
Exercise 11: 1. f; 2. d; 3. i; 4. h; 5. g; 6. a; 7. c; 8. e; 9. b; 10. j

13 *More strange names.* Fingerspell the name of each strange town name, and explain where it is located.

1. Pumpkin Center, Missouri
2. Plain Dealing, Louisiana
3. Notrees, Texas
4. Left Hand, West Virginia
5. Loco, Oklahoma
6. Boring, Maryland
7. Mary's Igloo, Alaska
8. Buttermilk, Kansas

14 *At the library.* What books are available in the Deaf Studies section of your library? Fingerspell the title and author's name in a complete sentence.

1. *In This Sign,* Joanne Greenberg
2. *Sign and Culture,* William Stokoe
3. *When the Mind Hears,* Harlan Lane
4. *American Deaf Culture,* Sherman Wilcox
5. *The Week the World Heard Gallaudet,* Jack R. Gannon
6. *Deaf History Unveiled,* John Van Cleve
7. *Forbidden Signs,* Douglas C. Baynton
8. *Train Go Sorry,* Leah Hager Cohen
9. *Deaf Like Me,* Thomas & James Spradley
10. *For Hearing People Only,* Matthew Moore

15 *Giving directions.* Select vocabulary from Column A, B, and C to create a complete sentence.

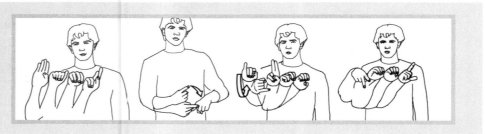

Example

The bank is at the intersection of June and Pool.

Column A	Column B		Column C

Column A

1. Hospital
2. Restaurant
3. Grocery store
4. Post Office
5. Library
6. Bookstore
7. Cafeteria
8. Fire station
9. Bank
10. Hotel

Column B

Pool	Beauregard
Edgar Avenue	Palm Drive
Pierce Street	Third Avenue
June	Stone Way
Post	Pacific Lane
Paseo Padre Pkwy.	Guelph Street
Carrington Blvd.	Dillon Blvd.
St. Clair	Wexler Ave.

Column C

16 *Foreign places.* Fingerspell each name quickly and clearly.

1. Paris, France
2. Berlin, Germany
3. Warsaw, Poland
4. Shanghai, China
5. Lima, Peru
6. Kobe, Japan
7. Tel Aviv, Israel
8. Montreal, Canada
9. Oaxaca, Mexico
10. London, England
11. Lhasa, Tibet
12. Cairo, Egypt
13. Perth, Australia
14. Nassau, Bahamas
15. Bangkok, Thailand
16. Nairobi, Kenya
17. Santiago, Chile
18. Istanbul, Turkey
19. Dakar, Senegal
20. Johannesburg, South Africa

17 *More famous movies.* Fingerspell each name clearly and quickly. Keep your hand in one position.

1. Armageddon
2. Romeo & Juliet
3. Dead Poets Society
4. Gone With the Wind
5. Back to the Future
6. The Exorcist
7. Apollo 13
8. Life is Beautiful
9. Jurassic Park
10. Star Wars
11. Casablanca
12. Bridge Over the River Kwai

18 *Fingerspelled words.* These words are generally fingerspelled. Learn to spell them quickly and clearly.

1. ceramics
2. pottery
3. cavity
4. antique
5. film
6. chopsticks
7. landscape
8. tropical
9. shadow
10. python

19 *Handshape drills.* Practice fingerspelling each letter combination until your hand becomes used to the shapes.

1	2	3	4	5	6	7	8	9	10
rye	lint	yon	mink	vest	Deon	crab	pork	batch	Juan
Ray	dint	yen	Manx	west	neon	Cruz	fork	watch	Joan
Ryan	mint	Yang	Mark	best	Cleo	cramp	cork	match	jolt
roam	hint	ylang	muck	chest	rodeo	crawl	work	catch	Jones
rind	Clint	Yolanda	Mickey	priest	Romeo	Creole	Bork	latch	Joshua

20 *Fingerspelling challenge.* Can you spell these words quickly and clearly, and understand them when spelled to you?

1. cash
2. cashew
3. travel agent
4. travelogue
5. asphalt
6. asparagus
7. money order
8. Montego

Unit 10

1 *Fingerspelled foods.* Many foods are fingerspelled in ASL. Practice spelling each quickly and clearly.

1. ham
2. tuna
3. yogurt
4. soy
5. enchilada
6. beef
7. casserole
8. squash
9. cake
10. pasta
11. jelly
12. ravioli
13. veal
14. pork chops
15. corn
16. chow mein
17. chili
18. rice
19. carrot
20. broccoli

2 *Popular cheeses.* Fingerspell the name of each cheese quickly and clearly.

1.	Cheddar	5.	Provolone	9.	Mozzarella
2.	Swiss	6.	Jarlsberg	10.	Parmesan
3.	cottage cheese	7.	Havarti	11.	Blue cheese
4.	Brie	8.	Gouda	12.	Ricotta

3 *Companies.* Every year Fortune 500 publishes a list of the best companies to work for. Fingerspell the name of the company and explain what kind of business it does.

1. Xilinx **(tech)**
2. Whole Foods Markets **(foods)**
3. Marriott International **(hotel)**
4. New York Times **(news)**
5. Washington Mutual **(bank)**
6. REI **(camping)**
7. Harley Davidson **(motorcycles)**
8. Starbucks **(coffee)**
9. General Mills **(food)**
10. Lenscrafters **(glasses)**

4 *Business acronyms.* Fingerspell an acronym to a partner, who will fingerspell its meaning to you. Switch roles for 9–16.

1.	IBM	5.	HP	9.	NBDA	13.	CBS
2.	NAD	6.	LCSW	10.	PBS	14.	FBI
3.	ABC	7.	NBC	11.	CIA	15.	ASLTA
4.	CPA	8.	RID	12.	MFT	16.	CDC

Marriage and Family Therapist
National Association of the Deaf
Centers for Disease Control
International Business Machines
Central Intelligence Agency
Public Broadcast Station
Hewlett Packard
National Broadcast Channel

Registry of Interpreters for the Deaf
Certified Public Accountant
National Black Deaf Advocates
Federal Bureau of Investigation
Central Broadcast Station
Licensed Clinical Social Worker
American Sign Language Teacher's Association
American Broadcast Corporation

I Want to Know . . .

I see Deaf people using signs instead of fingerspelling names. Why can't I?

When referring to the name of a street or other location that would be known by everyone participating in the conversation, signs will sometimes be substituted for fingerspelling. For example, if *Church Street* is a major road or a frequently used address, the words *church* and *street* may be signed rather than fingerspelled. Substitute signs only when you are certain everybody in the conversation is familiar with the context or if the same term is used repeatedly.

5 *Kitchen spice rack.* All the names of spices and herbs are fingerspelled. Fingerspell each quickly and clearly, developing your rhythm as you go.

1. oregano	6. sage	11. mint	16. rosemary
2. allspice	7. bay leaf	12. dill	17. chili powder
3. thyme	8. anise	13. chives	18. mustard seed
4. ginger	9. celery seed	14. garlic	19. jalapeno
5. marjoram	10. paprika	15. nutmeg	20. cinnamon

6 *What is it?* Into what classification should each creature be grouped? Fingerspell or sign the name of a creature to a partner, who will state into which classification the creature belongs. Switch roles for 11–20. Answers are at the bottom of the page.

1. salmon	11. panda
2. Bengal tiger	12. killer whale
3. frog	13. prawn
4. truffle	14. lizard
5. lobster	15. mushroom
6. snake	16. anaconda
7. bottlenose dolphin	17. salamander
8. leatherback turtle	18. yeast
9. squirrel	19. tuna
10. red snapper	20. alligator

> **Classifications**
>
> crustacean
> fish
> fungus
> amphibian
> mammal
> reptile

7 *Being specific.* Fingerspelling is often used to add clarification when needed. First sign the general meaning (such as *tree*) and then fingerspell the particular variety you have in mind (*oak*). Use this pattern with the signs provided for the following exercise.

1. cabin	5. toolshed	9. sequoia	13. tuberculosis
2. eucalyptus	6. meningitis	10. chrysanthemum	14. redwood
3. asthma	7. evergreen	11. lodge	15. shack
4. palm	8. hibiscus	12. ebola	16. bougainvillea

8 *Types of trees.* Fingerspell the name of each tree quickly and clearly.

1. juniper	5. olive	9. magnolia
2. aspen	6. willow	10. lilac
3. hickory	7. sycamore	11. cypress
4. maple	8. pecan	12. dogwood

9 *Famous chefs.* Fingerspell the name of each chef quickly and clearly.

1. Julia Child
2. Martin Yan
3. Wolfgang Puck
4. James Beard

5. Nigella Lawson
6. Todd English
7. Paul Prudhomme
8. Sheila Lukins

9. Jacques Pepin
10. Alice Waters
11. Emeril Lagasse
12. Nathalie Dupree

10 *Future plans.* Complete each sentence by filling in the blanks with a name and field of study or occupation. You may need to modify a sign using the Agent Marker. An example is provided.

June is majoring in nursing because she wants to be a nurse.

1. _____ _____ is majoring in _____.
2. _____ is not majoring in _____.
3. _____ _____ is not majoring in _____.
4. _____ is majoring in _____. He or she wants to design buildings.

5. _____ will major in _____ or _____.
6. _____ _____ wants to become a _____.
7. _____ is not majoring in _____.
8. _____ is majoring in _____. He or she teach _____.

11 *More occupations.* Sign each sentence in ASL, fingerspelling the underlined terms.

1. My sister is studying <u>architecture</u>. She wants to be an <u>architect</u>.
2. <u>Kesia</u> is a <u>dermatologist</u> at a hospital.
3. I enjoy sports. I will study <u>kinesiology</u> in college.
4. <u>Cheryl Beauchamp</u> works at the police station. She's a <u>parole officer</u>.
5. <u>Trevor Reynolds</u> is studying <u>molecular</u> biology. He wants to be a teacher.

12 *Trouble letters.* The following words and names contain one or more trouble letters. Fingerspell each column quickly, developing speed and rhythm as you go.

1	2	3	4	5	6	7	8	9	10
nuzzle	Basho	warp	Capra	Seiko	Kramer	Yueh	Prevost	Graham	Sheffie
huzzah	shopper	Warsaw	madcap	seize	Kress	Kyushu	pre-law	granny	shellac
buzzard	Tishon	Warren	Cape Breton	Seijman	Kremlin	Ilyusha	predict	gracious	Sherpa
muezzin	shoeshine	warranty	Capricorn	seismic	krypton	yuppie	preamble	grand jury	Arthur Ashe

13 *Foods & shapes.* The context is food; based on the letters and shapes provided, fingerspell the whole term. The answers are at the bottom of the page.

1. `S` ☐ ☐ ☐ `I`
2. ☐ `N` ☐
3. `C` ☐ ☐ `D` ☐ `R`
4. `P` ☐ ☐ `T` ☐

5. `W` ☐ `L` ☐ ☐ ☐
6. ☐ ☐ `C` ☐ ☐ `N` `I`
7. `H` ☐ ☐ ☐ ☐ ☐ `W`
8. ☐ `P` `I` `N` ☐ ☐ `H`

14 *At the restaurant.* Sign each sentence in ASL, fingerspelling the underlined terms.

1. Do you like <u>key lime</u> pie?
2. We want <u>quesedillas</u> and <u>salsa</u> for the <u>appetizer</u>.
3. No, I don't want <u>carrots</u> with the <u>zucchini</u>.
4. I feel like <u>pastry</u> for dessert. Do you want some <u>strudel</u>?
5. Do you want a <u>grilled</u> cheese sandwich or <u>minestrone</u> soup?

15 *Famous zoos.* Explain in a complete ASL sentence where each zoo is located.

1. Bronx Zoo **(New York)**
2. Knowland Park Zoo **(Oakland, California)**
3. Riverbanks Zoo **(Columbia, South Carolina)**
4. San Diego Zoo **(California)**
5. National Zoo **(Washington, D.C.)**
6. Henry Doorly Zoo **(Omaha, Nebraska)**
7. Woodland Park Zoo **(Seattle, Washington)**
8. Audubon Nature Institute **(New Orleans, Louisiana)**
9. Prospect Park **(Brooklyn, New York)**
10. Cincinnati Zoo & Botanical Garden **(Cincinnati, Ohio)**

16 *Fingerspelled occupations.* Many of these terms may be expressed using signs. Fingerspell each word quickly and clearly.

1. CEO
2. architect
3. notary
4. glazier
5. anesthesiologist
6. chef
7. midwife
8. longshoreman
9. tailor
10. orderly
11. consultant
12. hygienist

17 *Animals.* Many animal names are fingerspelled. Fingerspell each word quickly and clearly.

1. sea lion
2. ferret
3. lemur
4. hawk
5. badger
6. porpoise
7. lynx
8. cheetah
9. polar bear
10. jaguar
11. condor
12. meerkat
13. otter
14. swan
15. prairie dog
16. lemming

Answer Key:
Exercise 13: 1. salami; 2. tuna; 3. cheddar; 4. pasta; 5. walnuts; 6. zucchini; 7. honeydew; 8. spinach

18 *Fingerspelled words.* These words are generally fingerspelled. Learn to spell them quickly and clearly.

1. biscuit	3. cavity	5. peer	7. pan	9. motel
2. peas	4. antique	6. marble	8. olive	10. granite

19 *Handshape drills.* Practice fingerspelling each letter combination until your hand becomes used to the shapes.

1	2	3	4	5	6	7	8	9	10
Gere	jinx	Wade	oar	doe	Delia	Hugo	prop	model	skid
Gary	Jill	Dade	oak	shoe	Liang	Hugh	prom	yodel	Trask
Gina	Jax	Eades	Oahu	coe	Liann	Huff	probe	motel	skill
Guam	Juno	fade	Oates	Loeb	Celia	hula	prodigy	hotel	skull
Igor	Jiang	made	Oakley	Loew	liable	humid	prompt	hostel	skimp

20 *Fingerspelling challenge.* Can you spell these words quickly and clearly, and understand them when spelled to you?

1. cauliflower	3. brisket	5. truffle	7. treasurer
2. cornflower	4. basket	6. shuffle	8. presenter

I Want to Know . . .

Plural or Possessive "S"

Occasionally names of stores or companies include an apostrophe s, as in "Macy's." Sign the apostrophe s by turning the final S handshape inward after fingerspelling the name, similar to the Dollar Twist movement. You do not need to "draw" an apostrophe. Practice fingerspelling the following: Dillard's. Cabela's. Chef's. Magellan's. Hecht's

More Fingerspelling Activities

1   *The ABCs.* Complete each task by fingerspelling at a sustained pace from start to finish.

    1. fingerspell the alphabet: A–Z
    2. fingerspell the alphabet: Z–A
    3. fingerspell the vowels: A, E, I, O, U
    4. fingerspell the consonants: B, C, D, F, G, H, J, K, L, M, N, P, Q, R, S, T, V, W, X, Y, Z

2   *Acrostics.* Fingerspell a word beginning with the letter shown, following the example.

EXAMPLE:

I	N	D	I	A
i	n	d	i	a
n	i	i	n	n
v	g	s	v	n
e	h	c	a	e
s	t	l	x	
t		i		
		d		

   1. F O R E S T   **6.** S L I C K   **11.** C I T R U S
   2. R H I N O   **7.** F A Z E   **12.** W H E A T
   3. H E A R T   **8.** Y E L L O W   **13.** A R C H E R Y
   4. C O N T E M P T   **9.** D R A B   **14.** P A P E R
   5. K I M O N O   **10.** M A Y O R   **15.** T R O P H Y

3   *Pangrams.* A pangram is a sentence that uses at least every letter of the alphabet. Fingerspell the pangrams, including very brief pauses between words.

    1. Brick quiz whangs jumpy veldt fox.
    2. The quick brown fox jumps over the lazy dog.
    3. The five boxing wizards jumped quickly.
    4. Hick Jed wins quiz for extra blimp voyage.
    5. A large fawn jumped quickly over white zinc boxes.
    6. Five wine experts jokingly quizzed sample chablis.
    7. Pack my box with five dozen liquor jugs.
    8. How quickly daft jumping zebras vex.

Can you make your own pangram? What words would you use?

4   *Palindromes.* A palindrome is a word or sentence that has the same meaning when read left to right, or right to left, as in the example of E Y E. Fingerspell each palindrome below, focusing on clarity and developing a rhythm.

1. racecar
2. Madam, I'm Adam.
3. never odd or even
4. Some men interpret nine memos.

5. Don't nod.
6. No trace, not one cartoon.
7. May a moody baby doom a yam?
8. Anne, I vote more cars race Rome to Vienna.

5   *Is it a rule or not?* The "i before e" rule is often broken. Fingerspell each word quickly and clearly.

I before E,
Except after C,
Or when sounded as A,
As in neighbor or weigh.

Words following the IE rule		Words that break the IE rule	
beige	receipt	albeit	efficient
ceiling	priest	ancient	protein
conceive	receive	being	reimburse
feign	shield	caffeine	science
field	sleigh	conscience	seize
inveigh	weight	deign	species

6   *Acrostic story.* Create a story by fingerspelling a word beginning with each letter of the alphabet, following the example.

A	B	C	D	E	F	G	H	I	J	K	L	M	N	O	P	Q	R	S	T	U	V	W	X	Y	Z

A	b	C
l	o	a
e	u	r
x	g	o
	h	l
	t	

- work alone, with a partner, a group, or the entire class
- you may use the *period* sign after your word to ensure the story makes sense
- for an additional challenge, select a story topic before beginning

7 *Homonyms.* Part of fingerspelling fluency is being able to spell the word correctly and avoiding common mistakes hearing spellers make. Since Deaf people read English instead of relying on the sound of a word, it is key that you spell the correct word when needed. Fingerspell each group of words clearly and quickly.

1. A	2. B	3. C	4. D	5. E	6. F	7. G	8. H
acts	Barry	cache	days	earn	facts	gnawed	halve
ax	berry	cash	daze	urn	fax	nod	have
axe	bury						
		capital	die	eyelet	fair	grate	hangar
aisle	bases	capitol	dye	islet	fare	great	hanger
I'll	basis						
isle	basses	Chile	discussed		fairy	groan	herd
		chili	disgust		ferry	grown	heard
assent	board	chilly					
ascent	bored						

9. I	10. J	11. K	12. L	13. M	14. N	15. O	16. P
idol	jam	knead	lacks	made	naval	oar	pail
idle	jamb	need	lax	maid	navel	or	pale
						ore	
in	jewel	knight	lead	moose	none		passed
inn	joule	night	led	mousse	nun	one	past
						won	
		know	leased	muscle			presence
		no	least	mussel			presents

17. Q	18. R	19. S	20. T	21. U	22. V	23. W	24. Y
quarts	racket	sachet	tacks	Unix	vain	waist	yoke
quartz	racquet	sashay	tax	eunuchs	vane	waste	yolk
					vein		
quince	rain	scene	Thai	use		ware	you'll
quints	reign	seen	tie	ewes	vial	wear	yule
	rein				vile	where	
		sighs	threw				
		size	through				

8 *Rare spellings.* Can you fingerspell these rare spellings clearly and quickly?

Words ending in -shion
1. cushion
2. fashion

Words with -uu
9. vacuum
10. continuum

Words ending in -dous
3. tremendous
4. horrendous
5. hazardous
6. stupendous

Words with 5 vowels in a row
11. queueing

Words with A, E, I, O, U in order
12. abstemious
13. facetious
14. acheilous
15. caesious
16. annelidous
17. arsenious

Words ending in -gry
7. angry
8. hungry

9 *The Greek alphabet.* Fingerspell the names of the Greek letters clearly and quickly.

1. alpha	**9.** iota	**17.** rho
2. beta	**10.** kappa	**18.** sigma
3. gamma	**11.** lambda	**19.** tau
4. delta	**12.** mu	**20.** upsilon
5. epsilon	**13.** nu	**21.** phi
6. zeta	**14.** dsi	**22.** chi
7. eta	**15.** omikron	**23.** psi
8. theta	**16.** pi	**24.** omega

10 *A group of ...* What is a group of animals or birds called? Complete the sentence using the information provided.

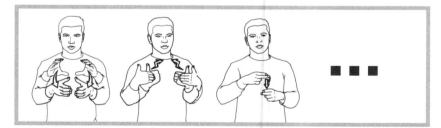

1. giraffes **(tower)**	8. jellyfish **(smack)**	15. parrots **(company)**
2. lions **(pride)**	9. kangaroos **(troop)**	16. cats **(clowder)**
3. monkeys **(troop)**	10. pigs **(drift)**	17. elephants **(herd)**
4. squirrels **(dray)**	11. birds **(flight)**	18. bluejays **(party)**
5. owls **(parliament)**	12. turtles **(bale)**	19. penguins **(colony)**
6. crocodiles **(bask)**	13. flies **(business)**	20. turkeys **(rafter)**
7. sharks **(shiver)**	14. swans **(bevy)**	

Commonly Fingerspelled Terms

A.A. (degree)	Coke	jam	quiz
account	comet	January	recipe
air	comics	jeans	recycle
all	condo	job	rent
Antarctica	context	juice	sale
April	cool	July	scholarship
apt (apartment)	corn	June	season
Asia	DA (disabled)	kill	September
ASL	debit	laser	sidewalk
August	December	law	snack
Ave. (avenue)	deli	lazy	so
B.A. (degree)	den	LCSW (degree)	soon
back	dept. (department)	league	sorority
bakery	did (for emphasis only)	leg	space
bank	disc	M.A. (degree)	spam
BBQ	dog	mall	spice
beach	DVD	March	street
block	early	May	studio
Blvd. (boulevard)	easy	mayo	style
box	email	miles	sunburn
bride	ex	Miss	sure
broil	fact	mortgage	tax
bulb	February	Mr.	toy
burn	feet	Mrs.	truck
bus	fix	MSW (degree)	TTY
bush	fly (insect)	nap	tub
busy	font	news	tuition
but	fool	no	TV
byte	foot	notes	universe
cable	frat (fraternity)	November	van
campus	fresh	October	what (for emphasis only)
car	fruit	off	when (for emphasis only)
carrot	fun	oh	why (for emphasis only)
cash	gallery	ok	wow
casserole	garden	only	xray
cavity	go	or	yes (for emphasis only)
CD	grade	out	zoo
celery	great	over	
ceramics	groom	own	
chance	HC (handicapped)	park	**Other fingerspelled**
cheap	hopeless	Ph.D. (degree)	**terms include:**
chess	human	pizza	
civilization	hurt	planet	States & provinces
clay	ice	pottery	foods
club	if	pro	names of places
Co. (company)	intramural	puppy	technical terms

Numbers

Each activity is designed to develop the skills you need to sign and understand signed numbers. By practicing numbers alone or with a partner and participating in activities during your ASL class, you will learn to sign numbers clearly and confidently.

Note: The numbers in illustrations have been created from left to right, for greater ease of use and comprehension when looking at the illustration. However, the hand moves <u>away</u> from the body when signing numbers.

Numbers: Do's and Don'ts

· Don't jerk, bounce, or move your hand.

· Keep your elbow down, close to your side.

· Hold your hand to the side of your chest, not in front of your face.

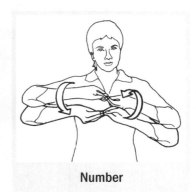

Number

Unit 1

1 *Palm orientation.* Use the correct orientation for the following numbers.

1. 7	**7.** 1	**13.** 4	**19.** 2	**25.** 7
2. 5	**8.** 6	**14.** 7	**20.** 7	**26.** 5
3. 0	**9.** 2	**15.** 1	**21.** 4	
4. 1	**10.** 9	**16.** 0	**22.** 1	
5. 10	**11.** 7	**17.** 5	**23.** 6	
6. 3	**12.** 3	**18.** 3	**24.** 3	

2 *How many?* Sign the number of shapes in each box using the correct handshape and palm orientation.

1.

4.

7.

10.
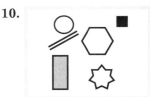

2.

5.

8.

11.

3.

6.
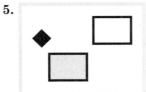

9.

12.

ASL Numbers 0–10

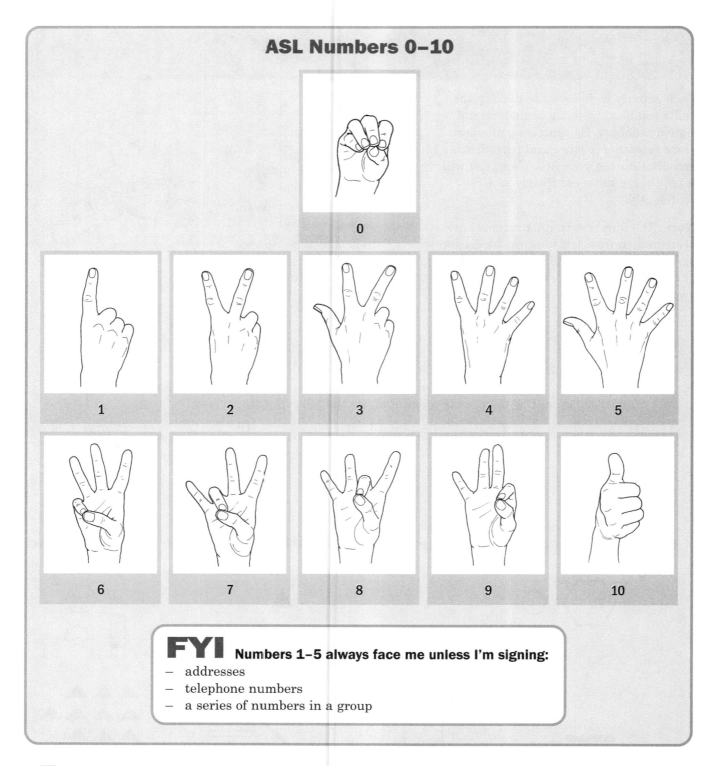

FYI **Numbers 1–5 always face me unless I'm signing:**
- addresses
- telephone numbers
- a series of numbers in a group

3 *Number challenge.* Focus on developing rhythm and maintaining a consistent speed start to finish.

1. sign numbers 0–10 without looking at your hand and without making a mistake
2. sign numbers 10–0 without looking at your hand and without making a mistake
3. sign the even numerals
4. sign the odd numerals

4 *Trouble numbers.* Develop speed and accuracy for each set of numbers.

__1__	__2__	__3__	__4__	__5__	__6__	__7__	__8__	__9__	__10__
0	8	3	6	3	8	7	3	1	6
3	5	3	8	3	8	6	5	3	7
3	1	7	0	3	7	3	7	7	3
7	1	7	3	3	3	0	6	8	0

Accent Steps

Avoid using the *w* sign when you want the numeral 3! While the letter O and the number 0 share the same handshape, confusion rarely occurs unless you're not paying attention to the signed context.

5 *Patterns.* Fill in the missing number that completes the pattern. Sign each number clearly. Answers are at the bottom of the page.

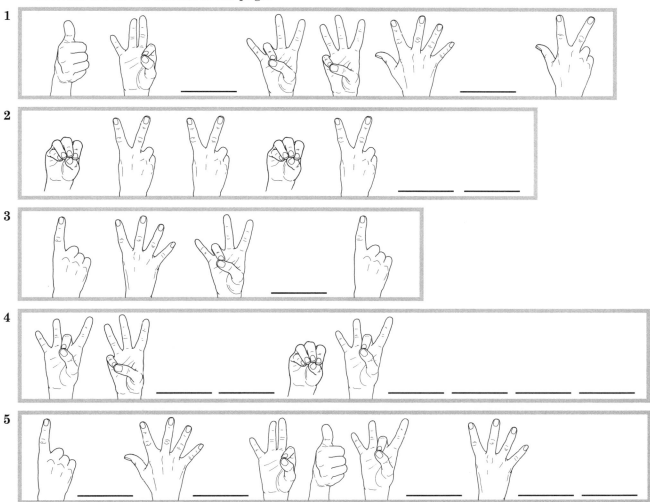

6   *Addition.* **Sign the correct answer to each problem. Answers are at the bottom of the page.**

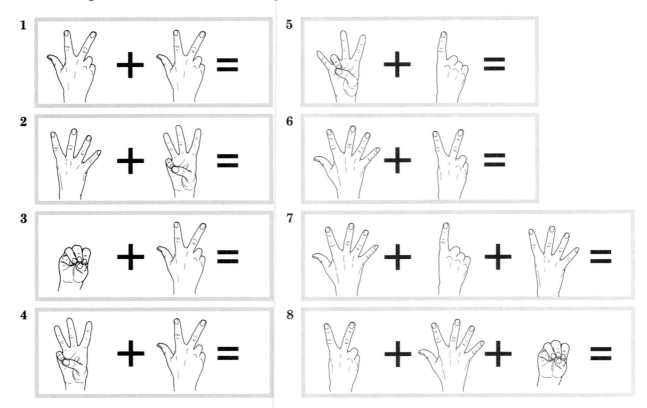

7   *How many is that?* **What number does each word refer to? Fingerspell the word and sign the correct number. Answers are at the bottom of the page.**

1. quint	**4.** quad	**7.** pair	**10.** mono	**13.** hexa
2. sept	**5.** triad	**8.** sext	**11.** deci	**14.** uno
3. duo	**6.** a	**9.** null	**12.** octo	**15.** pente

I Want to Know . . .

Why are numbers 1–5 different than the rest?

How would you sign the band name U2 or not be confused when talking about the strength of sunblock UV-32? To avoid confusion between the number 2 and the letter V as well as other meanings sharing handshapes, numbers 1–5 are twisted inward. When you sign several numbers in a series, the context is clear that you're using numbers, which is why 1–5 face outward in telephone numbers and addresses. This difference is less obvious when signing a number not surrounded by others. ASL students tend to think the inward / outward orientation doesn't matter, but it does.

8 | *Subtraction.* Sign the correct answer to each problem.

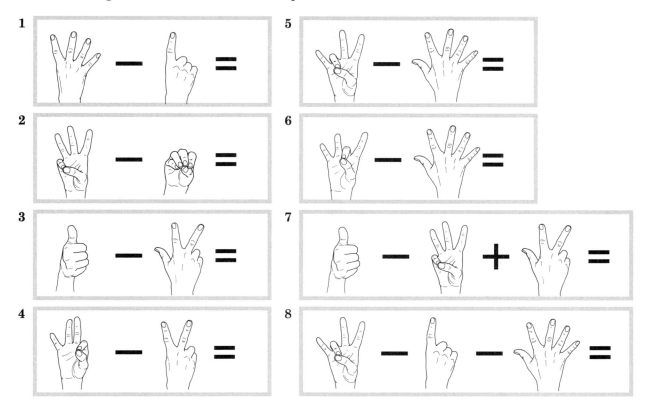

9 | *What number are you?* You and a Deaf friend are waiting for your number to be called. Explain in a complete sentence which numbers are being called. Follow the example below.

He or she is number two.

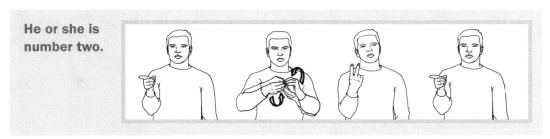

1. We are number 8.
2. She's number 3.
3. I'm number 4.
4. They're number 7.

5. Are you number 4?
6. He's number 6.
7. You are number 2, I'm number 5.

8. We're number 10.
9. They're number 3.

10 | *Number drill.* Develop speed and accuracy for each set of numbers.

1	2	3	4	5	6	7	8	9	10
9	0	6	8	6	2	6	8	1	7
4	2	7	2	3	9	2	10	3	9
5	3	10	1	0	7	4	4	2	6
3	1	4	7	4	10	1	5	5	10

Unit 2

1 *Numbers 11–20.* Develop accuracy with each number.

1. 20	**7.** 17	**13.** 11	**19.** 19	**25.** 20
2. 11	**8.** 18	**14.** 15	**20.** 13	**26.** 11
3. 16	**9.** 12	**15.** 18	**21.** 12	
4. 13	**10.** 20	**16.** 16	**22.** 19	
5. 15	**11.** 13	**17.** 17	**23.** 15	
6. 16	**12.** 14	**18.** 20	**24.** 18	

2 *Number challenge.* Focus on developing rhythm and maintaining a consistent speed start to finish.

1. sign numbers 11–20 without looking at your hand or without making a mistake
2. sign numbers 0–20 without looking at your hand or without making a mistake
3. sign the even numbers 0–20
4. sign the odd numbers 0–20

3 *Vertical drills.* Develop speed and accuracy for each column of numbers. Hold your hand higher than the regular fingerspelling location and move your hand slightly lower with each number, to show the column.

1	2	3	4	5	6	7	8	9	10
11	9	8	0	19	11	17	6	9	3
20	12	7	5	15	12	18	16	11	13
15	10	17	10	16	13	19	8	13	5
14	18	18	11	8	14	20	18	15	15
15	19	9	15	4	15	1	9	17	7
13	20	19	20	2	16	2	19	19	17

11	12	13	14	15	16	17	18	19	20
5	20	15	12	3	19	18	11	13	4
6	19	15	12	11	19	3	5	16	19
11	18	14	13	4	17	3	18	15	15
12	17	14	15	12	15	18	9	15	14
7	16	14	15	20	13	17	20	14	16
8	15	15	11	5	19	16	10	13	17
15	12	16	18	16	14	13	18	17	13
5	4	20	14	19	18	16	11	20	15
19	0	6	11	14	20	19	12	6	17
11	17	16	12	17	3	18	10	16	18

ASL Numbers 11—20

 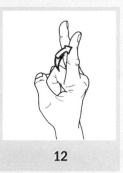

11 12

The numbers 11 and 12 are formed by flicking the necessary fingers up from the S handshape. Flick the fingers once.

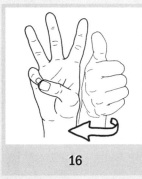 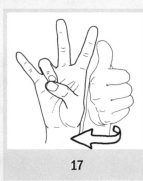 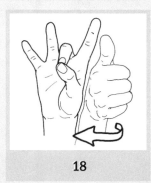

13 14 15

Numbers 13, 14, and 15 involve opening and closing their hand-shapes twice. Note the thumb is not extended for the number 14, unlike 13 and 15.

 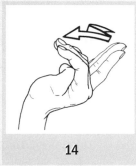 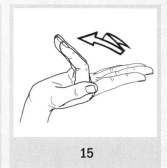 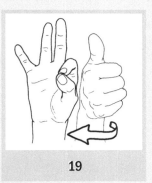

16 17 18 19

Numbers 16, 17, 18, and 19 are made by combining the number 10 with 6, 7, 8, and 9. Hold the number 10 handshape inward, and as you move your wrist outward add the second number. Think of these numbers as 10 and 6, 10 and 7, 10 and 8, 10 and 9.

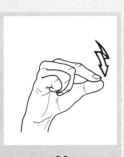

20

Tap your index finger and thumb together twice for the number 20.

4 *Horizontal drills.* In the previous exercise you signed the numbers to show a vertical column. Adapt the technique while signing numbers in a horizontal row. Develop speed and accuracy for each set of numbers. Pause briefly between each number.

1. 12, 13, 14, 15, 16, 18	**5.** 11, 6, 18, 12	**9.** 15, 20, 17, 18, 19, 6
2. 3, 4, 5, 10, 20	**6.** 20, 9, 14, 18, 19	**10.** 11, 14, 17, 20, 19, 5
3. 18, 19, 10, 11, 12	**7.** 16, 15, 3, 17, 4	**11.** 13, 12, 15, 14, 17, 16
4. 0, 4, 12, 17, 7, 19	**8.** 13, 19, 12, 20, 17	**12.** 20, 14, 12, 11, 18, 19

5 *Shape drills.* Sign the following number sets following the patterns shown, applying the same principle you used for the previous exercises.

1.
```
15   12   17
11        20
16        13
19        18
12   18   14
```

2.
```
16   10   15
12        20
17        18
20        12
14   17   11
```

3.
```
12   17   14   10
20             18
18             16
16             15
11   13   18   12
```

4.
```
11   12   13   14
19             14
18             16
17             17
16   20   19   18
```

5.
```
     12
16        10
19        14
  15    20
     17
```

6.
```
     13
20        15
12        17
  13    11
     14
```

7.
```
     17
11        19
15        10
18        14
     17
```

8.
```
     11
   16  17
  13     20
15   14   19
```

9.
```
     10
  14 16
 19    15
20     13
17  19  11
```

10.
```
     12
   16 19
 15     12
10       16
18   14   10
```

Accent Steps

Think visually when signing numbers. If you were describing an athlete's jersey number, where would you place the numbers? That's right — in front of your chest!

I Want to Know . . .

Do numbers 16-19 have to include the number 10?

Some Deaf people sign the numbers 16, 17, 18, and 19 without beginning with the number 10. You will not see this variant used as often as the style shown on page 69. In the general style, the signer says 10 (plus) 6 to mean 16 and follows the pattern up to 19. While the number 10 is not made with the variant style of numbers 16 through 19, the wrist flick conveys the number 10. Become familiar with both styles and follow the system used by your local Deaf community.

ASL Numbers 21–30

Learning ASL numbers 0–30 present the most difficulty for students because of the many patterns and exceptions that must be remembered. Numbers 21–30 present another series of patterns. Before you begin, review the ASL numbers you've learned so far:

1. Numbers 1–5 face inward (unless in a sequence of other numbers).
2. Numbers 6–10 always face outward.
3. Numbers 11–12 flick upward from an S handshape.
4. Numbers 13–15 wave the fingers back and forth. Note the thumb is not open for 14.
5. Numbers 16–19 are made by forming the number 10 plus 6, 7, 8, and 9.
6. Number 20 taps the index finger and thumb together.

Numbers 21–29 all use the L handshape as a base, like saying "20 and 1." Numbers 22 and 25 are exceptions to this pattern.

21

The palm must face down for number 22. Numbers 33, 44, 55, follow this pattern. Numbers 66, 77, 88, and 99 also face down but not as much.

22

23

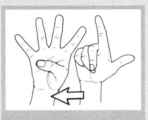

24

25

There are two ways to sign the number 25. The one shown here is most common, though some use the L handshape followed by the number 5.

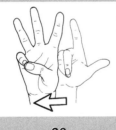

26

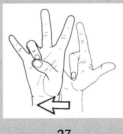

27

28

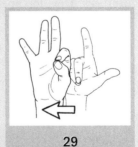

29

30

Close the 3 handshape into 0 to form 30.

6 *Attendance.* Explain in a complete sentence how many students are learning ASL in each class. An example is provided.

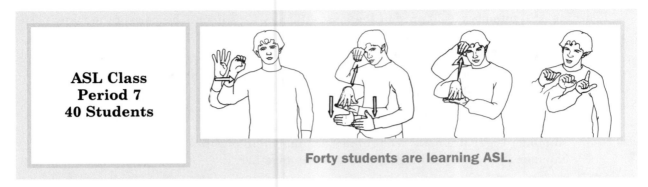

**ASL Class
Period 7
40 Students**

Forty students are learning ASL.

1.
ASL Class Period 1
30 Students

4.
ASL Class Period 4
23 Students

2.
ASL Class Period 2
28 Students

5.
ASL Class Period 5
22 Students

3.
ASL Class Period 3
24 Students

6.
ASL Class Period 6
8 Students

7 *Trouble numbers.* Develop speed and accuracy for each set of numbers.

1	2	3	4	5	6	7	8	9	10
22	29	30	21	29	28	22	23	29	27
28	23	23	28	20	25	27	27	26	23
25	21	25	27	30	21	29	26	20	22
23	24	20	24	27	22	21	23	22	29
20	26	22	22	22	29	20	28	25	30

11	12	13	14	15	16	17	18	19	20
3	8	16	11	8	2	16	7	20	19
13	18	26	22	18	12	6	27	21	9
23	28	19	25	28	22	26	17	22	12
5	10	29	29	4	14	28	30	23	11
15	20	15	19	14	24	29	24	25	22
25	30	25	18	24	30	27	15	27	23

8 *When is it?* You and a Deaf friend are making plans to go to a local Deaf event. Use the calendar to help you explain when the Deaf event will be held. An example is provided. Note that the sign for *event* is the same as *what's up*.

The Deaf event is on Tuesday, the 15th.

1

2

3

4

5

6

7

8

9

10

11

12

9 *Horizontal drills.* Sign each row of numbers quickly and accurately, filling in the blank with the missing number.

1. 29, 27, 25, ___, 21, 19
2. 18, 19, ___, 21, ___
3. 15, 20, ___, 30
4. 5, 10, ___, ___, 25, 30
5. 30, 27, 24, ___, ___
6. 17, ___, 23, 26, ___

7. 3, ___, 6, 9, 11, ___
8. 30, 29, ___, 27, ___
9. 11, 22, 11, ___, ___
10. 18, ___, 20, ___, 22
11. 3, 6, 12, ___
12. 4, 8, ___, 16, ___, ___

13. 19, ___, 23, ___, 27, ___
14. 18, 20, ___, 24, ___, 28, ___
15. 14, 18, ___, 26, ___
16. 25, 26, ___, 28, ___, ___
17. 6, ___, 16, 21, ___,
18. 9, 12, ___, 18, 21, ___, 27

10 *Number drill.* Develop speed and accuracy for each set of numbers.

1	2	3	4	5	6	7	8	9	10
12	27	4	20	4	23	21	18	9	22
20	24	12	27	19	11	16	22	13	23
18	21	24	30	27	9	19	27	24	25
15	11	30	3	25	17	2	29	28	28
13	19	15	10	21	22	29	12	30	29
29	17	23	15	20	28	0	16	3	14

11	12	13	14	15	16	17	18	19	20
14	28	6	5	7	23	18	3	15	14
20	25	13	18	29	21	27	29	28	24
30	23	28	22	26	25	26	24	27	26
10	22	30	23	12	29	29	23	16	28
8	19	29	30	19	20	21	20	0	4
12	8	27	17	25	27	23	21	30	9

ASL Numbers 1–30 Review

Can you:

1. Sign the numbers 0–30 quickly, without making a mistake?
2. Understand the numbers 0–30 when signed to you?
3. Identify the numbers you struggle to sign and understand?
4. Explain the number patterns for numbers 0–30?

Answer the following:

1. These numbers always face inward, unless in a series.
2. The L handshape is used with these numbers.
3. These numbers involve wiggling one or more fingers.
4. The 10 handshape is incorporated into these numbers.
5. These numbers always face down.

Unit  3

1 *Numbers 31–100.* Develop accuracy with each number.

1. 39	**7.** 60	**13.** 44	**19.** 55	**25.** 80
2. 85	**8.** 99	**14.** 73	**20.** 81	**26.** 62
3. 52	**9.** 36	**15.** 50	**21.** 34	**27.** 63
4. 63	**10.** 100	**16.** 32	**22.** 64	**28.** 95
5. 71	**11.** 90	**17.** 84	**23.** 75	**29.** 48
6. 58	**12.** 94	**18.** 47	**24.** 48	**30.** 28

2 *Number challenge.* Focus on developing rhythm and maintaining a consistent speed start to finish.

1. sign numbers 0–100 without looking at your hand or making a mistake
2. sign the even numbers 0–100
3. sign the odd numbers 0–100
4. sign the numbers that face downward
5. sign the numbers that move towards the body
6. sign the numbers that move away from the body

3 *Number exceptions.* Develop accuracy with each number.

1. 66	**7.** 78	**13.** 96	**19.** 44	**25.** 23
2. 67	**8.** 79	**14.** 97	**20.** 55	**26.** 25
3. 68	**9.** 86	**15.** 98	**21.** 13	**27.** 67
4. 69	**10.** 87	**16.** 99	**22.** 14	**28.** 98
5. 76	**11.** 88	**17.** 22	**23.** 15	**29.** 69
6. 77	**12.** 89	**18.** 33	**24.** 21	**30.** 76

4 *Vertical drills.* Develop speed and accuracy for each column of numbers. Hold your hand higher than the regular fingerspelling location and move your hand slightly lower with each number, to show the column.

1	2	3	4	5	6	7	8	9	10
88	67	23	77	69	86	6	62	23	35
52	92	17	8	25	24	75	86	5	17
100	43	18	23	4	0	18	2	100	4
49	21	3	84	29	97	76	94	57	61
25	50	99	36	33	36	20	89	65	76
19	83	87	48	90	44	66	15	88	89

I Want to Know . . .

Are using the number exceptions really important?

As you learned with the difference between the number 2 and the letter V, these number exceptions have developed over time for purposes of clarity. In some cases incorporating movement into number signs makes them more comfortable to sign or easier to move on to another sign in a conversation. It will take time, practice, and effort to become comfortable with the number exceptions, but it is important to be able to understand them when signed to you.

ASL Numbers 31–100

Numbers 31–99 are signed the way they are written: 3 1, 3 2, 3 3, and so on, with a few exceptions. Avoid signing numbers the way they are spoken, as in 30 1, 30 2, et cetera. Reminder: Numbers 33, 44, 55 face the floor, and 66, 77, 88 and 99 are signed at a slightly higher angle.

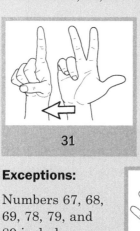

31

39

40

50

Exceptions:

Numbers 67, 68, 69, 78, 79, and 89 include a specific movement towards the body.

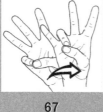

67

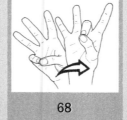

68

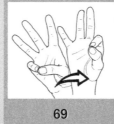

69

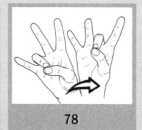

78

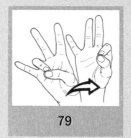

79

89

Exceptions:

Numbers 76, 86, 87, 96, 97, and 98 include a specific movement away from the body.

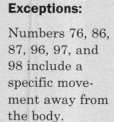

76

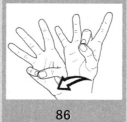

86

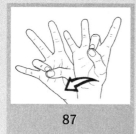

87

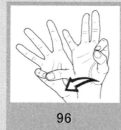

96

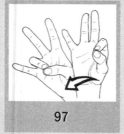

97

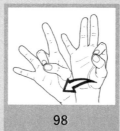

98

100

Form the 100 sign by changing the number 1 into the letter C. As you make the letter C, move the handshape towards your torso.

5 *Hundreds practice.* Practice signing each number clearly.

1. 100	**4.** 400	**7.** 700
2. 200	**5.** 500	**8.** 800
3. 300	**6.** 600	**9.** 900

6 *What page is that?* In a complete sentence, explain what to do with each page. Use the suggested vocabulary and the example if needed.

We need to read page 40.

1. 10	**6.** 82, 83	**11.** 96	**16.** 389	**21.** 212
2. 94	**7.** 100	**12.** 105	**17.** 525	**22.** 99, 100
3. 76	**8.** 40	**13.** 240	**18.** 423	**23.** 375
4. 20, 21, 22	**9.** 52, 53	**14.** 175	**19.** 941	**24.** 500
5. 14, 15, 16	**10.** 65, 75, 85	**15.** 322	**20.** 753	**25.** 855

ASL Numbers 100–999

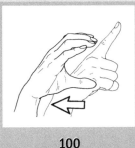

100

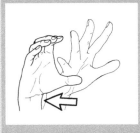

500

Numbers 100–900 use the *hundred* sign paired with a particular number. When signing mixed numbers such as 510, sign them the way they are spoken: Five hundred ten. For numbers beyond 999, avoid using the construct 11 hundred or 13 hundred. You will learn how to use that feature in Unit 4.

7 *Mixed numbers.* Develop speed and accuracy for each column of numbers. Hold your hand higher than the regular fingerspelling location and move your hand slightly lower with each number, to show the column.

1	**2**	**3**	**4**	**5**	**6**	**7**	**8**	**9**	**10**
1	11	21	31	41	51	61	71	81	91
2	12	22	32	42	52	62	72	82	92
3	13	23	33	43	53	63	73	83	93
4	14	24	34	44	54	64	74	84	94
5	15	25	35	45	55	65	75	85	95
6	16	26	36	46	56	66	76	86	96
7	17	27	37	47	57	67	77	87	97
8	18	28	38	48	58	68	78	88	98
9	19	29	39	49	59	69	79	89	99
10	20	30	40	50	60	70	80	90	100

11	**12**	**13**	**14**	**15**	**16**	**17**	**18**	**19**	**20**
101	111	121	131	141	151	161	171	181	191
102	112	122	132	142	152	162	172	182	192
103	113	123	133	143	153	163	173	183	193
104	114	124	134	144	154	164	174	184	194
105	115	125	135	145	155	165	175	185	195
106	116	126	136	146	156	166	176	186	196
107	117	127	137	147	157	167	177	187	197
108	118	128	138	148	158	168	178	188	198
109	119	129	139	149	159	169	179	189	199
110	120	130	140	150	160	170	180	190	200

21	**22**	**23**	**24**	**25**	**26**	**27**	**28**	**29**	**30**
201	211	221	231	241	251	261	271	281	291
202	212	222	232	242	252	262	272	282	292
203	213	223	233	243	253	263	273	283	293
204	214	224	234	244	254	264	274	284	294
205	215	225	235	245	255	265	275	285	295
206	216	226	236	246	256	266	276	286	296
207	217	227	237	247	257	267	277	287	297
208	218	228	238	248	258	268	278	288	298
209	219	229	239	249	259	269	279	289	299
210	220	230	240	250	260	270	280	290	300

31	**32**	**33**	**34**	**35**	**36**	**37**	**38**	**39**	**40**
301	311	321	331	341	351	361	371	381	391
302	312	322	332	342	352	362	372	382	392
303	313	323	333	343	353	363	373	383	393
304	314	324	334	344	354	364	374	384	394
305	315	325	335	345	355	365	375	385	395
306	316	326	336	346	356	366	376	386	396
307	317	327	337	347	357	367	377	387	397
308	318	328	338	348	358	368	378	388	398
309	319	329	339	349	359	369	379	389	399
310	320	330	340	350	360	370	380	390	400

41	42	43	44	45	46	47	48	49	50
401	411	421	431	441	451	461	471	481	491
402	412	422	432	442	452	462	472	482	492
403	413	423	433	443	453	463	473	483	493
404	414	424	434	444	454	464	474	484	494
405	415	425	435	445	455	465	475	485	495
406	416	426	436	446	456	466	476	486	496
407	417	427	437	447	457	467	477	487	497
408	418	428	438	448	458	468	478	488	498
409	419	429	439	449	459	469	479	489	499
410	420	430	440	450	460	470	480	490	500

8 *Email.* Fill in the blanks with numbers or letters to complete the email address. Sign the address in a complete sentence. An example is provided.

Her email address is rae@nd.com.

1. 21sharon@___.edu
2. __7@neville.com
3. ___@k12.ca.us
4. johnb45@___.___
5. barbara___@horizon2.net
6. rex@129.com

7. aslstudent8@___.___.___
8. pp23@___.edu
9. gadgets@100toys.com
10. ___@fed4.gov
11. account95@___.bank
12. kp392@___.edu

13. lori17@emailcanada.ca
14. ___@2favoriteshow.tv
15. tyrells@4city.___
16. ___@8want.info
17. ___76@yahoo.___
18. ___@67.___

9 *IP addresses.* Sign each IP address clearly.

1. 12.223.27.14
2. 184.16.19.221
3. 18.10.254.43
4. 33.29.38.67

5. 14.28.50.12
6. 78.39.17.221
7. 11.68.69.40
8. 187.77.94.94

9. 90.86.35.19
10. 37.17.10.25
11. 12.12.38.54
12. 8.34.26.38

I Want to Know . . .

How do I know when to use the *hundred* sign?

When you see a number like 794 standing alone, it's likely you pronounce it as seven hundred ninety four, and it would be signed the same way. But when you see the same number paired with another, like 794-2, you would pronounce it seven nine four dash two - and this is the same way it is signed. Just remember that if numbers are in groups you usually don't need to use the *hundred* sign.

10 *What is today's date?* Follow the example to sign each date in a complete sentence.

Today's date is February 9th.

1. April 23	8. September 27	15. March 22	22. April 19
2. October 31	9. July 5	16. July 7	23. September 1
3 January 25	10. February 12	17. December 10	24. January 28
4. March 14	11. November 18	18. May 21	25. June 15
5. August 29	12. June 30	19. August 9	
6. May 24	13. October 3	20. January 16	
7. December 13	14. August 31	21. November 7	

11 *Addresses.* Sign each address clearly. When signing a sequence of numbers, such as telephone numbers or addresses, simply sign each number the way they are written. For three-digit sequences like 244, don't sign 200 44 but 2 4 4. See the Accent Step below for related information.

1. 575 Sunrise Court	9. 2185 Castiglione Way	17. 719 Emerson Court
2. 31 Henderson Way	10. 8 Brickell Way	18. 4597 Highpoint Way
3. 148 Medford Avenue	11. 544 Shenandoah Place	19. 7634 East 84th
4. 16939 Sycamore	12. 48708 Creekwood Drive	20. 108 Alvarado Blvd.
5. 5447 Village Common	13. 8024 Kilcare Road	21. 5418 6th Avenue North
6. 3924 Red Rock Terrace	14. 5439 Crow Canyon	22. 6523 Lexington Avenue
7. 6090 Joaquin Street	15. 89223 Revere Avenue	23. 7004 Middlefield Loop
8. 32206 Almaden Blvd.	16. 167 Mesa Corner	24. 1055 El Camino Real

Accent Steps

With four-digit series you can sign the numbers individually or group them into pairs. For example, you could sign 4850 as 4 8 50 or 48 50. However, don't do this with longer addresses! The general rule is to sign numbers the way they are written, not heard.

FYI You don't need to fingerspell the -th, -st, or -nd as part of a name like West 152nd Street.

12 *Area codes.* Use the information provided to explain where each area code is found. Since the numbers are in a series, don't flip your wrist for area codes including the numbers 1–5.

<u>1</u>	<u>2</u>	<u>3</u>	<u>4</u>
201 (New Jersey)	650 (California)	260 (Indiana)	901 (Tennessee)
202 (Washington, DC)	651 (Minnesota)	262 (Wisconsin)	903 (Texas)
203 (Connecticut)	659 (Alabama)	267 (Pennsylvania)	904 (Florida)
204 (Manitoba)	660 (Missouri)	269 (Michigan)	906 (Michigan)
205 (Alabama)	662 (Mississippi)	270 (Kentucky)	907 (Alaska)
206 (Washington)	667 (Maryland)	276 (Virginia)	913 (Kansas)
207 (Maine)	678 (Georgia)	480 (Arizona)	937 (Ohio)
208 (Idaho)	689 (Florida)	503 (Oregon)	939 (Puerto Rico)
209 (California)	701 (North Dakota)	505 (New Mexico)	970 (Colorado)
210 (Texas)	702 (Nevada)	508 (Massachusetts)	985 (Louisiana)

FYI You don't need to use the *hundred* sign for area codes. Sign them the way they are written.

13 *Telephone numbers.* Sign each set of telephone number clearly and quickly. Since the numbers are in a series, don't flip your wrist for the numbers 1–5. Remember that you can divide the last four numbers into groups of two.

<u>1</u>	<u>2</u>	<u>3</u>	<u>4</u>	<u>5</u>
823-8092	793-1010	481-1600	266-7503	538-9400
264-1104	538-8884	698-6721	582-4345	733-8118
295-0205	657-6741	792-3350	790-9221	788-3452
838-4647	582-4667	803-8855	485-2953	226-6485
713-9553	351-8524	493-2222	346-6400	670-1118
249-9941	924-5469	526-8328	354-3210	792-0234
581-1312	490-6537	750-4492	518-1293	560-9375
377-9205	252-0505	886-7614	657-1782	248-8200
945-9733	622-6220	441-1140	484-1747	490-1125
795-4231	725-0077	301-5462	312-0466	888-9166
651-9790	481-5070	662-6298	582-8498	829-6360
781-5291	882-3921	963-5521	490-7902	309-3233
733-8275	778-5325	317-8777	651-1881	441-1139
278-7788	299-7066	559-1011	222-4051	307-9871
616-2314	623-9778	656-7823	786-1639	588-1620
213-1592	796-9323	267-3200	949-5319	820-1707
337-0467	453-4747	825-5467	793-0492	356-0322
744-0802	803-1239	352-3203	204-9555	764-3711
583-1654	489-6881	595-9542	612-3041	522-4967
414-3134	653-2093	603-2901	907-2987	481-2056

14 *More mixed numbers.* Develop speed and accuracy for each column of numbers. Hold your hand higher than the regular fingerspelling location and move your hand slightly lower with each number, to show the column.

<u>1</u>	<u>2</u>	<u>3</u>	<u>4</u>	<u>5</u>	<u>6</u>	<u>7</u>	<u>8</u>	<u>9</u>	<u>10</u>
501	511	521	531	541	551	561	571	581	591
502	512	522	532	542	552	562	572	582	592
503	513	523	533	543	553	563	573	583	593
504	514	524	534	544	554	564	574	584	594
505	515	525	535	545	555	565	575	585	595
506	516	526	536	546	556	566	576	586	596
507	517	527	537	547	557	567	577	587	597
508	518	528	538	548	558	568	578	588	598
509	519	529	539	549	559	569	579	589	599
510	520	530	540	550	560	570	580	590	600

<u>11</u>	<u>12</u>	<u>13</u>	<u>14</u>	<u>15</u>	<u>16</u>	<u>17</u>	<u>18</u>	<u>19</u>	<u>20</u>
601	611	621	631	641	651	661	671	681	691
602	612	622	632	642	652	662	672	682	692
603	613	623	633	643	653	663	673	683	693
604	614	624	634	644	654	664	674	684	694
605	615	625	635	645	655	665	675	685	695
606	616	626	636	646	656	666	676	686	696
607	617	627	637	647	657	667	677	687	697
608	618	628	638	648	658	668	678	688	698
609	619	629	639	649	659	669	679	689	699
610	620	630	640	650	660	670	680	690	700

<u>21</u>	<u>22</u>	<u>23</u>	<u>24</u>	<u>25</u>	<u>26</u>	<u>27</u>	<u>28</u>	<u>29</u>	<u>30</u>
701	711	721	731	741	751	761	771	781	791
702	712	722	732	742	752	762	772	782	792
703	713	723	733	743	753	763	773	783	793
704	714	724	734	744	754	764	774	784	794
705	715	725	735	745	755	765	775	785	795
706	716	726	736	746	756	766	776	786	796
707	717	727	737	747	757	767	777	787	797
708	718	728	738	748	758	768	778	788	798
709	719	729	739	749	759	769	779	789	799
710	720	730	740	750	760	770	780	790	800

<u>31</u>	<u>32</u>	<u>33</u>	<u>34</u>	<u>35</u>	<u>36</u>	<u>37</u>	<u>38</u>	<u>39</u>	<u>40</u>
801	811	821	831	841	851	861	871	881	891
802	812	822	832	842	852	862	872	882	892
803	813	823	833	843	853	863	873	883	893
804	814	824	834	844	854	864	874	884	894
805	815	825	835	845	855	865	875	885	895
806	816	826	836	846	856	866	876	886	896
807	817	827	837	847	857	867	877	887	897
808	818	828	838	848	858	868	878	888	898
809	819	829	839	849	859	869	879	889	899
810	820	830	840	850	860	870	880	890	900

41	**42**	**43**	**44**	**45**	**46**	**47**	**48**	**49**	**50**
901	911	921	931	941	951	961	971	981	991
902	912	922	932	942	952	962	972	982	992
903	913	923	933	943	953	963	973	983	993
904	914	924	934	944	954	964	974	984	994
905	915	925	935	945	955	965	975	985	995
906	916	926	936	946	956	966	976	986	996
907	917	927	937	947	957	967	977	987	997
908	918	928	938	948	958	968	978	988	998
909	919	929	939	949	959	969	979	989	999
910	920	930	940	950	960	970	980	990	

15 *Skills review.* Sign each item quickly and clearly.

1. Addresses

Their address is 5256 Glenmoor Drive.
His address is 47 Talbot Lane.
My pager address is travis10@67blue.com.
We live at 88651 Le Conte Way.
Her email address is butterfly24@44pi.net.

2. Dates

July 30	December 14
October 11	April 8
February 16	September 27
November 29	May 23
August 25	January 15

3. Mixed Numbers

45	33	55
66	87	68
76	44	617
50	972	800
100	523	760

4. Telephone

231-3988
796-9523
885-0450
539-6767
644-3949

5. Using Numbers

Please study pages 245-255.
My telephone number is (   ) ___ - _____.
My email address is _____.
My birthday is _____ __.

ASL Numbers 31–999 Review

Can you:

1. Sign numbers 31–999 without making a mistake?
2. Understand the numbers 31–999 when signed to you?
3. Identify the numbers you struggle to sign and understand?
4. Explain the number patterns and exceptions?

Answer the following:

1. When do you use the *hundred* handshape? When do you not?
2. Explain how to sign the numbers 67, 68, 69, 76, 78, 79, 86, 87, 89, 96, 97, 98.
3. What are two different examples of a number series?
4. What is an example of a series of numbers signed the way they are written?
5. Explain the different ways you can and cannot sign this number: 8254.

Unit 4

1 *Numbers 1,000–1,000,000.* Develop accuracy with each number.

1. 1,000	**7.** 18,000	**13.** 4,255	**19.** 21,000	**25.** 845,000
2. 2,000	**8.** 50,000	**14.** 9,021	**20.** 972,140	**26.** 17,000
3. 10,000	**9.** 7,525	**15.** 11,292	**21.** 17,800	
4. 25,000	**10.** 100,000	**16.** 27,465	**22.** 4,670	
5. 3,200	**11.** 500,000	**17.** 725,000	**23.** 1,500	
6. 5,500	**12.** 250,000	**18.** 89,330	**24.** 1,000,000	

2 *Number challenge.* Focus on developing rhythm and maintaining a consistent speed start to finish.

1. sign the numbers 10–100 in increments of 10
2. sign the numbers 100–1,000 in increments of 100
3. sign the numbers 1,000–10,000 in increments of 1,000
4. sign the numbers 10,000–100,000 in increments of 10,000
5. sign the numbers 100,000–1,000,000 in increments of 100,000

3 *Vertical drills.* Develop speed and accuracy for each column of numbers. Hold your hand higher than the regular fingerspelling location and move your hand slightly lower with each number, to show the column.

1	**2**	**3**	**4**	**5**	**6**	**7**	**8**	**9**	**10**
94	70	11	62	44	80	21	76	23	17
940	704	110	622	440	800	215	767	237	177
1,940	1,704	1,110	1,622	4,400	8,000	2,155	7,676	2,370	1,777
10,940	10,704	11,100	16,220	44,400	88,000	21,550	76,767	23,705	17,777
109,000	107,004	111,000	162,200	444,000	888,000	215,500	767,767	237,500	177,777
1,000,000	1,500,000	3,000,000	4,600,000	2,050,000	1,745,400	1,250,322	9,000,001	4,201,000	6,030,300

4 *How many?* Ask a partner how many people live in each city. Your partner will respond using the information provided. An example is provided.

How many people live in Chicago?

1. San Francisco (728,921)	**5.** Regina, Saskatchewan (195,000)	**9.** Boise, Idaho (185,787)
2. Austin, Texas (656,562)	**6.** Leesburg, Florida (15,956)	**10.** Detroit, Michigan (951,270)
3. Dutch Flat, California (344)	**7.** Nome, Alaska (9,196)	**11.** Flagstaff, Arizona (52,894)
4. New York City (8,008,278)	**8.** Atlanta, Georgia (2,960,000)	**12.** Madawaska, Maine (4,890)

ASL Numbers 1,000–1,000,000+

Numbers between 1,000 and 1,000,000 and higher follow the established pattern for ASL numbers with the addition of the *thousand* sign. Based on the number of times the hand taps the palm, the *thousand* sign can mean *million, billion, trillion,* or larger.

When using the *thousand* sign, remember:

- do not twist the hand for numbers 1,000–5,000
- when signing numbers that use commas, sign them the way they are spoken
- the *thousand* sign works like a comma

1,000   **1,000,000**

Example 1: 1,540

Divide the number into its components.

Example 2: 11,021

Divide the number into its components. Notice no sign is needed for the hundreds place.

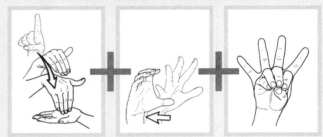

Example 3: 110,000

Divide the number into its components.

Example 4: 1,550,514

Divide the number into its components.

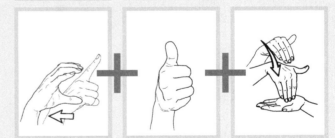

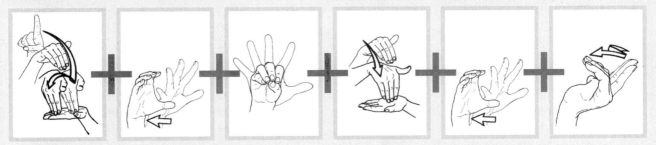

5 *Signing the year.* Sign the date the same way it is written, without commas: 2 0 0 8 instead of using the *thousand* sign. Because the date is in a series of numbers, do not flick your wrist for years including the numbers 1–5. Follow the examples as shown.

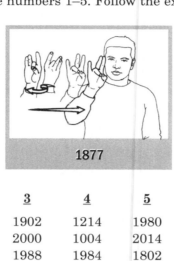
1877

2005

<u>1</u>	<u>2</u>	<u>3</u>	<u>4</u>	<u>5</u>	<u>6</u>	<u>7</u>	<u>8</u>	<u>9</u>	<u>10</u>
1998	2009	1902	1214	1980	1667	1936	1987	1992	1179
2008	1655	2000	1004	2014	2032	1883	1003	1873	1928
1865	1430	1988	1984	1802	1981	1300	1943	1789	2065
1954	1987	1991	1600	2003	1945	2019	1919	1925	1866
1978	1974	1860	1763	1987	1911	1897	1844	2002	1914
1983	2001	1530	2005	1862	1805	1908	2004	1863	2009
2000	1955	2006	1689	1401	2001	1777	1977	1940	1392
1987	1812	1979	1866	2000	1523	1490	1962	1659	1511
1962	1909	1853	1907	1743	1909	1930	1859	1491	1946
1776	2010	1999	2011	1966	1825	1982	1963	2000	1985

<u>11</u>	<u>12</u>	<u>13</u>	<u>14</u>	<u>15</u>	<u>16</u>	<u>17</u>	<u>18</u>	<u>19</u>	<u>20</u>
1908	1654	1982	1998	1567	1986	1929	1828	1980	2013
1879	1100	1977	2008	1391	1992	1852	1730	2011	1931
2010	1297	1829	1865	1988	2013	2002	1872	1903	1968
1981	1921	1923	1954	2006	1292	1973	1876	1934	1960
1994	1905	2036	1978	1602	1700	1980	1930	1402	1998
1988	1569	1517	1983	1993	1904	1824	1739	1989	1740
1989	2008	1619	2000	1815	1697	1982	1820	1748	1542
1641	1765	2025	1987	1905	1888	1831	1038	2005	1750
1885	1670	1722	1962	1711	2000	1948	1029	1049	1900
1732	1038	1044	1776	2002	1543	2019	1738	1950	2003

<u>21</u>	<u>22</u>	<u>23</u>	<u>24</u>	<u>25</u>	<u>26</u>	<u>27</u>	<u>28</u>	<u>29</u>	<u>30</u>
1901	1925	1698	1944	1998	1980	1013	1873	2004	1746
1492	2003	2002	2001	1763	1849	1947	1059	1804	1092
1800	1954	2023	1899	1982	1630	1938	2017	1796	1594
1912	1989	1955	1892	1329	1984	1840	1071	1780	2007
1840	2001	1319	1841	1502	1250	1762	1890	1233	1641
1906	1499	1968	1937	1840	2003	1831	1874	1509	1850
1993	1843	1913	1942	1847	1948	1484	1482	2007	1899
2020	1987	2017	1804	2009	1841	1592	1849	1988	1200
1970	1920	1876	1549	2010	1185	2022	1730	1965	2004
2002	1993	1407	2020	1161	1290	2004	1634	1847	1831

6 *What's the date?* Follow the example to sign each date. Practice alone or with a partner as desired. Recall that dates using the numbers 1–5 must face in because they are not in a series with other numbers.

What is today's date?
Today is April 5, 2005.

1. February 5, 1989	**6.** January 17, 1990	**11.** August 30, 1960	**16.** November 9, 1976
2. May 28, 2009	**7.** April 13, 2001	**12.** June 11, 1999	**17.** June 4, 1984
3. September 15, 1993	**8.** July 7, 1974	**13.** September 20, 2003	**18.** December 31, 2007
4. March 1, 1975	**9.** December 21, 1982	**14.** March 23, 1988	**19.** May 16, 1992
5. October 11, 2000	**10.** November 4, 2011	**15.** July 8, 2010	**20.** February 22, 1987

Accent Steps

Nobody is sure how years like 2015 will be signed: Will it be 20 15, 2 0 1 5, or 2 0 15? Until then, sign dates beyond 2009 the way you prefer.

FYI If date is written 10/22/09, sign the entire date as October 22, 2009.

7 *Using dates.* Sign the following sentences in ASL. For now, don't worry about signs for *was* or how to use the past or future tenses.

1. Today is Thursday, April 14.
2. My brother was born July 5, 1979.
3. I have an ASL test on Wednesday the 4th.
4. The twins were born May 17, 1998.
5. I will celebrate New Year's Eve on December 31.
6. Yesterday was October 3, 2005.
7. Tomorrow will be January 1, 2009.
8. My family moved here in 2002.
9. My niece was born March 20, 2000.
10. I was born on _____.

8 *From first to last.* Use the Listing & Ordering Technique for each set of numbers. Listing numbers this way can be used when you want to emphasize the particular order of numbers. An example is provided.

4, 12, 10

The first number is 4, the second is 12, and the third is 10.

1. 33, 27
2. 422, 18, 1000
3. 84, 63, 99, 7
4. 18, 25, 800, 650
5. 1,200, 140
6. 0, 88, 230, 312, 16
7. 9,500, 100, 102

8. 63, 55, 56, 443, 890
9. 17, 93, 100,000
10. 52,000, 90,000
11. 6,704, 633, 543
12. 24, 25, 26, 27, 28
13. 125,000, 15,000, 25,000
14. 67, 68, 69, 76, 78

15. 79, 86, 87, 89, 96
16. 730, 4,934,502
17. 62, 90, 849
18. 10, 277, 455, 821, 10
19. 17, 18, 29, 30, 21
20. 120,000, 240,000

9 *What's the sign for and?* Use Shoulder-Shifting to sign each group of numbers. For each number, orient your shoulders in a separate direction. This is the best way to sign *and*.

1	2	3	4	5
12, 4	8, 7	75, 76, 77	19, 25, 79	24, 109, 245
2, 3	130, 10	35, 0	60, 17	59, 88, 200, 201
1, 1	67, 63	1,500, 99, 17	5, 4, 7	98, 110, 11, 9
22, 27	5, 11, 14	81, 91, 101	850, 900	46, 5, 8, 86
100, 1,000	90, 100	66, 50	1,000, 10,000	2, 50, 93, 14

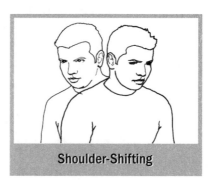

Shoulder-Shifting

10 *Shoulder-Shifting & listing.* Use either technique where necessary to sign the following sentences in ASL.

1. I have 3 sisters and 1 brother.
2. She has 2 brothers named Jeff and Jason.
3. The first four numbers are 8, 13, 14, and 15.
4. She has 16 fish, and he has 2 dogs.
5. First, go to room 8. Second, go to room 9. Then, go to room 11.
6. My family is small. I have 1 brother and 1 sister.
7. My school has 3 ASL classes. One has 20 students, the other has 30, and the third has 18.
8. I have a large family. I have 3 brothers, 4 aunts, and 9 cousins.
9. My family has 4 dogs, 3 cats, and 2 fish.
10. Remember these telephone numbers: 555-8900, 324-0544, 888-7124, and 545-7890.

11 *Signing age.* All age signs originate at the Age Spot, and can be made in one of the two ways shown here. Both formats can be used for ages 1–99, but only the Age + Number form is used for ages higher than 100. Remember that age signs already incorporate "years old", so don't add separate signs for these words. The signs for 13, 14, and 15 years old are exceptions to the rule. Touch the Age Spot with the fingertips of the 13, 14, or 15 number sign and move the hand down and away from your body, similar to the sign two years old in the example. Remember to include the regular finger movements for 13, 14, and 15 once located in the final position.

Age Spot + Number

Age+Number

Use either Age format

1	**2**	**3**	**4**	**5**	**6**	**7**	**8**	**9**	**10**
14	23	6	27	16	25	34	15	18	87
3	30	13	18	30	1	56	12	57	39
19	25	49	10	76	47	20	49	33	32
22	24	22	7	26	50	17	99	29	22
60	12	11	13	37	20	21	18	14	24
82	98	9	91	2	42	68	22	23	100

Use the Age + Number format

11	**12**	**13**	**14**	**15**	**16**	**17**	**18**	**19**	**20**
1	7	13	19	25	31	37	43	49	55
2	8	14	20	26	32	38	44	50	56
3	9	15	21	27	33	39	45	51	57
4	10	16	22	28	34	40	46	52	58
5	11	17	23	29	35	41	47	53	59
6	12	18	24	30	36	42	48	54	60

21	**22**	**23**	**24**	**25**	**26**	**27**	**28**	**29**	**30**
61	67	73	79	85	91	97	103	109	115
62	68	74	80	86	92	98	104	110	116
63	69	75	81	87	93	99	105	111	117
64	70	76	82	88	94	100	106	112	118
65	71	77	83	89	95	101	107	113	119
66	72	78	84	90	96	102	108	114	120

Use the Age Spot + Number format

31	**32**	**33**	**34**	**35**	**36**	**37**	**38**	**39**	**40**
1	7	13	19	25	31	37	43	49	55
2	8	14	20	26	32	38	44	50	56
3	9	15	21	27	33	39	45	51	57
4	10	16	22	28	34	40	46	52	58
5	11	17	23	29	35	41	47	53	59
6	12	18	24	30	36	42	48	54	60

41	**42**	**43**	**44**	**45**	**46**	**47**	**48**	**49**	**50**
61	67	73	79	85	91	97	44	1	7
62	68	74	80	86	92	98	55	2	8
63	69	75	81	87	93	99	66	3	9
64	70	76	82	88	94	11	77	4	10
65	71	77	83	89	95	22	88	5	11
66	72	78	84	90	96	33	99	6	12

12 *Multiple ages.* Use Shoulder-Shifting to sign each set of ages.

1	2	3	4	5	6	7	8	9	10
2, 3	19, 67	1, 4	83, 36	10, 20	78, 81	32, 19	20, 100	12, 14, 4	23, 18
12, 18	30, 23	90, 30	12, 13	11, 13	20, 27	6, 15	17, 30	29, 22	15, 16
20, 21	15, 28	54, 22	6, 5	26, 31	16, 21	38, 50	2, 7, 3	17, 5	44, 69
49, 53	6, 17	34, 30	1, 3, 4	30, 28	65, 40	45, 47	16, 32	56, 60	5, 9, 18, 20
33, 34	3, 8	17, 16	18, 24	5, 1, 9	4, 29	76, 67	40, 12	71, 18	15, 6, 7, 9

13 *How old is it?* State how old each item is, based on the information shown. Generally, it is acceptable to sign *years old* when talking about an object. An example is provided.

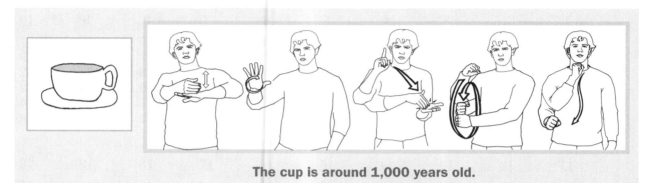

The cup is around 1,000 years old.

1. **5,500 years old**
2. **1896**
3. **1980's**
4. **4.5 billion years old**

14 *How many?* Use the correct ASL pronoun for the following phrases.

1. The five of us.
2. Us two.
3. Those three.
4. These five.
5. Us four.
6. You and I.
7. These two.
8. Those six.
9. The three of us are going.
10. The ten of us are going.
11. The twenty of them are going.
12. The two of us aren't going, but the three of them are.

ASL pronoun: Us-four

15 *Skills review.* Sign each item quickly and clearly.

1. Numbers	2. Dates	3. Mixed Numbers	4. Shoulder-Shifting	5. Age
1,000	January 4, 1955	2013, 2013	16, 32, 64	33
35,000	May 22, 2009	7, 7, 7	28, 12	100
100,000	October 31, 1998	800 years old	8, 7, 7	25
755,500	February 17, 1975	52 years old	38, 22	5
1,000,000	August 8, 2014	Those two	14, 29	19
2,000,000,000	April 23, 2006	Us two	1, 3	30

ASL Numbers 1,000–1,000,000+ Review

Can you:

1. Sign numbers between 1,000 and 1,000,000,000?
2. Understand large numbers signed to you?
3. Identify the numbers you struggle to sign and understand?
4. Explain how age, years, and counting numbers differ?

Answer the following:

1. What are three different examples of ASL pronouns?
2. How do you sign *billion* or *trillion*? How do you know?
3. What does Shoulder-Shifting do? Give two examples of Shoulder-Shifting.
4. What is the difference between 2,005 and 2005? How are they signed?
5. How are age numbers signed? When do you sign *years old*? When do you not?

Unit 5

1 *Numbers.* Develop accuracy with each number, applying the skills you've learned.

1. 668	**8.** 1912	**15.** 67, 68	**22.** 86, 87
2. 1,432	**9.** 101,000	**16.** 1988	**23.** 2009
3. 1942	**10.** 785-3812	**17.** 16 million	**24.** 2,302
4. 30, 31	**11.** 2812 Oak	**18.** 15,000	**25.** 651-2213
5. 22 years old	**12.** 10,000	**19.** 1805	**26.** 19 years old
6. 1,156	**13.** 1999	**20.** 7 years old	
7. 8, 11, 13	**14.** 14,900	**21.** 11,430	

2 *Room numbers.* Make a complete sentence using each room number. An example is provided.

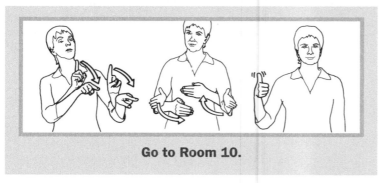

Go to Room 10.

1. Room 228	**6.** Room 500	**11.** Room 414	**16.** Room 3-A
2. Room 3488	**7.** Room 89	**12.** Room 9805	**17.** Room 90
3. Room 5	**8.** Room 3	**13.** Room 66-B	**18.** Room 607
4. Room 59	**9.** Room 25	**14.** Room 21345	**19.** Room 38402
5. Room 23	**10.** Room 64	**15.** Room 49R	**20.** Room 5820

3 *Telecommunications hub.* You are responsible for creating a database for access information at your school. Explain what's available for each room in a complete sentence. Fingerspell *video mail* and *voice mail.*

	Room	Instructor	Telephone	I.P. Address	Video Mailbox	Voice mailbox	Visual bell
1.	4	Deaf	435-6554	4.167.12.68	14-C	none	needs
2.	37	Hearing	435-0034	4.166.14.70	none	yes, 106	yes
3.	98	Deaf	435-2306	4.166.21.80	84A	none	broken
4.	54	Hard of hearing	435-1216	4.167.44.65	none	yes, 110	yes
5.	18	Hearing	435-7896	4.167.13.56	none	yes, 118	no
6.	5	Hearing	435-5644	4.166.34.34	15A	yes, 094	yes
7.	88	Deaf	435-3333	4.167.56.78	8B	none	needs
8.	60	Deaf	435-7000	4.166.66.04	9B	none	yes
9.	19	Hard of hearing	435-4322	4.167.90.43	18A	yes, 012	yes
10.	20	Deaf	435-7533	4.166.78.90	17C	none	yes

4   *Enrollment.* In a complete sentence explain how many students attend each school.

1. University of California, Berkeley **(23,205)**
2. Rice University **(4,202)**
3. Hillsdale College **(1,200)**
4. Carnegie Mellon University **(8,514)**
5. Notre Dame **(11,311)**
6. Culinary Institute of America **(2,028)**
7. Rutgers University **(51,868)**
8. Palomar College **(32,109)**
9. Johns Hopkins University **(5,690)**
10. Academy of Art College **(5,208)**
11. Xavier University **(3,994)**
12. Embry-Riddle Aeronautical University **(4,502)**
13. Washington State University, Pullman **(16,202)**
14. Lincoln University **(4,101)**
15. Gallaudet University **(2,014)**
16. Quincy College **(4,401)**
17. George Mason University **(15,851)**
18. Vanderbilt University **(10,300)**
19. Rhode Island School of Design **(1,920)**
20. New York University **(38,188)**

5   *Schools for the Deaf.* Are any of these schools for the Deaf near you? Where is your local school for the Deaf? Sign the following addresses quickly and clearly.

1. Colorado School for the Deaf and the Blind
   33 North Institute Street
   Colorado Springs, Colorado 80903-3599

2. Texas School for the Deaf
   1102 South Congress Avenue
   Austin, Texas 78704-1728

3. Minnesota State Academy for the Deaf
   615 Olof Hanson Drive
   Faribault, Minnesota 55021

4. American School for the Deaf and the Blind
   139 North Main Street
   West Hartford, Connecticut 06107

5. California School for the Deaf
   39350 Gallaudet Drive
   Fremont, California 94538

6. New Mexico School for the Deaf
   1060 Cerrillos Road
   Santa Fe, New Mexico 87505

7. New York School for the Deaf
   555 Knollwood Road
   White Plains, New York 10603

8. Kentucky School for the Deaf
   303 South Second Street
   Danville, Kentucky 40422

9. Washington School for the Deaf
   611 Grand Boulevard
   Vancouver, Washington 98661

10. 47, The ASL and English School
    225 East 23rd Street
    New York, New York 10010

6   *How many?* Explain each fact in a complete sentence.

1. Telephone book: 985 pages
2. White House: 32 bathrooms, 132 rooms
3. Steps in the Statue of Liberty: 354
4. People living in Canada: 32,233,955
5. Palace of Versailles: 1,300 rooms
6. Steps in the Eiffel Tower: 2,731
7. Pentagon: 284 bathroom, 16,250 lights, 22,354 doors
8. People living in the United States: 293,027,571
9. Books in the New York library: 39,729,724
10. Pet birds: 4,121,004

7 *Graduation.* Explain each person's graduation class in a complete sentence. The two ways of signing a class year are provided.

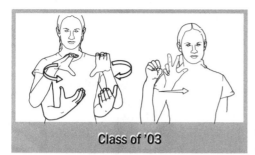

Class of '03

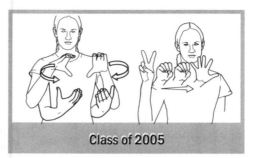

Class of 2005

1. Stephanie ... class of 1972
2. Jared ... class of 1999
3. Doug ... class of 2010
4. Esperanza ... class of '09
5. Gloria ... class of '77
6. Chris ... class of 1998

7. Jose ... class of '06
8. Alex ... class of 2001
9. Theo ... class of 1990, Sara ... class of 1991
10. Clarence ... class of 1988
11. Marsha ... class of '92 ... Scott ... class of '93
12. Ahmed ... class of 1976, Cara ... class of 1995

8 *Since when?* The sign *since* is often used for topics including dates and general periods of time. Substitute the words *since* or *for* with *since*. Sign each phrase below in ASL.

1. Since 1988
2. For 5 years
3. Since May 3
4. Since 1991
5. For 5 days
6. Since April

7. Since 2001
8. For 7 years
9. Since 1600
10. For 250 years
11. Since the winter
12. Since studying

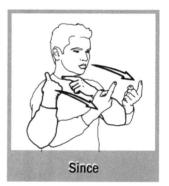

Since

9 *How long has it been?* Use *since* to sign the following sentences. For now, don't worry about how to sign the past tense. An example is shown.

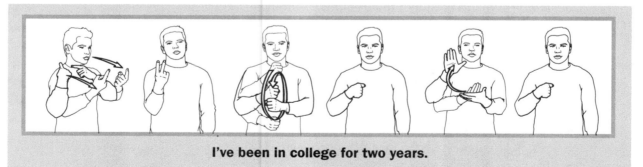

I've been in college for two years.

1. We've been studying ASL for _____ year/s.
2. I've known my friend Sean for _____ year/s.
3. I've been in high school for 3 years.
4. Since 1817, Deaf people have had schools for the Deaf.
5. They've been married for 10 years.

6. I've been in _____ for _____ year/s.
7. Since graduation I've been working.
8. For 22 years I've had my license.
9. We've been friends for 11 years.
10. Since I was little I've been shy.

10 *What time is it?* Signs referring to the time of hour originate at the Time Spot. When the time includes both the hour and minute, the hour sign begins at the Time Spot and the minute sign begins where the hour number stops. You don't need to add 0 0 after an hour sign if no minutes follow.

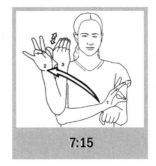

7:15

3:00

Hours & Minutes

1	2	3	4	5	6	7	8	9	10
1:00	1:15	1:30	1:45	1:05	1:10	1:20	1:25	1:40	1:50
2:00	2:15	2:30	2:45	2:05	2:10	2:20	2:25	2:40	2:50
3:00	3:15	3:30	3:45	3:05	3:10	3:20	3:25	3:40	3:50
4:00	4:15	4:30	4:45	4:05	4:10	4:20	4:25	4:40	4:50
5:00	5:15	5:30	5:45	5:05	5:10	5:20	5:25	5:40	5:50
6:00	6:15	6:30	6:45	6:05	6:10	6:20	6:25	6:40	6:50
7:00	7:15	7:30	7:45	7:05	7:10	7:20	7:25	7:40	7:50
8:00	8:15	8:30	8:45	8:05	8:10	8:20	8:25	8:40	8:50
9:00	9:15	9:30	9:45	9:05	9:10	9:20	9:25	9:40	9:50
10:00	10:15	10:30	10:45	10:05	10:10	10:20	10:25	10:40	10:50
11:00	11:15	11:30	11:45	11:05	11:10	11:20	11:25	11:40	11:50
12:00	12:15	12:30	12:45	12:05	12:10	12:20	12:25	12:40	12:50

Mixed Hours & Minutes

11	12	13	14	15	16	17	18	19	20
8:15	2:19	4:18	1:07	8:14	12:13	7:22	6:27	3:53	9:43
12:00	11:59	10:14	8:14	12:38	9:04	10:51	1:04	5:31	4:19
10:05	5:26	9:07	12:01	9:16	5:16	1:49	4:37	2:46	6:06
6:06	9:41	1:58	2:25	4:57	11:54	4:16	8:23	6:17	10:14
2:20	8:04	8:34	9:19	1:41	7:39	11:28	10:16	10:18	1:14
4:14	10:19	3:46	3:44	10:09	4:57	5:12	12:00	8:48	12:03
9:44	3:20	12:29	10:37	2:59	1:19	9:56	3:12	4:49	2:29
10:12	6:34	6:01	11:21	7:14	10:47	12:29	5:43	1:12	7:17
2:29	11:11	2:43	7:04	11:44	8:29	2:04	9:51	7:29	3:48
7:43	1:28	5:16	5:26	6:12	6:13	6:17	2:39	12:27	5:57
5:14	4:19	7:56	4:11	5:36	3:23	8:53	11:14	9:23	8:21
3:09	7:22	11:14	2:19	3:28	2:48	3:42	7:42	11:09	11:14

Time Phrases

21	22	23
4 p.m.	2 o'clock	3 on the nose
8 a.m.	quarter til 5	10 past 5
5 on the dot	12:15 a.m.	6:15 p.m.
half past 10	9 o'clock	half past 8

24	25	26
6 a.m.	0100 hours	2:45 p.m.
9 o'clock	7:20 a.m.	half past 9
3:30 exactly	quarter til 8	4 and a quarter
quarter after 7	11 o'clock	quarter til 7

Accent Steps

Time Tips: Deaf people rarely fingerspell a.m. or p.m. when referring to the time of day. Instead, sign *morning* or *evening* after the time sign.

11 *Minutes.* When there is no hour sign paired with a minute sign, follow the pattern shown here. While numbers 1–5 do not face inward for hour signs, they do for minutes.

Minute

35 minutes

1	2	3	4	5	6	7	8	9	10
10	50	12	120	30	17	11	22	25	3
15	9	59	25	15	33	34	10	10	18
8	4	35	39	29	11	54	4	18	26
2	33	13	13	46	19	18	18	45	45
25	28	29	19	51	5	39	27	50	60
30	29	57	40	3	16	41	49	30	120
5	49	15	51	8	17	30	31	15	20
9	20	19	26	28	29	21	3	10	15
12	18	1	18	17	40	12	8	5	10
45	5	6	39	32	55	8	20	1	5

12 *Seconds.* Similar to how minutes are signed in ASL, seconds are shown by pairing a number with a finger-spelled abbreviation shown to the right.

Second

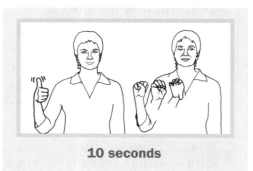

10 seconds

1	2	3	4	5	6	7	8	9	10
33	48	18	16	3	100	75	14	19	27
12	29	25	29	13	5	44	46	28	38
60	12	60	40	27	16	30	92	47	91
54	40	54	32	25	28	21	14	75	53
39	53	39	22	54	16	33	49	32	44
57	3	18	25	39	15	8	31	4	51
84	21	4	17	30	48	74	5	90	4
23	22	68	49	65	23	68	39	51	18
15	9	2	57	67	54	88	51	44	12
4	10	45	44	80	42	32	2	36	10

13 *Telling time.* Change the following numbers by adapting them to the Time Spot or adding the *minute* and *seconds* signs.

<u>1</u>	<u>2</u>	<u>3</u>	<u>4</u>	<u>5</u>	<u>6</u>	<u>7</u>	<u>8</u>	<u>9</u>	<u>10</u>
2	30	44	2	6	30	5	33	30	48
19	14	10	19	16	22	9	66	20	26
45	3	7	33	30	7	19	52	14	3
6	8	29	56	43	18	28	3	5	9
12	18	40	7	12	65	34	29	3	17
8	22	60	10	5	40	54	12	18	45
56	5	33	9	27	3	39	60	6	5
92	12	8	29	8	9	8	32	20	49
44	11	14	40	23	15	16	15	22	33
9	49	9	55	3	24	15	4	10	20

14 *Using time.* Explain each of the schedules below in complete ASL sentences.

1. **Train Schedule**

Arrives	Departs
5:45 a.m.	6:00 a.m.
9:30 a.m.	9:50 a.m.
1:45 p.m.	3:00 p.m.
5:00 p.m.	5:25 p.m.
10:15 p.m.	10:45 p.m.

2. **Tuesday Class Schedule**

	Begins	Finishes
ASL	9:00 a.m.	11:30 a.m.
Math	2:15 p.m.	3:45 p.m.
Deaf history	6:00 p.m.	9:00 p.m.

3. **Movie Schedule**

	Starts	Ends
Matinee	5:45	7:45
	7:00	9:30
	8:15	9:40
Last	10:00	12:10

4. **Plane Schedule**

Arrivals		Departures	
New York	3:12 p.m.	London	7:15 a.m.
Chicago	4:09 p.m.	Montreal	8:44 a.m.
Houston	4:33 p.m.	Albuquerque	9:45 a.m.
Los Angeles	5:17 p.m.	Miami	12 noon

5. **Wednesday Class Schedule**

	Begins	Finishes
Engl.	10:00 a.m.	11:15 a.m.
ASL	1:00 p.m.	3:20 p.m.
Bio.	6:00 p.m.	10:00 p.m.

15 *Skills review.* Sign each item quickly and clearly.

1. Time	2. Numbers	3. Classes	4. Since	5. Populations
3:00	Room 44	Class of 2002	1997	1,455,200
8:04 a.m.	Room 23	Class of '71	2000	718,000
6:45 p.m.	Room 11	Class of '98	1540	13,512
half past 5	Room 1077	Class of 2016	2005	4,986
10 seconds	Room 245	Class of 1994	1978	16,000
25 minutes	Room 689	Class of '67	1999	25,000

Unit 6

1   *Numbers.* Develop accuracy with each number, applying the skills you've learned.

1.	9:45	**8.**	1955	**15.**	8:00	**22.**	May 4
2.	2004	**9.**	4:13 p.m.	**16.**	67	**23.**	1993
3.	1,377	**10.**	9, 10	**17.**	54 years old	**24.**	10,500
4.	6:16 a.m.	**11.**	510	**18.**	2 million	**25.**	22 years old
5.	15 minutes	**12.**	April 3, 1901	**19.**	7:35 a.m.	**26.**	3:40 p.m.
6.	4 years old	**13.**	12,544	**20.**	1989		
7.	98,000	**14.**	1998	**21.**	533-0210		

2   *How many?* State the number of people who play each sport, using the information provided.

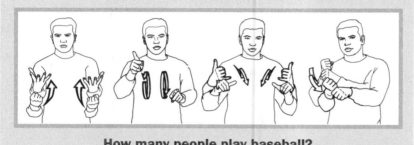

How many people play baseball?

1. bowling **(44,800,000)**
2. ice skating **(921,500)**
3. football **(3,140,000)**
4. volleyball **(2,390,000)**
5. baseball **(15,480,000)**
6. snowboarding **(432,000)**
7. swimming **(16,974,000)**
8. basketball **(11,020,000)**
9. biking **(23,112,000)**
10. softball **(5,630,000)**
11. hockey **(1,688,000)**
12. water polo **(592,000)**
13. soccer **(14,590,000)**
14. golf **(16,045,800)**
15. gymnastics **(1,240,000)**

*Source: Wikipedia

3   *Olympic records.* Use the information provided to sign a complete sentence.

Summer Games

1. 100 meter run, Justin Gatlin (9.85 seconds)
2. 5,000 meter run, Hicham Guerrouj (13 minutes, 14.38 seconds)
3. Marathon, Stefano Baldini (2 hours, 10 minutes, 55 seconds)
4. 50 meter freestyle swimming, Gary Hall Jr. (21.93 seconds)
5. 200 meter butterfly swimming, Michael Phelps (1 minute, 54.04 seconds)

Winter Games

6. downhill skiing, Fritz Strobl (1 minute, 39.13 seconds)
7. bobsledding, Andre Lange (3 minutes, 7.51 seconds)
8. cross-country skiing 18.6 miles, Christian Hoffmann (1 hour, 11 minutes, 31 seconds)
9. snowboarding slalom, Ross Rebagliati (2 minutes, 3.96 seconds)
10. speed skating, 5,000 meters, Claudia Pechstein (6 minutes, 46.91 seconds)

4 *Where the crowds are.* Explain the capacity of each stadium, and what it is used for. Fingerspell the underlined terms. An example of how to use CL: 5 is shown below.

Large crowds go there to watch football.

1. 61,500 – <u>New Soldier Field</u>, football
2. 82,957 – <u>Telstra</u> Stadium, soccer
3. 32,000 – <u>Wimbledon</u> Stadium, tennis
4. 17,104 – <u>Pengrowth Saddledome</u>, hockey
5. 72,515 – <u>Lambeau Field</u>, football

6. 168,000 – <u>Daytona International Speedway</u>, auto racing
7. 56,000 – <u>Dodger</u> Stadium, baseball
8. 107,501 – <u>Michigan</u> Stadium, college football
9. 9,500 – <u>Patriot Center</u>, gymnastics
10. 17,483 – <u>HP Pavilion</u>, ice skating

5 *Then & Now.* When referring to future or past dates like "In the year ..." in ASL, you must first indicate the relative distance of the date from the present. The four tense markers of *distant past, past, distant future,* and *future* fulfill this function. Select the past or future tense marker that best describes the year shown. Notice you must include the *year* sign. An example is provided.

Tense Markers

 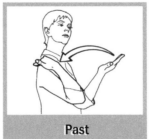 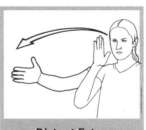 

| Distant Past | Past | Distant Future | Future |

In 2050...

1. In 1776	6. In 2003	11. In 1979	16. Back in 1990	21. In 1998
2. In 2100	7. In 1929	12. In 2012	17. In 2006	22. Back in 1910
3. In 1999	8. In 2010	13. In 800	18. In 3000	23. In 2020
4. In 2005	9. In 2004	14. In 2200	19. Back in 1100	24. In 2015
5. In 1989	10. In 1950	15. In 1210	20. 1866	25. In 1700

6 *The Rule of 9: Age.* The Rule of 9 refers to a feature of ASL in which numbers 1–9 are incorporated into signs for specific meanings. You learned part of the Rule of 9 with the signs for age, but the concept of including number is also used for time, days, weeks, and more. Sign the following correctly.

Signing Age: Ages 1–9

1	2	3	4	5	6	7	8	9	10
1	9 years old	8	9, 4	4 years old	8	3, 2, 8	8 years old	7, 3	4
2	5 years old	4	3, 7	9 years old	1	1, 5, 5	4 years old	1, 4	1
3	7 years old	1	2, 1	3 years old	4	9, 2, 5	1 year old	5	9
4	2 years old	9	8, 5	7 years old	3	6, 1, 3	9 years old	9	8
5	8 years old	3	9, 3	2 years old	9	5, 8, 2	7 years old	2, 4, 6	3
6	6 years old	2	7, 2	5 years old	7	4, 1, 9	2 years old	8, 7	5
7	1 year old	7	1, 4	8 years old	5	7, 9, 4	6 years old	7	7
8	3 years old	6	6, 7	1 year old	6	2, 9, 1	3 years old	1, 3	2
9	4 years old	5	4, 5, 7	6 years old	2	7, 6, 4	5 years old	2, 9	6

Signing Age: Ages higher than 9

1	2	3	4	5	6	7	8	9	10
10	45	55	100	32	30	70	13	31	17
22	88	81	10	103	25	87	20	43	29
34	11	41	14	53	28	98	45	15	15
17	20	33	95	84	41	83	68	71	93
18	26	21	27	14	65	23	98	20	14
11	19	29	48	38	79	91	46	48	12
15	43	37	70	19	31	82	72	85	49
19	66	50	33	50	40	28	60	50	54

7 *The Rule of 9: Time.* The Rule of 9 refers to a feature of ASL in which numbers 1–9 are incorporated into signs for specific meanings. Sign the following time numbers correctly.

Signing Time: 1:00–9:00

1	2	3	4	5	6	7	8	9	10
1	7 o'clock	3:00	6	8 a.m.	6	3 o'clock	7 p.m.	4:15	8:45
2	2 o'clock	8:00	9	4 a.m.	2	8 o'clock	1 p.m.	8:10	1:15
3	8 o'clock	2:00	3	1 a.m.	7	1 o'clock	5 p.m.	9:00	5:30
4	1 o'clock	4:00	1	9 a.m.	5	6 o'clock	9 p.m.	1:10	2:10
5	5 o'clock	9:00	4	7 a.m.	9	2 o'clock	2 p.m.	3:30	7:30
6	9 o'clock	7:00	2	3 a.m.	1	4 o'clock	6 p.m.	7:45	6:45
7	3 o'clock	5:00	5	5 a.m.	3	7 o'clock	3 p.m.	2:20	3:15
8	6 o'clock	6:00	7	2 a.m.	4	5 o'clock	4 p.m.	5:05	4:20
9	4 o'clock	1:00	8	6 a.m.	8	9 o'clock	8 p.m.	6:50	9:30

Signing Time: Times higher than 9:00

1	2	3	4	5	6	7	8	9	10
10:00	11:22 a.m.	10:01	11:10	11:04 p.m.	10 p.m.	12:05	half past 10	11:05	11:45
11:00	10:43 a.m.	10:05	11:13	11:10 p.m.	11 a.m.	10:13	10 til 11	11:10	11:50
12:00	12:00 a.m.	10:02	11:25	11:58 p.m.	10:10	12:45	quarter to 12	11:15	11:55
11:45	10:15 a.m.	10:04	11:33	11:27 p.m.	10:47	11:02	5 past 10	11:20	10:15
11:12	11:59 a.m.	10:03	11:49	11:19 p.m.	10:34	12:55	quarter after 10	11:25	10:25
10:50	10:55 a.m.	10:06	11:50	11:49 p.m.	11:41	12:09	quarter til 11	11:30	10:35
11:04	11:00 a.m.	10:07	11:22	11:31 p.m.	11:22	10:41	half past 12	11:35	10:45
12:30	12:44 a.m.	10:08	11:13	11:23 p.m.	10:57	11:51	10 past 11	11:40	10:50

8 *The Rule of 9: Hours*. The Rule of 9 refers to a feature of ASL in which numbers 1–9 are incorporated into signs for specific meanings. Notice in the examples below that the number sign is included into the sign for *hour*, changing the meaning. Sign the following hour numbers correctly.

Hour, 1 hour

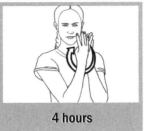

4 hours

Signing Hours: Hours 1–9

1	2	3
1 hour	4 hours	7 & 2 hours
2 hours	1 hour	6 & 4 hours
3 hours	9 hours	1 & 2 hours
4 hours	6 hours	8 & 3 hours
5 hours	3 hours	2 & 5 hours
6 hours	8 hours	7 & 8 hours
7 hours	2 hours	3 & 5 hours
8 hours	5 hours	2 & 9 hours
9 hours	7 hours	4 & 7 hours

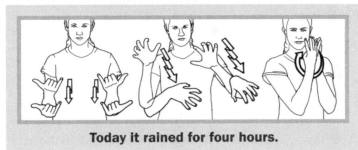

Today it rained for four hours.

Signing Hours: More than 9 hours

1	2	3
10 hours	16 hours	30 hours
11 hours	72 hours	45 hours
12 hours	50 hours	34 hours
15 hours	14 hours	21 hours
18 hours	86 hours	10 hours
20 hours	40 hours	17 hours
22 hours	33 hours	28 hours
24 hours	100 hours	104 hours
48 hours	13 hours	68 hours

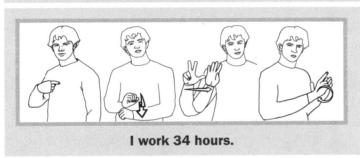

I work 34 hours.

9 *The Rule of 9: Minutes*. While the *minute* sign once followed the Rule of 9, over time its use has changed. When incorporating a number with *minute* you may sign it either in your palm or at the end of your index finger. However, for numbers nine or higher use a number sign followed by *minute*, shown below.

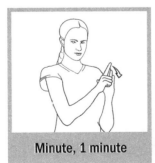

Minute, 1 minute

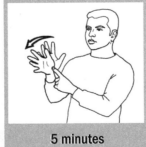

5 minutes

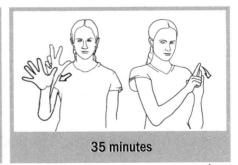

35 minutes

1. 1 minute
2. 2 minutes
3. 3 minutes
4. 4 minutes
5. 5 minutes

6. 6 minutes
7. 7 minutes
8. 8 minutes
9. 9 minutes
10. 10 minutes

11. 15 minutes
12. 20 minutes
13. 30 minutes
14. 45 minutes
15. 50 minutes

16. 60 minutes
17. 25 minutes
18. 105 minutes
19. 55 minutes
20. 120 minutes

10 *The Rule of 9: Days.* Follow the Rule of 9 when signing about the number of days, though you may choose not to for numbers beyond 5. For numbers higher than 9, follow a number sign with the sign for *day*.

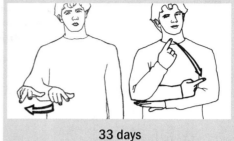

Three days	33 days

<u>1</u>	<u>2</u>	<u>3</u>	<u>4</u>	<u>5</u>	<u>6</u>	<u>7</u>	<u>8</u>	<u>9</u>	<u>10</u>
1 day	15 days	3 days	7 days	1 day	17 days	1 day	300days	9 days	12 days
2 days	20 days	8 days	14 days	12 days	7 days	4 days	18 days	7 days	3 days
3 days	25 days	14 days	21 days	4 days	55 days	8 days	2 days	6 days	4 days
4 days	30 days	12 days	28 days	8 days	14 days	12 days	8 days	18 days	8 days
5 days	35 days	114 days	35 days	2 days	1 day	16 days	365 days	36 days	15 days
6 days	40 days	85 days	42 days	20 days	8 days	20 days	1 day	76 days	21 days
7 days	45 days	52 days	49 days	3 days	5 days	24 days	6 days	152 days	1 day
8 days	50 days	444 days	56 days	5 days	1,000 days	28 days	19 days	304 days	6 days
9 days	55 days	76 days	63 days	6 days	10 days	32 days	4 days	608 days	7 days
10 days	60 days	5 days	70 days	9 days	14 days	36 days	6 days	1,216 days	2 days

11 *The Rule of 9: Weeks.* The Rule of 9 applies to *weeks*. For numbers higher than nine, pair the number sign with *week*. An example is provided.

Last year I stayed for two weeks. Now I will stay for 15 weeks.

1. 1 week	**5.** 8 weeks	**9.** 2 weeks	**13.** 10 weeks	**17.** 6 weeks
2. 3 weeks	**6.** 12 weeks	**10.** 7 weeks	**14.** 52 weeks	**18.** 25 weeks
3. 4 weeks	**7.** 15 weeks	**11.** 5 weeks	**15.** 18 weeks	**19.** 33 weeks
4. 6 weeks	**8.** 20 weeks	**12.** 9 weeks	**16.** 4 weeks	**20.** 100 weeks

I Want to Know . . .

Why can't larger numbers follow the Rule of 9?

ASL numbers 1–9 are easy to see and don't require additional movement, unlike numbers such as 11, 25, or 100. Combining signs that involve movement into number signs would be awkward and cumbersome! But note that the Rule of 9 and the *minute* sign have changed over time, so perhaps others will as well.

12 *The Rule of 9: Months.* The Rule of 9 applies to *months.* For numbers higher than nine, pair the number sign with *month.* Complete the sentence below using the correct form of *month.*

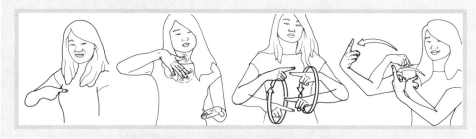

I've been studying sign language for ...

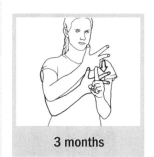

3 months

1. 1 month	**8.** 8 months	**15.** 35 months	
2. 2 months	**9.** 9 months	**16.** 44 months	
3. 3 months	**10.** 10 months	**17.** 100 months	
4. 4 months	**11.** 12 months	**18.** 104 months	
5. 5 months	**12.** 15 months	**19.** 88 months	
6. 6 months	**13.** 20 months	**20.** 97 months	
7. 7 months	**14.** 23 months		

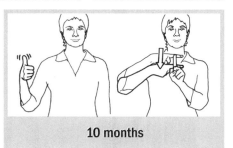

10 months

13 *The Rule of 9: Years.* The Rule of 9 does not apply to *year* aside from a small group of specific signs. The general pattern is to follow a number with the *year* sign unless signing about the recent past or future.

3 years

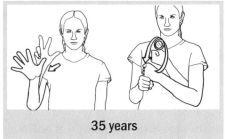

35 years

FYI

Numbers 1–5 should face inward.

Past tense

1 year ago, 2 years ago, and *3 years ago* follow this pattern:

1 year ago

Future tense

In *1 year,* in *2 years,* in *3 years,* in *4 years,* in *5 years* follow this pattern:

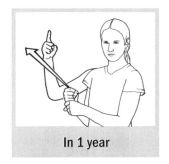

In 1 year

1. 1 year	**6.** 10 years	**11.** 7 years	**16.** 15 years
2. 3 years	**7.** 1 year ago	**12.** 2 years	**17.** in 1 year
3. 5 years	**8.** 2 years from now	**13.** 2 years ago	**18.** 3 years from now
4. 6 years	**9.** in 4 years	**14.** 3 years ago	**19.** 100 years
5. 8 years	**10.** 25 years	**15.** 4 years	**20.** 50 years

14 *Using the tenses.* Many signs in ASL incorporate the Rule of 9 and the past or future tenses, as you saw with *year* in Exercise 13. Signs establishing tense may go before or after a number sign depending on the context. If you introduce a new topic or use the future tense, the tense sign should come first. This applies to: *Minute, hour, day, month,* and *year.* Only *week* can incorporate the Rule of 9 and tense in a single sign.

Ago

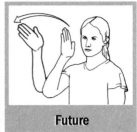
Future

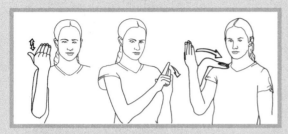
15 minutes ago.

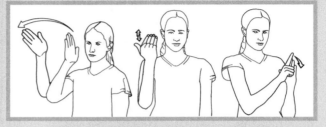
In 15 minutes.

2 weeks ago. / **In 1 week.**

**1 month ago. /
Last month.**

**In 3 months. /
3 months from now.**

Past & Future Tenses: Use *ago* and *future* as required.

1. in 5 years	5. 3 hours ago	9. in 10 years	13. in 3 minutes	17. 7 years ago
2. 3 weeks ago	6. in an hour	10. in 3 weeks	14. last week	18. in 4 days
3. 2 months ago	7. 4 years ago	11. 30 minutes ago	15. next year	19. in 9 hours
4. in 5 minutes	8. in a month	12. 6 months ago	16. in 5 seconds	20. 25 minutes ago

15 *Skills review.* Sign each item quickly and clearly.

1	2	3	4	5
3 hours	4 days ago	in 4 weeks	1,680,000	4 days old
10 days	in 6 hours	70,000	15 years old	5 seconds
4 minutes	6 weeks ago	10 years	15 minutes ago	7:45 p.m.
2 months	in 4 months	21 minutes	in 15 minutes	22,400
5 weeks	6 days	6 hours	7 months ago	821
6 years	12 years	8 weeks ago	3 weeks ago	in 2 months
25 seconds	15,954	2 years from now	in 5 weeks	7 weeks ago
15 minutes	9 years old	in 12 minutes	100 years from now	last year
next week	143,230	18 years old	12 months ago	23 weeks
8 days	18 months	15 years ago	in 3 months	14 days

Unit 7

1   *Numbers.* Develop accuracy with each number, applying the skills you've learned.

1. 5 days	**8.** 8:11 a.m.	**15.** 42 million	**22.** 6:17 a.m.
2. 1985	**9.** 5 hours	**16.** 5:05 p.m.	**23.** Class of '92
3. 9:30 p.m.	**10.** in 2 weeks	**17.** 18 years old	**24.** 20 minutes ago
4. 2 months	**11.** 2004	**18.** 12,500	**25.** 25 years old
5. 1,435	**12.** 2,004	**19.** 120 minutes	**26.** 8 hours
6. 10/12/05	**13.** 3 minutes	**20.** 4 weeks ago	
7. 7 years old	**14.** in a week	**21.** 899-0420	

2   *Wake-up times.* Following the example, explain whether one wakes up early or late.

I set my alarm for 6:30. I wake up early.

1. 5:15 a.m.	**5.** 2:40 p.m.	**9.** 4:00 a.m.	**13.** 11:55 a.m.	**17.** 4:50 a.m.
2. 11:45 p.m.	**6.** 11:00 a.m.	**10.** 11:00 p.m.	**14.** 12:05 p.m.	**18.** 9:00 a.m.
3. 7:00 a.m.	**7.** 1:30 p.m.	**11.** 7:20 a.m.	**15.** 1:00 a.m.	**19.** 10:30 p.m.
4. 10:30 a.m.	**8.** 12:30 a.m.	**12.** 5:00 a.m.	**16.** 8:49 p.m.	**20.** 6:15 a.m.

3   *Bed time.* Based on the provided information, explain when each person goes to sleep. Use the *around* and *between* signs as needed, as well as Shoulder-Shifting if necessary. An example is provided.

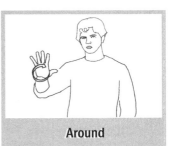

Around

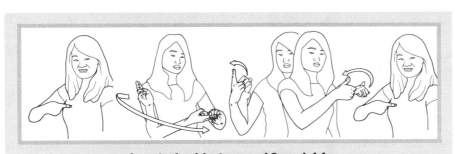

I go to bed between 10 and 11.

Between (10 & 11)

1. around 11	**7.** around 9	**13.** 1:30 a.m.	
2. 10:15	**8.** 11:00	**14.** around 10	
3. between 11, 12	**9.** midnight	**15.** around 12	
4. around 7:30	**10.** between 10, 10:45	**16.** 11:45	
5. between 9:30, 10	**11.** around 1 a.m.	**17.** between 2, 3 a.m.	**19.** between 11, 11:30
6. between 10, 11:30	**12.** between 9, 10	**18.** 9:50	**20.** between 9, 9:30

4 *How much time do you need to do the following activities?* In a complete sentence, state how long you think it takes to do each activity. An example is provided.

I need 5 minutes to eat.

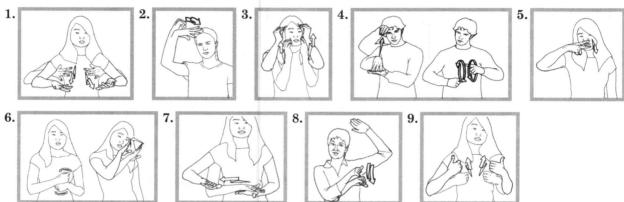

5 *Grouping details.* Organize the following information into groups by month, number, and year. Use the Spatial Organization Technique shown below.

1. 1999	**5.** October	**9.** March	**13.** September	**17.** 500
2. January	**6.** 20	**10.** 23	**14.** 2000	**18.** 1985
3. 150	**7.** 2004	**11.** 1,000	**15.** 31	**19.** February
4. 275	**8.** 2005	**12.** August	**16.** 425	**20.** May

6 *More grouping.* Organize the following information into groups by using the Spatial Organization Technique. How many spatial groups will you have?

<u>1</u>	<u>2</u>	<u>3</u>	<u>4</u>
6:45 a.m.	7:30 a.m.	5 minutes	2 hours
3 minutes	10 minutes	2001	10:45 p.m.
5:00 p.m.	9:15 p.m.	6 hours	8:00 a.m.
4 hours	12 hours	11:20 p.m.	15 minutes
1990	4:10 a.m.	30 minutes	1 hour

7 *Odds & Evens.* Organize the following information into groups of even and odd numbers using the Spatial Organization Technique.

1	**2**	**3**	**4**	**5**
2	100	23	40	500
5	250	21	33	1,000
8	8	18	100	303
7	101	3	95	91
10	83	10	20	37
11	67	11	22	30
12	90	5	17	17
14	4	6	19	5

Accent Steps

When using spatial organization to group information, you don't need to make the *group* sign repeatedly. Before signing the information, shift your shoulders towards the area where you first established the group.

8 *Activities.* What do you do at particular times of the day? Complete each sentence in ASL. An example is provided.

I go to class every morning at 7:15.

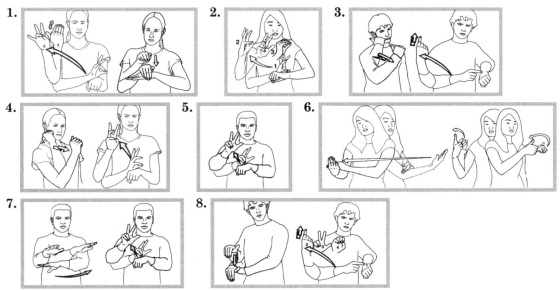

9 *Nap time.* Studies show napping is important to overall health for all people. Use the information below to explain how much nap time each person should have. Fingerspell *nap* or use the *sleep* sign.

1. grandma, age 78, 1 hour nap
2. woman, age 29, 15 minute nap
3. baby, age 6 months, 5 1 hour naps
4. teenager, age 15, 20 minute nap
5. boy, 3 years old, 2 hour nap
6. man, age 45, 30 minute nap
7. great-grandpa, age 94, 2–3 hour nap
8. teenager, age 13, 40 minute nap
9. woman, age 19, 20–30 minute nap
10. girl, 5 years old, 2–3 hour nap

10 *How long was I asleep?* Combine information from each column to create a sentence explaining how long each person was asleep. Follow the example as shown.

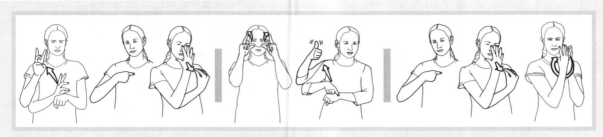

I went to bed at 6:00, and woke up at 10:00. I slept for 4 hours.

Name		Went to bed		Woke up	
1. Robin	**6.** Amanda	11:30	midnight	8:00	3:00
2. Dane	**7.** Chuck	10:00	6:30	12:00	10:45
3. Jennifer	**8.** James	9:45	1:00	6:15	7:10
4. Sarah	**9.** Theresa	7:00	10:30	4:00	9:15
5. Matt	**10.** Brandon	8:50	11:15	7:30	noon
		12:00	3:00	9:45	1:30

11 *Life in the future.* What do you think you'll be doing in the future? Use your imagination to sign a complete sentence explaining your expectations, following the example.

I will have a house by the year 2050. / In 2050, I will have a house.

1. 2015	**5.** 2017	**9.** 2007	**13.** Thanksgiving 2007
2. 2009	**6.** 2050	**10.** Fall 2006	**14.** Spring 2012
3. 2025	**7.** Summer, 2009	**11.** 2020	**15.** Winter 2013
4. 2008	**8.** Fall 2011	**12.** 2030	**16.** 2008

12 *Life in the past.* What were you doing at the following dates and times? Use your imagination to sign a complete sentence using the past tense.

1. 2 days ago	**6.** 5 years old	**11.** 2 years ago	**16.** December 31, 1999
2. 1998	**7.** Fall 2005	**12.** 8 hours ago	**17.** 5 minutes ago
3. Summer 2000	**8.** 6 months ago	**13.** 3 weeks ago	**18.** 6:00 a.m. today
4. last week	**9.** yesterday	**14.** 1 month ago	**19.** 4 months ago
5. 10 years ago	**10.** July 4, 2002	**15.** 12 years old	**20.** yesterday afternoon

13 *Recurring activities.* Sign each sentence in ASL, following the example.

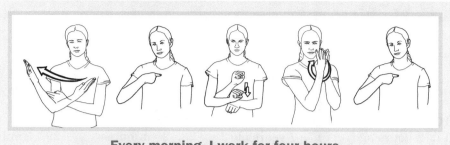

Every morning, I work for four hours.

1. They swim every day between 8:00 and 9:15.
2. I read every night for 2 hours.
3. On Fridays I work out for 3 hours.
4. We start work at 10:00 a.m. on Tuesdays.
5. On Wednesday evenings my ASL class begins at 6:30.
6. I have soccer practice starting at 7:45 on Saturdays.
7. On Tuesdays we work together for 5 hours.
8. Every year we have 2 weeks for vacation.
9. I eat dinner every night at 7:00.
10. During the weekends I study for 4 hours, 2 hours on Saturday, and 2 hours on Sunday.

14 *Available time.* Suggest activities that can be done in the amount of time provided below, following the example.

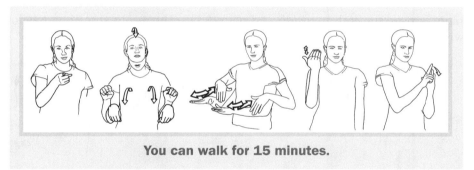

You can walk for 15 minutes.

1. 5 hours
2. 4 days
3. 10 minutes
4. 2 hours
5. 3 weeks
6. 1 year
7. 48 hours
8. 3 days
9. 5 minutes
10. half hour
11. 2 minutes
12. 15 minutes
13. 1 hour
14. 1 week
15. 8 hours
16. 45 minutes
17. 5 days
18. 4 hours
19. 25 minutes
20. 3 hours

15 *Skills review.* Sign each item quickly and clearly.

1	2	3	4	5
33.231.45C	2 hours, 5 minutes	3 weeks	1 million	798-4322
145 days	3-Aug-02	5 hours	22 years old	410 Tera Lane
10 minutes	in 1 week	in 3 months	3	4,799
88 seconds	5:30 a.m.	2 years ago	3 years ago	between 7 & 8 p.m.
3 weeks	72 hours	12,000,000	3 weeks ago	12 hours
4 days	510-0782	6 hours	in 3 months	5 hours
21,233,000	166.16.05.3	100	25 minutes	8 minutes
1999	94538	499-2862	in 4 months	2 minutes
in 8 hours	4:45 p.m.	7:15 a.m.	10-Sep-09	4 years
10 years ago	7 months	2 weeks ago	14 days	4 years ago

Unit 8

1 *Numbers.* Develop accuracy with each number, applying the skills you've learned.

1. in 10 hours	**7.** 55.2	**13.** 3:30 a.m.	**19.** 765-1421	**25.** 6:45 p.m.
2. 2003	**8.** 5 minutes	**14.** 23	**20.** 11/4/04	**26.** 7 days ago
3. 11,500	**9.** 8 weeks	**15.** 1991	**21.** 5 hours	**27.** 33
4. 3 days	**10.** 7 months	**16.** 1,991	**22.** 157	**28.** 510-39-0241
5. 9:30 a.m.	**11.** 2 hours ago	**17.** 7 years old	**23.** 23 minutes	**29.** 1 million
6. May 1, 1999	**12.** 1 year ago	**18.** 200,000	**24.** between 4 & 5	**30.** 17.22.032

2 *Body facts.* Sign each sentence below in ASL. Fingerspell the underlined terms.

1. people have around 100,000 hairs on their head
2. in 1 year, people blink around 84,000,000 times
3. people tend to fall asleep in 7 minutes
4. the heart beats 37,000,000 times a year
5. people with red hair tend to have freckles
6. people have 4,600 <u>taste buds</u> on their tongue
7. adults have 32 teeth, but children have 20
8. people have around 75 trillion body <u>cells</u>
9. people tend to have brown, blue, <u>hazel</u>, or green eyes
10. people drink around 16,000 <u>gallons</u> of water

3 *Weights.* The *weigh* sign is used for both to *weigh* and *pound.* Use the *weigh* sign shown below to state the following weights.

To weigh

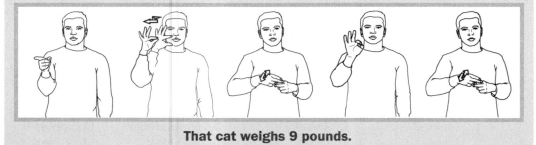

That cat weighs 9 pounds.

1. 2 pounds	**6.** 150 lbs.	**11.** 225 pounds	**16.** My dog weighs 32 pounds.	**20.** The cat weighs 7 pounds.
2. 10 pounds	**7.** 112 pounds	**12.** 15 pounds		
3. 100 pounds	**8.** 500 lbs.	**13.** 137 pounds	**17.** 75 pounds	
4. 1,000 lbs.	**9.** 94 pounds	**14.** 200 lbs.	**18.** 17 lbs.	
5. 11 pounds	**10.** 188 lbs.	**15.** 2.2 pounds	**19.** 259 pounds	

4 *Population.* Use the census chart to explain the population composition of the United States.

1. Black
2. Asian
3. White
4. Indian
5. Mixed
6. Hispanic
7. Native American
8. Arab

Population of the United States

Black/African American 37,098,946	Arab 1,422,000
Native American 2,786,652	Hispanic/Latino 39,898,889
Indian 1,899,599	Caucasian 234,196,357
Asian 11,924,912	Mixed race 4,307,575

Source: United States Census Bureau, 2004

5 *Signing height.* The words feet and inches are used to describe height in English. In ASL, sign *height* using a number handshape in front of the forehead that moves slightly away from the head. When signing *feet* and *inches*, the number handshape moves downward as it changes to the second number. Separate signs for feet or inches is not needed. This technique applies only to people's height.

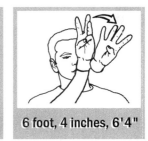

| 5'9" | 6 foot, 4 inches, 6'4" |

1.	5'	**5.**	4'10"	**9.**	5'2"	**13.**	5'9"
2.	3 foot	**6.**	5 foot 3	**10.**	6'0"	**14.**	6 foot 5 inches
3.	6'1"	**7.**	7 foot	**11.**	5'6"	**15.**	7'10"
4.	5'11"	**8.**	6'4"	**12.**	5 foot 8	**16.**	5 foot

17. 5'1"
18. 6'7"
19. 5 foot, 5 inches
20. 5 feet, 2 inches

6 *More height.* Sign the following sentences in ASL, using the height technique properly. Remember the format for describing people: General information first, followed by specific details.

1. I'm 5'5" and she's 5'7".
2. My father is 6'1".
3. My mother is 5'6".
4. He's 6'2" and I'm 5'9".
5. I have 3 brothers: Adam is 5'11", Scott is 6'0", and Bill is 5'10".

6. He's tall — he's 7'4".
7. My sister Lisa is 5 feet, 6 inches tall.
8. Janet is 5'2", and her sister is 5'3".
9. Michael Jordan is 6'6".
10. He stands 6 feet, 2 inches.

7 *Heights of objects: Trees.* The example below shows you how to sign the height of an object. Notice that *feet* is fingerspelled but again, there is no separate sign for tall or height. The sign *measure* shows you are signing about an object, not a person. In a complete sentence, explain how tall each type of tree grows.

To measure

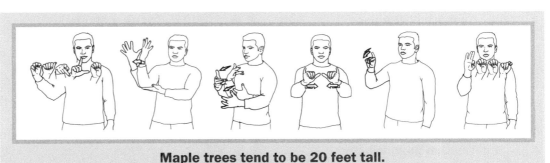

Maple trees tend to be 20 feet tall.

1. ash, 75'
2. red maple, 50'
3. cypress, 125'
4. white spruce, 100'
5. redwood, 300'
6. mayhaw, 20'
7. dogwood, 9'
8. magnolia, 65'

9. sawtooth oak, 40'
10. red maple, 70'
11. fir, 60'
12. giant sequoia, 275'
13. pine, 30'
14. aspen, 80'
15. myrtle, 11'
16. red pine, 75'

8 *Heights of objects: Mountains.* Signing the elevation of a mountain resembles signing the height of an object, though the sign *elevation* is used instead of *measure*. Sign the following elevations in a complete sentence. Remember to use the *mountain* sign instead of fingerspelling *mount*. See below for an example.

The mountain's elevation is 18,000 feet. / The mountain is 18,000 feet high.

1. Mt. McKinley: 20,320'
2. Mt. Batu: 14,131'
3. Mt. Sajama: 21,391'
4. Mt. Jaya: 16,500'
5. Mt. Everest: 29,035'
6. Mt. Zupo: 13,120'
7. Tent Peak: 24,165'
8. Mt. Ararat: 16,804'
9. Mt. Rainier: 14,410'
10. Mt. Solo: 20,492'
11. Mt. Fuji: 12,387'
12. Mt. Shasta: 14,162'
13. Mt. Kilimanjaro: 19,340'
14. Mt. Hood: 11,239'
15. K2: 28,250'
16. Mt. Fairweather: 15,300'

9 *Rivers.* How long is each river? Sign the name of the river and its length in a complete sentence. Fingerspell *mile*.

1. Mississippi: 2,340 miles
2. St. Lawrence: 800 miles
3. Yukon: 1,979 miles
4. Klamath: 250 miles
5. Nile: 4,160 miles
6. Danube: 1,776 miles
7. Yangtze: 3,964 miles
8. Amazon: 4,000 miles
9. Missouri: 3,710 miles
10. Colorado: 1,450 miles
11. Congo: 2,900 miles
12. Indus: 1,800 miles
13. Mekong: 2,700 miles
14. Thames: 210 miles
15. Rio Grande: 1,900 miles
16. Hudson: 306 miles

10 *Astronomy 101.* What can you say about each planet? Sign a complete sentence including all the information provided.

	Planet Name	1 year equals	Miles from sun	Miles from Earth
1.	Mercury	88 days	43,400,000	48,000,000
2.	Venus	225 days	67,700,000	23, 700,000
3.	Earth	365 days	94,500,000	—
4.	Mars	687 days	154,900,000	33,900,000
5.	Jupiter	4,332 days	507,400,000	366,000,000
6.	Saturn	10,759 days	941,100,000	743,000,000
7.	Uranus	30,685 days	1,866,000,000	1,605,000,000
8.	Neptune	60,188 days	2,824,000,000	2,676,000,000
9.	Pluto	90,465 days	4,538,000,000	3,669,000,000

11 *Medical conditions.* How many people in the United States and Canada have each condition? Fingerspell the underlined terms.

1. <u>high cholesterol</u>, 37 million
2. <u>diabetes</u>, 18.2 million
3. <u>allergies</u>, 56.2 million
4. <u>AIDS</u>, 1.1 million
5. <u>arthritis</u>, 70 million
6. <u>Alzheimer's</u>, 4.5 million
7. <u>depression</u>, 13–14 million
8. <u>cancer</u>, 13 million
9. <u>ADHD</u>, 11 million
10. <u>schizophrenia</u>, 2.2 million
11. blindness, 1.3 million
12. deaf / hard of hearing, 7–8 million

Source: The National Institutes of Health

12 *Health statistics.* Complete the sentence using the information provided, following the example. Fingerspell the underlined terms.

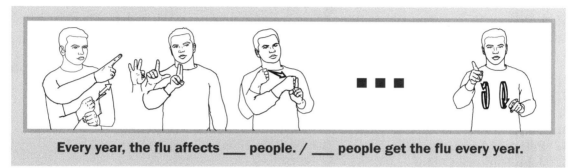

Every year, the flu affects ___ people. / ___ people get the flu every year.

1. <u>breast cancer</u>, 140,400
2. <u>flu</u>, 42,150,000
3. <u>stroke</u>, 167,000
4. break arm, 880,000
5. <u>lung cancer</u>, 173,770
6. heart <u>attack</u>, 1,000,000
7. <u>pneumonia</u>, 4,376,000
8. chicken pox, 3,800,000
9. <u>asthma</u>, 17,000,000
10. <u>salmonella</u>, 40,000
11. <u>Lyme</u> disease, 23,000
12. <u>rabies</u>, 4,322

Source: The National Institute of Health

13 *How long?* Explain in a complete sentence how long you've been ill. Use the *since* sign instead of *for*.

1. 8 weeks
2. Tuesday evening
3. last weekend
4. this morning
5. 4 days
6. 2 hours
7. Thursday morning
8. 2 days
9. yesterday afternoon, 3 p.m.
10. 3 weeks ago
11. 4 hours
12. 10 minutes

14 *Exercise Tips.* How long does it take to burn 150 calories? Sign a complete sentence for each activity.

1. playing football, 30 minutes
2. dancing fast, 16 minutes
3. raking leaves, 30 minutes
4. washing windows, 1 hour
5. bicycling, 5 miles
6. walking, 6 miles
7. swimming, 20 minutes
8. shoveling snow, 15 minutes
9. playing basketball, 20 minutes
10. sleeping, 9 hours
11. running, 10 minutes
12. jumping rope fast, 8 minutes

Source: U.S. Dept. of Health and Human Services

15 *Skills review.* Sign each item quickly and clearly.

<u>1</u>	<u>2</u>	<u>3</u>	<u>4</u>	<u>5</u>
13,455 miles	30 minutes	1,233,000	30 years old	5'4, 110 pounds
180 pounds	150 years	22 million	5'11	3 minutes
6 days	12 months	6 feet tall	2,300 feet high	6'5, 240 pounds
4 hours	5 months	10 minutes	400,000	2,543,233

Unit 9

1 *Numbers.* Develop accuracy with each number, applying the skills you've learned.

1. 2 hours	**7.** 2 months	**13.** 4:45 p.m.	**19.** 1992	**25.** 2 days ago
2. 5'3"	**8.** 3 days ago	**14.** 8 weeks	**20.** 7:30 a.m.	**26.** 5:00 p.m.
3. 23 lbs.	**9.** 1,250	**15.** in 1 month	**21.** 6 hours	**27.** 90 feet high
4. 5 days	**10.** in 3 years	**16.** next week	**22.** 12 days	**28.** 140,000
5. 200 miles	**11.** 5 minutes	**17.** 415-2323	**23.** 215 pounds	**29.** 2 weeks ago
6. 8 years old	**12.** 10 pounds	**18.** 22 feet high	**24.** 5'9"	**30.** 890-1129

2 *Tall buildings.* Sign a complete sentence based on the information provided. Use the *floor* sign as needed.

Building Name	Feet / Height	Stories
1. Taipei 101	1,650	101
2. Sears Tower	1,450	110
3. CN Tower	1,815	n/a
4. Empire State Building	1,250	102
5. Petronas Tower	1,483	88
6. John Hancock Center	1,127	100

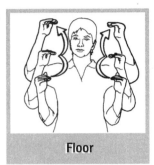

Floor

3 *Populations.* Based on the table below, what can you say about each city's population? Sign a complete sentence using the information provided.

City	Population 1975	Population 2000	Population 2015
1. Tokyo	26,615,000	34,450,000	36,214,000
2. New York	15,880,000	17,846,000	19,717,000
3. Shanghai	11,443,000	12,887,000	12,666,000
4. Los Angeles	8,926,000	11,814,000	12,904,000
5. Boston	2,666,000	2,918,000	3,166,000
6. Chicago	6,749,000	6,951,000	7,386,000

Source: United Nations & U.S. Census

4 *More populations.* Use the Listing and Ordering Technique to rank each location in a complete sentence by its population.

1. Madison, Wisconsin	221,000	**4.** Frankfort, Kentucky	27,400
Norfolk, Virginia	244,600	Las Vegas, Nevada	527,900
Bellevue, Washington	112,400	Columbus, Ohio	730,900
2. Cameron, Missouri	10,300	Kingston, Ontario, Canada	112,700
Fort Lee, New Jersey	37,300	Deer Park, New York	28,500
Deming, New Mexico	14,600	**5.** Kearns, Utah	35,700
Blackfoot, Idaho	10,800	Coos Bay, Oregon	15,400
3. Toccoa, Georgia	9,300	Fort Collins, Colorado	126,900
Chapais, Quebec, Canada	1,800	Elsmere, Delaware	5,800
Elwood, Indiana	9,300	**6.** Waterville, Maine	15,900
Opelousas, Lousiana	22,800	Plano, Texas	245,900
		St. Paul, Minnesota	278,900
		Kallispell, Montana	17,000

Source: The World Gazetteer

5 *Dollars & cents.* Signing money is first determined by the type of money being signed about: Cents-only amounts, dollar-only amounts, or mixed figures including both dollars and cents.

Signing: Cents

When a number sign is made after touching the area of your temple called the Money Spot, the number formed becomes a *cent* sign. This is an example of a combined sign where the sign for *cent* is incorporated into the amount, as if saying *cent one, cent two*, and so on. Touch the Money Spot first before making a number sign, or touch the number sign itself to the Money Spot as in the example. Signs for *penny, nickel, dime, quarter,* and *half-dollar* are made by showing their monetary amount.

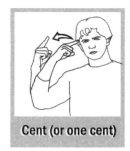

Cent (or one cent)

1	2	3	4	5	6	7	8	9	10
1 cent	penny	10¢	4 cents	3¢	1 quarter	6¢	1 dime	5¢	20 cents
2 cents	nickel	55¢	50 cents	25¢	16 cents	10¢	10 cents	25¢	45 cents
3 cents	dime	60¢	2 cents	63¢	25 cents	5¢	1 penny	60¢	30 cents
4 cents	quarter	23¢	19 cents	5¢	5 cents	49¢	1 cent	50¢	2 pennies
5 cents	20 cents	4¢	30 cents	10¢	2 pennies	56¢	1 nickel	5¢	1 dime
6 cents	12 pennies	1¢	95 cents	7¢	15 cents	65¢	5 cents	33¢	80 cents
7 cents	65 cents	99¢	65 cents	22¢	5 cents	100¢	1 quarter	10¢	84 cents
8 cents	80 cents	60¢	1 cent	14¢	1 nickel	2¢	25 cents	22¢	25 cents
9 cents	3 cents	30¢	10 cents	4¢	1 dime	8¢	50 cents	15¢	1 quarter
10 cents	half-dollar	7¢	15 cents	10¢	20 cents	4¢	half-dollar	4¢	1 nickel

Signing: Dollars

There are two forms used to sign a monetary amount that does not include cents. For dollar amounts up to $9.00, the wrist is flicked inward, so the sign shows both the amount and the concept of *dollars*. For amounts higher than $9,00, you must add the *dollar* sign after a number.

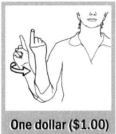
One dollar ($1.00)

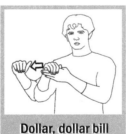
Dollar, dollar bill

34 dollars / $34.00

1	2	3	4	5	6	7	8	9	10
1 dollar	$11.00	$100	3 bucks	$8	4 bucks	$12.00	8 dollars	$18	$5.00
2 dollars	$13.00	$1,000	12 dollars	$900	$100,000	$84.00	5 dollars	$9	$30
3 dollars	$15.00	$250	15 dollars	$43	3 dollars	$120.00	$50	$25	$4
4 dollars	$17.00	$60	1 dollar	$103	$80.00	$77.00	3 bucks	$100	4 bucks
5 dollars	$19.00	$30	100 bucks	$81	11 bucks	$1,400.00	24 dollars	$68	4 dollars
6 dollars	$21.00	$99	2 dollars	$67	20 dollars	$200.00	$60.00	$92	$150.00
7 dollars	$23.00	$800	188 bucks	$30	$3,200	$54.00	5 bucks	$483	8 dollars
8 dollars	$25.00	$320	4 dollars	$10	90 dollars	$3.00	5 dollars	$202	25 dollars
9 dollars	$27.00	$480	80 bucks	$19	$450.00	$90.00	$75.00	$135	2 bucks
10 dollars	$29.00	$500	2 dollar bill	$3	half-dollar	$15.00	$40	$43	10 dollars

Signing: Dollars and cents

After signing a dollar amount, sign the cents value. You do not need to touch the Money Spot when cents follow a dollar amount or add the *dollars* sign (see Examples A and B). Some people do include the *cent* and *dollar* signs for amounts larger than $9.00 or for emphasis (see Example C). You should become familiar with each way of signing mixed monetary amounts. Do not follow Example C when signing a cent amount only.

A.

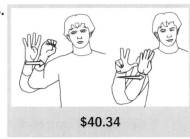

$1.34

B.

$40.34

C.

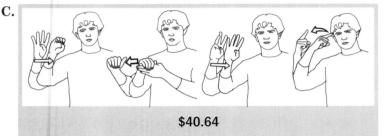

$40.64

1	2	3	4	5	6	7	8	9	10
$10.30	$201.30	$55.60	$21.10	$88.40	$0.25	$14.35	$15.60	$25.40	$17.80
$4.99	$19.95	$4.00	$0.45	$301.10	$4.00	$90.51	$45.23	$1.89	$50.50
$101.10	$49.50	$32.30	$9.00	$55.00	$23.25	$3.00	$0.85	$49.76	66¢
$43.50	$21.95	$3.25	$12.96	$90.87	$40.00	$0.35	$187.02	$515.89	$23.60
$10.25	$23.25	$10.90	$1.10	$1.25	$0.85	$775.25	$1,040.20	$90.40	$0.40
$15.90	$3.99	$2.00	2¢	$7.00	$412.80	88¢	50¢	$2.00	$91.15
$1.99	$320.90	$19.45	$65.00	$19.23	50¢	$2.00	$12.00	$66.90	$1,290.20
$80.05	$93.35	$3.00	$0.10	$45.80	$6.50	$9.99	$67.90	$943.12	$60.40
$33.20	$50.15	$17.30	$40.00	$10.27	40¢	$12.50	27¢	$0.45	$74.23
$45.36	$1.98	$24.00	$0.95	$9.00	$0.83	20¢	$2,350.11	$51.30	$5.00

6 *Neighborhood rents.* How much do people pay to rent a 1-bedroom apartment? Use the sign *every-month* for *rent.* Why do you think the sign is the same? Sign a complete sentence based on the information provided.

1. San Francisco $1,652.00
2. Philadelphia $922.50
3. El Paso $513.00
4. Miami $830.10
5. United States $780.25
6. Chicago $959.00
7. Greensboro $592.00
8. Los Angeles $913.75
9. Denver $717.43
10. San Jose $1,448.00
11. New York $1,588.09
12. Tulsa $466.50
13. Washington, DC $914.00
14. Houston $582.65
15. Memphis $543.02

Every month / Rent

Source: Statistical Abstract of the United States

7 *Famous zip codes.* Explain in a complete sentence using the information provided where each zip code is located. Fingerspell *zip* and *code,* as well as underlined terms.

1. 90210, Beverly Hills, Los Angeles
2. 20002, White House, Washington, DC
3. 60611, Magnificent Mile, Chicago
4. 10001, Manhattan, New York City
5. 33139, Ocean Drive, Miami Beach
6. 96815, Diamond Head, Hawaii
7. 81611, Aspen, Colorado
8. 70116, French Quarter, New Orleans
9. 57760, center of the United States, Castle Rock, South Dakota
10. 02360, Plymouth Rock, Massachusetts

8 *Exchange rates.* Complete the sentence using the information provided. Fingerspell the underlined terms.

1. 103 <u>yen</u> (Japan)
2. 45 <u>rupee</u> (India)
3. 1.18 dollar (Canada)
4. 596 <u>peso</u> (<u>Chile</u>)
5. .54 <u>pound</u> (England)
6. 11.4 <u>peso</u> (Mexico)
7. 6.24 <u>pound</u> (Egypt)
8. 188 <u>forint</u> (<u>Hungary</u>)
9. 3 <u>zloty</u> (<u>Poland</u>)
10. .77 <u>euro</u> (<u>Europe</u>)

An American dollar is worth ...

11. 4.39 <u>shekel</u> (<u>Israel</u>)
12. 6 <u>krone</u> (<u>Norway</u>)
13. 32 dollar (<u>Taiwan</u>)
14. 1,064 <u>won</u> (South <u>Korea</u>)
15. 38.8 <u>baht</u> (<u>Thailand</u>)

16. 8,973 <u>rupiah</u> (<u>Indonesia</u>)
17. 6 <u>rand</u> (South Africa)
18. 1.28 dollar (<u>Australia</u>)
19. 28.5 <u>ruble</u> (<u>Russia</u>)
20. 1,917 <u>bolivar</u> (<u>Venezuela</u>)

Source: Pacific Exchange Rate Service

9 *How much?* For the items below, explain what prices you think would be inexpensive or expensive. What would you pay?

1.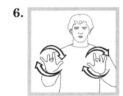
2.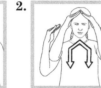
3.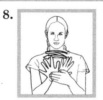
4.
5.

6.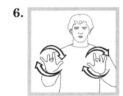
7.
8.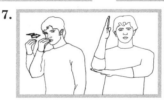
9.
10.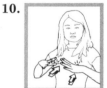

10 *More zip codes.* Sign each zip code clearly and quickly.

1	2	3	4	5	6	7	8	9	10
57101	04216	22306	92178	96703	12025	35572	18433	30339	50601
42603	62310	03224	76645	72201	51465	19954	33912	28052	21223
98119	87105	67730	15236	99546	34230	00680	21402	63545	75415
40006	30802	12241	07717	81657	99695	72855	47339	94539	56630

11 *Famous places.* Sign each address clearly and quickly.

1. Navy Pier
   600 E. Grand Avenue
   Chicago, IL 60611

2. Gateway Arch
   50 South Leanor K. Sullivan
   St. Louis, MO 63102

3. Mount Rushmore
   13000 Highway 244
   Keystone, SD 57751

4. The White House
   1600 Pennsylvania Avenue NW
   Washington, D.C. 20500

5. Fisherman's Wharf
   Pier 39
   San Francisco, CA 94105

6. Empire State Building
   350 5th Avenue
   New York, New York 10118

12 *Transportation schedules.* Explain each transit schedule clearly, using the correct signs for *arrive* and *depart*.

Transfer, change

Schedule

To take off

To take off (plane)

To arrive

To arrive (plane)

1. **Bus Schedule**
   Begins at 5:45 a.m.
   Stops at 11:45 p.m.
   Buses arrive and depart
   every 15 minutes on the hour.

2. **Flight Schedule**
   Departs / Arrives
   New York 7:45 / 9:15
   Atlanta 6:10 / 7:30
   Des Moines 8:16 / 11:20

3. **Subway Schedule**
   Begins 5:15 a.m.
   Ends 12:00 midnight
   Arrives at station every 4–8
   minutes. No service from
   9:15-9:40 p.m.

4. **Taxi Schedule**
   Costs $1.10 per mile
   Can get on / off at bus station, home, airport, school,
   business. No schedule.

5. **Train Schedule**
   Los Angeles to Tucson,
   leaves at 7:00, takes 6
   hours. Transfer trains in
   Phoenix. Costs: $133.20.
   Montreal to Niagara Falls,
   leaves at 4:30 and 10:00
   p.m., takes 4 hours. Costs:
   $84.00 Canadian dollars.

6. **Commute Options**
   – board bus at 7:11, ride
   for 12 minutes. Walk 2
   blocks to work.
   – take taxi, costs $7.10.
   – ride subway at 7:01,
   transfer at 7:15, walk 1
   block to work.
   – take 6:40 train to station, arrive at 7:05,
   board bus at 7:10, arrive
   at work 7:25 a.m.

13 *Deaf community addresses.* Sign each address quickly and clearly.

1. National Association of the Deaf
   814 Thayer Avenue
   Silver Spring, MD 20910
   301.587.1781
   http://www.nad.org

2. Gallaudet University
   800 Florida Avenue NE
   Washington, DC 20002
   202.651.5000
   http://www.gallaudet.edu

3. NTID
   52 Lomb Memorial Drive
   Rochester, NY 14623
   http://www.ntid.rit.edu

14 *More community addresses.* Use your imagination to sign a complete sentence that uses the address below.

1. Central Bank
   34403 Central Ave.
   Spanaway, WA 98002

2. Workout World
   1201 Bridge Street
   Annapolis, MD 21402
   – corner of Bridge & Vine

3. Fairview Post Office
   1802 Third Street
   – across from the grocery
     store

4. Shane & Shane Consulting
   12 Etruria Lane
   – upstairs, office #6
   – 788-1216

5. Engineers, Inc.
   45390 Olympic View
   Reston, VA 20901
   – next to 7-11

6. Colfax Police Dept.
   34 Old Gold Road
   – corner of Gold & Lark
   – bring money

7. Barnard Hall
   Vanderbilt University
   2201 West End Avenue
   Nashville, TN 37235

8. Gourmet Foods
   321 North Second Street
   San Jose, CA 95110
   – near the post office

15 *Skills review.* Sign each item quickly and clearly.

<u>1</u>	<u>2</u>	<u>3</u>	<u>4</u>	<u>5</u>	<u>6</u>	<u>7</u>	<u>8</u>	<u>9</u>	<u>10</u>
$8.50	3 hours	4 minutes	8 years old	1 hour	5 minutes	in 10 years	4 days	467-0976	15 cents
25 cents	10 minutes	100	4440 Oak	10.5	8 hours	$1,900	6 cents	2 weeks	$1.15
3 days	882-8910	$7	6'2	20 miles	5'11	6:45 a.m.	$889	6 hours	1:15 a.m.
5 miles	2,500	1 penny	1,000	$4.00	67	665-1267	5'3	3:50 p.m.	5 bucks
2	6 days	3 years ago	2 weeks	34 pounds	15,400 feet high	19 Pine St. 125 pounds	5,412	$400	25 years old

Unit 10

1 *Numbers.* Develop accuracy with each number, applying the skills you've learned.

1. $50.00	**7.** 15,143	**13.** $20.00	**19.** 6 months	**25.** 1,000 feet
2. 8:15	**8.** 6'4"	**14.** 8:54 p.m.	**20.** 25 cents	**26.** 2 months ago
3. 15 years old	**9.** ages 7, 2	**15.** 2 hours	**21.** 5 minutes	**27.** 50¢
4. 5¢	**10.** 3 weeks	**16.** 229 pounds	**22.** 3:15 a.m.	**28.** in 6 months
5. 2006	**11.** 97	**17.** dime	**23.** 5'4"	**29.** $150.30
6. Oct. 16	**12.** 14 days	**18.** 754-8743	**24.** 50,000	**30.** 10 cents

2 *Average salaries.* Use the given information to explain the average salary for each occupation. An example is provided.

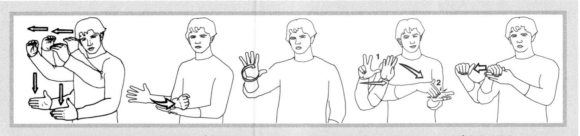

Teachers earn around $34,000. / A teacher's salary is around $34,000.

1. plumber, $29,610	**7.** CEO, $250,000+	**13.** engineer, $68,489
2. lawyer, $71,530	**8.** secretary, $23,320	**14.** farmer, $41,660
3. nurse, $36,920	**9.** doctor, $104,000+	**15.** software design, $84,356
4. factory, $14.38/hour	**10.** veternarian, $46,370	**16.** physicist, $65,000
5. mechanic, $34,056	**11.** waiter, $25,856	
6. accountant, $45,919	**12.** physical therapist, $38,000	Source: Statistical Abstract of the United States

3 *Time for a raise?* Below are the average salaries of selected occupations. In a complete sentence explain how much you think would be an appropriate salary for the position, and why.

1. day care, $22,300	**7.** babysitter, $6.00 /hour	**13.** chef, $34,000
2. coach, $31,500	**8.** armed services, $23,750	**14.** stay-at-home-mom, $0
3. banker, $89,322	**9.** artist, $14,012	**15.** police officer, $54,000
4. counselor, $29,400	**10.** president, $200,000	**16.** kindergarten teacher,
5. writer, $26,000	**11.** janitor, $19,200	$21,008
6. pro athlete, $8,750,000	**12.** pro actor, $1,200,000	

4 *Enrollment.* Research indicates that the more education one attains, the higher one's income. Using the information below, explain how many people attend each type of school.

1. preschool	4,273,000	**6.** college / university	12,523,000
2. kindergarten	7,213,000	**7.** training school	1,640,000
3. elementary	13,051,000	**8.** business / trade school	3,201,000
4. junior high / middle school	12,209,000	**9.** charter school	852,000
5. high school	16,423,000	**10.** private school	4,546,000

Source: U.S. Dept. of Education

5 *More occupations.* English uses the phrase "There are" to introduce a statement. ASL uses the sign *have* instead of separate signs for "there" and "are." Follow the example to sign a complete sentence using the information provided.

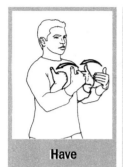

Have

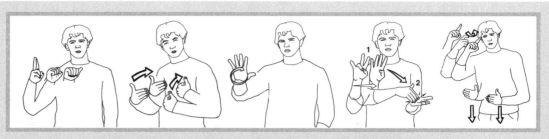

There are about 74,000 politicians in the United States.

1.	managers	10,772,000	**10.**	dentists	136,000
2.	real estate agents	306,000	**11.**	teachers	3,378,000
3.	engineers	1,572,000	**12.**	photographers	115,000
4.	doctors	612,000	**13.**	sales	11,818,000
5.	professional actors	71,000	**14.**	technicians	1,303,000
6.	college professors	606,000	**15.**	librarians	213,000
7.	professional athletes	58,000	**16.**	farmers	3,305,000
8.	bankers / tellers	2,397,000	**17.**	cashiers	2,019,000
9.	computer scientists	563,000	**18.**	administration	16,395,000

Source: U.S. Bureau of Labor Statistics

6 *At the grocery store.* Use the *cost* sign to make a complete sentence from the information provided.

1. watermelon, $2.00	**5.** cookies, $5.00	**9.** apple, .25
2. pineapple, $4.99	**6.** gum, .80	**10.** chicken, $2.95
3. steak, $7.20	**7.** can of soup, $1.50	**11.** eggs, $3.00
4. cereal, $3.99	**8.** milk, $2.39	**12.** soda, $4.50

To cost

7 *At the fruit stand.* Use the *weigh/pound* sign and basic math skills to sign the final price of each item in a complete sentence. Refer to the price guide as needed.

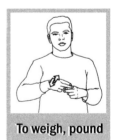

To weigh, pound

Fruit Stand Prices		
yellow apple .40 each	peach $1.50/lb	red apple $1.99/lb
banana .50/lb	grapes $2.99/lb	nectarine $1.00 each / $4.00/lb
cherry $2.00/lb	plum .50 each	orange $2.50/lb

1. 10 yellow apples	**5.** 4 lbs. oranges	**9.** 3 1/2 lbs. cherries	**13.** 3 plums
2. 2 lbs. cherries	**6.** 1 lb. grapes	**10.** 2 lbs. peaches	**14.** 1 lb. oranges
3. 1 lb. bananas	**7.** 3 nectarines	**11.** 1 lb. red apples	**15.** 5 nectarines
4. 5 plums	**8.** 1/2 lb. bananas	**12.** 4 yellow apples	**16.** 4 lbs. bananas

8 *Caloric information.* How many calories are there in each food item? Sign a complete sentence using the information provided, fingerspelling the word *calories*. Figures are for 3.5 oz servings or whole portions.

1. carrot, 34 cal.
2. lettuce, 13 cal.
3. ribs, 566 cal.
4. cheese, 216 cal.
5. water, 0 cal.
6. cheeseburger, 1,420 cal.
7. tomato, 17 cal.
8. spaghetti, 688 cal.
9. bread, 152 cal.
10. hot dog, 140 cal.
11. celery, 7 cal.
12. chicken enchilada, 323 cal.
13. mayo, 695 cal.
14. chocolate milk, 226 cal.
15. banana, 160 cal.
16. fish, 122 cal.

9 *The local restaurant.* You and some friends are eating out. Use the menu to select a meal. What will you order, and what will it cost?

1. Breakfast
   Meal & beverage
2. Lunch
   Meal, beverage, dessert
3. Dinner
   Meal, beverage, dessert

Breakfast	Lunch & Dinner	Dessert
2 eggs $1.95	salad $4.99	chocolate cake $2.00
bacon $1.50	vegetable soup $5.25	apple pie & ice cream $2.50
sausage $2.25	hamburger $7.95	strawberries $3.00
waffles $4.99	baked potato $3.99	**Beverages**
cereal $3.20	ravioli $6.95	milk .95
omelette $2.99	mac & cheese $6.00	coffee $1.50
cheese omelette $3.35	baked chicken $12.50	tea $1.10
fruit $5.00	carrots or peas $2.30	soda $2.00
pancakes & eggs $5.10	vegetarian lasagna $6.99	

10 *Ingredients.* How many ingredients can you name for each meal? Use the Listing and Ordering Technique to help explain the ingredients in each dish. An example is provided.

The sandwich has bread, turkey, and cheese on it.

1.   a. _____ b. _____ c. _____ d. _____

3.  a. _____ b. _____ c. _____ d. _____ e. _____

5.  a. _____ b. _____ c. _____

2. 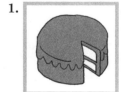 a. _____ b. _____ c. _____

4.   a. _____ b. _____ c. _____ d. _____ e. _____

6. a. _____ b. _____ c. _____ d. _____ e. _____ f. _____

11 *Prices.* The Consumer Price Index tracks the changes in prices from year to year. Based on the chart below, what can you say about each price?

Type	Year 1945	1990	1999	2002	2004	2006 (est.)
1. gas	.12	$1.16	$1.11	$1.51	$1.68	$2.30
2. weekly food	$8.00	$34.40	$41.60	$44.00	$46.10	$48.90
3. clothing, every 3 months	$9.15	$67.00	$104.30	$115.06	$127.00	$145.00
4. milk	.40	$1.45	$1.41	$1.66	$2.19	$2.37
5. bread	.10	.99	$1.10	$1.85	$2.01	$2.22
6. health care, every 3 months	$10.12	$43.20	$145.02	$166.40	$192.30	$218.00

12 *Business cards.* What does each business do? State the information found on each business card and explain what kind of business it is in complete sentences.

1.
Internal Revenue Service
1.800.829.1040
http://www.irs.gov

4.
Lawns & Trees
Joel Stevenson
cell phone: 566.7420
$50 /hour

7.
United States Postal Service
1.800.ASK.USPS

2.
Elisa Roberts, CEO
Computer Consulting
3090 Maxwell Drive
Silicon Valley, CA 94530
657.8930

5.
Dr. Rita Caler
399078 Liberty Ave.
Office 45A
Pediatrics

8.
Clothiers R Us
358 Supermall Road
Sales every day!

3.
Instant Photography
12 Aptos Way, #4
981.5543

6.
Plumbing 24/7, 365 days
Cheap rates!
Friendly people!

13 *Endangered species.* Explain in a complete sentence the name and remaining number of each endangered specie. Fingerspell the underlined terms or ask your ASL teacher for particular signs.

1. elephant, 50,000
2. black rhino, 2,500
3. manatee, 2,000
4. Hawaiian monk seal, 500
5. condor, 50
6. black ferret, 18
7. sea turtle, 500
8. bald eagle, 15,000
9. mountain gorilla, 700
10. grizzly bear, 10,000
11. river otter, 1,000
12. humpback whale, 12,500
13. panda, 800
14. tiger, 350
15. spotted dolphin, 900
16. white rhino, 6

14 *Animal facts.* Sign each fact in ASL, fingerspelling the underlined terms. Use the sign *pregnant* for "gestate" and *measure* for "inches."

1. a person can run 18 miles per hour (<u>mph</u>)
2. a cat can run 12 <u>mph</u>
3. a <u>cheetah</u> can run 46 <u>mph</u>
4. brown bears can weigh 1,700 pounds
5. dolphins sleep with one eye open
6. a giraffe's tongue is 21 inches long
7. <u>zebras</u> are white with black stripes

8. 6,000 years ago <u>greyhounds</u> were popular in <u>Egypt</u>
9. ants don't sleep
10. a baby <u>panda</u> weighs 6 <u>ounces</u>
11. a <u>mackerel</u> fish lays 500,000 eggs in 2 minutes
12. a female elephant gestates for 608 days

15 *Skills review.* Sign each item quickly and clearly.

1	2	3	4	5
$1.00	341 Pine	2 minutes	5,000 years ago	4 hours
6 days	6'1"	last week	5,000 years old	in 2 hours
4 weeks	5'11"	2 days	213-0776	$100.00
2,975	25	3 hours	2,009	5 months ago
20 cents	$90	700	$504.10	17,765 feet high
458-0967	4,100,000	91	3 weeks ago	6'7"
56.7	15 years old	$861	in 3 weeks	$76.50
$45.00	6,700	$5	quarter	$6
2 pounds	$376	3:45 a.m.	8:10 p.m.	18 years old
6 years old	50 cents	dime	2 pennies	9 million

More Number Activities

1 *Population changes.* Describe the population changes of the United States using the chart below.

	Year	Total Population
1.	1790	3,929,214
2.	1830	12,866,020
3.	1870	39,818,449
4.	1900	75,994,575
5.	1950	150,697,361
6.	1980	227,726,804
7.	1990	248,718,301
8.	2001	275,279,000
9.	2005	287,716,000 (estimated)
10.	2010	299,862,000 (estimated)

2 *Immigration.* How many people have immigrated to the United States?

	Year	Total Immigration
1.	1901–1910	8,795,000
2.	1911–1920	5,736,000
3.	1921–1930	4,102,000
4.	1931–1940	528,000
5.	1941–1950	1,035,000
6.	1951–1960	2,515,000
7.	1961–1970	3,322,000
8.	1971–1980	4,493,000
9.	1981–1990	7,338,000
10.	1991–2000	7,605,000
11.	2001–2004	4,165,703
12.	2005–2010	4,043,000 (estimated)

3 *Age distribution.* Use the chart below to explain the age distribution of the population.

	Year	Total Immigration
1.	Under 5 years of age	19,176,000
2.	5–9 years	20,550,000
3.	10–14 years	20,528,000
4.	15–19 years	20,220,000
5.	20–24 years	18,964,000
6.	25–34 years	39,892,000
7.	35–44 years	45,149,000
8.	45–54 years	37,678,000
9.	55–59 years	13,469,000
10.	60–64 years	10,805,000
11.	65–74 years	18,391,000
12.	75–84 years	12,361,000
13.	85–120 years	4,240,000

4   *State populations.* Use the chart below to explain how many people live in each area.

State	Population	State	Population
Alabama	4,447,000	North Dakota	642,000
Alaska	627,000	Ohio	11,353,000
Arizona	5,131,000	Oklahoma	3,451,000
Arkansas	2,673,000	Oregon	3,421,000
California	33,872,000	Pennsylvania	12,281,000
Colorado	4,301,000	Rhode Island	1,048,000
Connecticut	3,406,000	South Carolina	4,012,000
Delaware	784,000	South Dakota	755,000
Florida	15,982,000	Tennessee	5,689,000
Georgia	8,186,000	Texas	20,852,000
Hawaii	1,212,000	Utah	2,233,000
Idaho	1,294,000	Vermont	609,000
Illinois	12,419,000	Virginia	7.079,000
Indiana	6,080,000	Washington	5,894,000
Iowa	2,926,000	Washington, D.C.	572,000
Kansas	2,688,000	West Virginia	1,808,000
Kentucky	4,042,000	Wisconsin	5,364,000
Louisiana	4,469,000	Wyoming	494,000
Maine	1,275,000		
Maryland	5,296,000	**Canadian Province**	**Population**
Massachusetts	6,349,000	Alberta	2,964,807
Michigan	9,938,000	British Columbia	3,907,738
Minnesota	4,919,000	Manitoba	1,119,583
Mississippi	2,845,000	Newfoundland	512,930
Missouri	5,595,000	New Brunswick	729,498
Montana	902,000	Northwest Territories	37,360
Nebraska	1,711,000	Nova Scotia	908,007
Nevada	1,998,000	Nunavut	26,745
New Hampshire	1,236,000	Ontario	11,410,146
New Jersey	8,414,000	Prince Edward Island	135,294
New Mexico	1,819,000	Quebec	7,237,479
New York	18,976,000	Saskatchewan	978,933
North Carolina	8,049,000	Yukon	28,674

5   *In the past month...* Use the graph below to explain how many people participate in each activity every month.

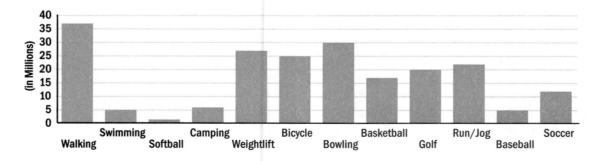

6 *Statistics.* Sign each sentence in ASL.

1. Every year, people ...

eat 37.8 pounds of cheese
watch 1,130 hours of television
see 16 movies at a theater
spend $83.00 on books
volunteer 6 hours

2. There are ...

9,210,000 milk cows in the United States
435,000,000 chickens in the United States
around 1,000,000 moose in Canada
528 million credit cards in the United States
18 million people who have digital cameras

3. Every year ...

2,103 Americans move to Canada
18,569 Canadians move to the
    United States
2.21 million people graduate from college
teenagers spend 13.1 billion dollars
people eat 523,000 organic eggs

4. Every year ...

44,000 people go to jail
19,277,000 people are pulled over by police
1,217,317 people take Advanced
    Placement exams
2.3 million people get married
1.23 million people get divorced

7 *Addresses.* Sign each address in ASL.

1. Centers for Disease Control
   1600 Clifton Road, N.E.
   Atlanta, GA 30333
   1-800-311-3435
   http://www.cdc.gov

2. Space Needle
   400 Broad Street
   Seattle, WA 98109
   206-905-2100
   http://www.spaceneedle.com

3. United States Department of Education
   400 Maryland Avenue, S.W.
   Washington, D.C. 20202-5621
   1-800-424-1616
   http://www.ed.gov

4. Social Security Administration
   6400 Security Boulevard
   Baltimore, MD 21235
   1-800-772-1213
   http://www.ssa.gov

5. Disneyland
   1313 Harbor Boulevard
   Anaheim, CA 92803
   714-999-4565
   http://www.disneyland.com

6. National Science Foundation
   4201 Wilson Boulevard
   Arlington, VA 22230
   703-292-5111
   http://www.nsf.gov

8 *Gestation periods & life span.* What can you say about each specie based on the table below?

	Specie	Gestation period	Approximate Life Span		Specie	Gestation period	Approximate Life Span
1.	Cat	2 months	16 years	9.	Cow	10 months	11 years
2.	Elephant	640 days	57 years	10.	Dog	2 months	17 years
3.	Human	9 months	77 years	11.	Monkey	164 days	23 years
4.	Mouse	3 weeks	3 years	12.	Horse	1 year	19 years
5.	Nightingale	15 days	3.8 years	13.	Dolphin	9 months	unknown
6.	Giant tortoise	1 month	177 years	14.	Lion	4 months	28 years
7.	Goldfish	4 hours	6 years	15.	Rabbit	1 month	4 years
8.	Spider	5 minutes	7 days	16.	Rat	3 weeks	3 years

9   *Average costs.* Sign each sentence in ASL.

1. A new DVD costs around $18.00.
2. 1 month of cable internet costs around $24.95.
3. A new truck costs around $21,490.00.
4. A soda costs .65 or $1.25.
5. It costs $9.00 to watch a movie.
6. A gallon of gas costs around $1.72.
7. A pound of oranges costs .99.
8. A candy bar costs $1.00.
9. A large pizza costs around $12.95.
10. A new house costs around $123,000 in the USA.
11. Americans owe around $3,102 on credit cards

12. People spend around $1,000 a year on clothes.
13. It costs around $300 to fly from L.A. to NYC.
14. A plasma television costs around $2,500.
15. Dinner for 4 at a restaurant costs around $40.00
16. A new computer costs around $700.00.
17. A gallon of milk costs around $2.50.
18. 1 pound of dog food costs around $1.89.
19. A cell phone costs around $30.00 each month.
20. A bottle of water costs around $1.00.

10   *Film facts.* What can you say about each film?

	Title	Year	Length	Cost to Make
1.	Gone With the Wind	1930	3 hours, 45 minutes	$3,700,000
2.	Titanic	1997	189 minutes	$208,000,000
3.	Star Wars	1977	121 minutes	$9.5 million
4.	To Kill a Mockingbird	1963	2 hours, 10 minutes	$2,122,000
5.	Jaws	1975	2 hours, 4 minutes	$8,000,000
6.	Lord of the Rings	2001	3 hours	$310 million
7.	Ben Hur	1959	3 hours, 50 minutes	$15,000,000
8.	Wizard of Oz	1939	1 hour, 41 minutes	$2,777,000
9.	Spiderman	2002	2 hours, 1 minute	$139,000,000
10.	Raiders of the Lost Ark	1981	115 minutes	$18 million

Glossing ASL

Historically there was no written form for American Sign Language. Transposing a three-dimensional language that uses space, non-manual signals, and motion as its primary characteristics onto paper is a daunting challenge. Only recently with the advent of SignWriting™ has ASL become a written language, though this system has not yet gained acceptance with most signers. Because ASL is not written, Deaf people have relied on the written formats of the spoken languages used around them. Thus, a Deaf person in the United States signs in ASL but writes in English, and depending on where he or she lives, a Deaf Canadian may sign in ASL and / or LSQ (Quebec Sign Language) and write both English and French. Over the years a written system has been developed by ASL teachers and researchers to translate signs into a basic form of English. Using one language to write another has its limitations but doing so can be a quick way to convey concepts. This system is called **glossing** ASL. Knowing how to gloss is not a requirement for learning ASL, but it can be a handy tool if you plan on continuing your ASL studies. An example of this system is shown below, followed by explanations of how to gloss ASL.

American Sign Language	ASL Gloss	English translation

wh   wh
YOU NAME WHAT YOU

What is your name?

b. State which facial expression accompanies the sign, phrase, or sentence

a. Translate each sign into an English equivalent

How to Gloss ASL

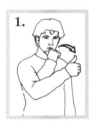

1. Every sign has one gloss. The English word and ASL gloss may not match exactly. See your glossary. Each gloss is always written in capitalized letters.

Example: TOMORROW

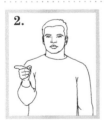

2. Using the index finger to point to a person or thing is called deixis. Abbreviate this with IX, and follow with another gloss or name of the person to whom you are pointing. You can also add he, she, or it in lower-case letters after IX, but add a hyphen if you do this.

Example: IX (or IX-he)

Example: IX MAN

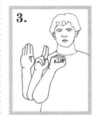

3. Fingerspelled words are preceded by fs-. Capitalize the fingerspelled term but not the fs-.

Example: fs-BUS

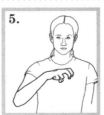

4. Many signs can't be glossed using just one English word. Use hyphens between each segment to show a single concept.

Example: GIVE-ME

5. Glossing classifiers requires two parts. Gloss the classifier with CL: and then add the concept described by the classifier in English.

Example: CL: Bent V
           "person sitting down"

6. When there are two or more parts to a single sign, use a + between each.

Example: SUN+SHINE

9. Raising the eyebrows to ask a yes / no question is written with a _q_ over the gloss.

Example:
$$\frac{q}{\text{YOU}}$$

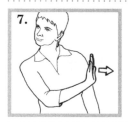

7. Possessive signs like his, hers, its, and theirs are preceeded by POSS. Add who is referred to in italics.

Example: POSS-*hers*

10. Write above the gloss the word mouthed by the lips for signs that have non-manual signals attached to them.

Example:
$$\frac{\text{cha}}{\text{CL: Claw}}$$

8. Non-manual signals formed by the eyebrows, head, and lips must be included.

First, draw a line above the glossed sentence. Specific descriptions for the non-manual signal are written above the glossed term that uses the NMS.

Example:
$$\frac{\text{confused}}{\text{ME DON'T-KNOW}}$$

When the same NMS is used throughout a sentence, such as the WH-Face or the Question-Maker, write the NMS at the beginning and end of the sentence.

Example:
$$\frac{\text{whq} \qquad\qquad \text{whq}}{\text{YOU NAME WHAT YOU}}$$

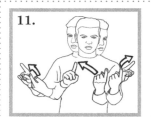

11. Use the ++ symbol for signs that are repeated or to show a recurring action.

Example: MEET-MANY-PEOPLE++

12. WH questions are shown by writing _whq_ over the gloss.

Example:
$$\frac{\text{whq}}{\text{WHERE}}$$

13. Specific facial expressions or other non-manual signals are written over the corresponding gloss.

Example:
$$\frac{\text{happy}}{\text{FACIAL-EXPRESSION}}$$

Glossing Tips

- Approach glossing as a labeling exercise: Label only what is signed and corresponding non-manual signals. Avoid adding English words that are not signed, like *is* and *are*.
- The gloss for each sign is found in the Glossing Index at the back of this book. Some signs can be translated into English different ways, but there is only one gloss for each sign.
- Glossed phrases and sentences should be accompanied with non-manual signals.
- Refer to the Glossary section to find exact glosses for vocabulary.
- When handwriting gloss, it is better to use print letters rather than cursive. Substitute cursive for italics where necessary.

Unit 1

1 *One-word glosses.* Follow the examples to gloss each sign correctly.

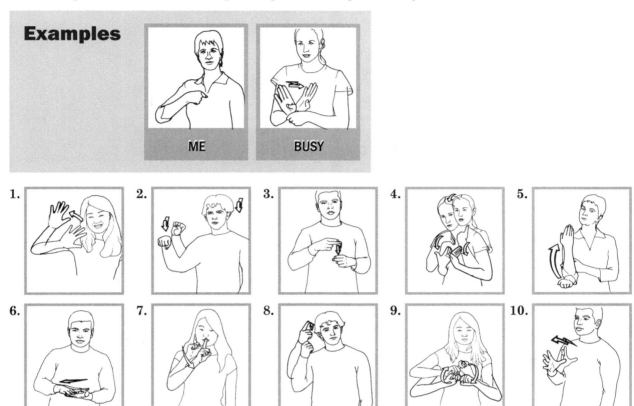

2 *Two- and three-word glosses.* Many signs in ASL can't be glossed by a single English word. Hyphens are used to connect each part. Match each sign with the correct gloss from the list provided.

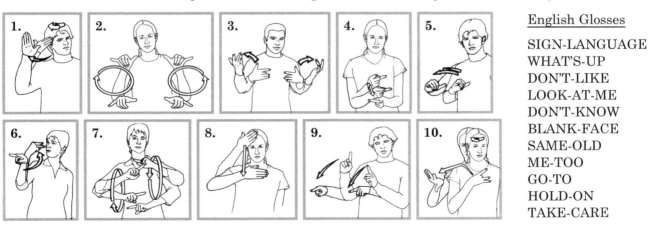

English Glosses

SIGN-LANGUAGE
WHAT'S-UP
DON'T-LIKE
LOOK-AT-ME
DON'T-KNOW
BLANK-FACE
SAME-OLD
ME-TOO
GO-TO
HOLD-ON
TAKE-CARE

3 *Glossing deixis.* Any time you point to a person or object, your index finger is glossed as IX, unless signing *me*, *you* or *they*. Sometimes other signs or a fingerspelled name follows deixis, but there may be instances when this information is not available. Unless given specific details, do not gloss deixis as *he*, *she*, or *it*. When the gender of a person referred to by IX is known, add -he, -she, or -it to the gloss. Follow the example below to write each signed phrase or sentence in ASL gloss and English.

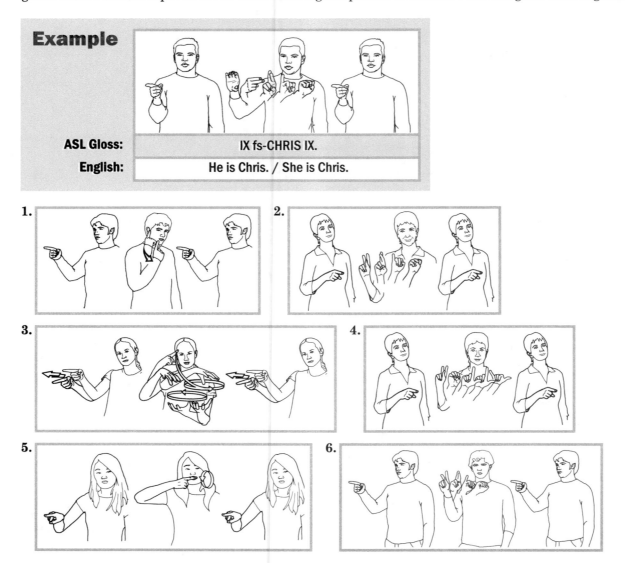

Example

ASL Gloss:	IX fs-CHRIS IX.
English:	He is Chris. / She is Chris.

4 *Gloss completion.* Complete the ASL glosses for each sign.

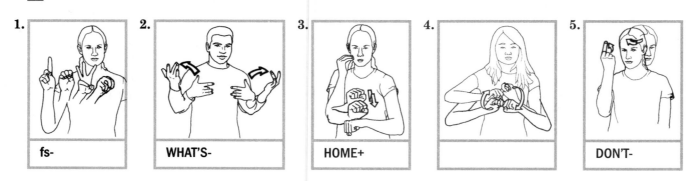

1. fs-
2. WHAT'S-
3. HOME+
4.
5. DON'T-

6. | **7.** | **8.**

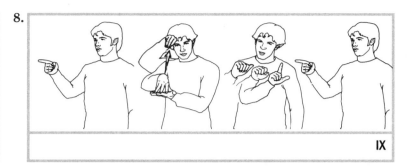

| - -VOICE | THANK- | IX |

5 *Non-manual signals.* Glossing is incomplete until facial expressions and other non-manual signals are included in the gloss. When adding non-manual signals, focus on what you do with your eyebrows, lips, facial expressions, and head while signing. These actions are added above the gloss. For now, focus only on adding *head nod*, *head shake*, *Question-Maker eyebrows*, *smile* and *frown* labels. Follow the examples to complete the gloss of each sign below.

Examples

NMS Labels:

1. smile
2. frown
3. head shake
4. head nod
5. q (Question-Maker)

Gloss: NICE   ME-MEET   YOU
NMS: smile   smile   smile

Glossed   __smile   smile__
sentence: NICE ME-MEET YOU

English: Nice to meet you.

Gloss: YOU   fs-KRIS   YOU
NMS: brows up   brows up   brows up
(brows up = Question-Maker)

Glossed   __q   q__
sentence: YOU fs-KRIS YOU

English: Are you Kris?

1. 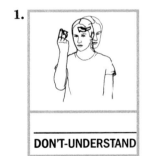 | **2.** 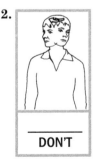 | **3.**  | **4.** 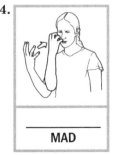 | **5.**  | **6.**

| DON'T-UNDERSTAND | DON'T | HI | MAD | QUESTION | YES |

6 *More deixis.* Sign the following glossed sentences in ASL.

1. ME NAME fs-SARA. IX-he NAME fs-SEAN IX-he.
2. IX LEARN SIGN-LANGUAGE IX.
3. IX WANT MEET YOU.
4. IX LAST NAME fs-COOPER IX.
5. fs-MARC DEAF. IX-he MY FRIEND IX-he.
6. IX-she NAME fs-TARA IX-she.
7. IX HARD-OF-HEARING IX.
8. IX-he BUSY IX-she.
9. IX-she NAME fs-RITA IX-she.
10. IX SICK IX.

Unit 2

1   *Glossing rules.* Gloss each sign correctly. Include non-manual signals if needed.

1. 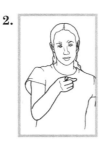   2.    3.    4.    5.    6.

2   *The WH-Face.* WH signs like *who*, *where*, *what*, *when*, and *why* are always accompanied by the non-manual signal known as the WH-Face. Other signs may also use the WH-Face if used in a WH sentence. Rather than writing WH-Face when glossing, use the abbreviation whq. Gloss the following WH signs after looking at the example.

Example

ASL Gloss:

whq		whq

YOU LEARN fs-ASL WHY

English:
Why are you learning ASL?

1.    2. 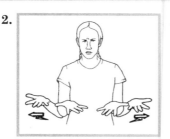   3. 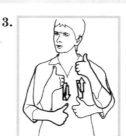   4.    5.

3   *Using non-manual signals.* Gloss each sign or NMS correctly. Write a short glossed sentence that includes the vocabulary sign or non-manual signal.

1. 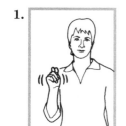   2. 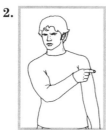   3.    4. 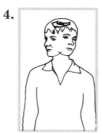   5.    6.

4 *Glossing directionality.* To gloss directional signs effectively, note the beginning and ending location of the sign. If the sign moves away from the body, the gloss tends to include *to* or *you*. If the sign moves towards the body, the gloss may include *me* or *here*. Complete the gloss that corresponds to the following directional signs.

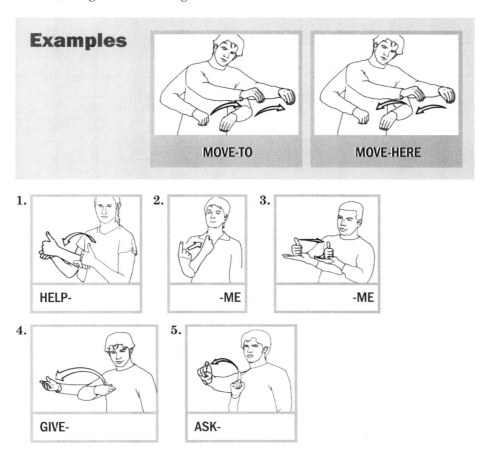

5 *Comparisons.* In this exercise, write both glossed and English versions of the ASL sentence, including non-manual signals. Note that *huh* and the Question-Maker NMS are often interpreted into English as "Do you..."

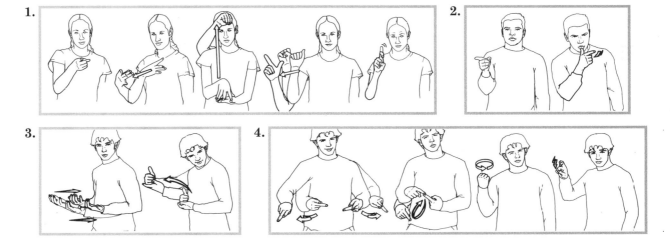

6 *Non-manuals.* Insert the appropriate non-manual signals into each glossed sentence.

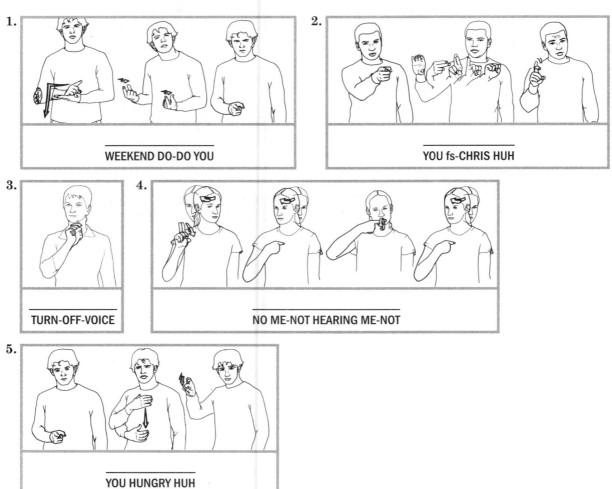

1. WEEKEND DO-DO YOU

2. YOU fs-CHRIS HUH

3. TURN-OFF-VOICE

4. NO ME-NOT HEARING ME-NOT

5. YOU HUNGRY HUH

Unit 3

1 *Review.* Gloss each sign correctly.

1.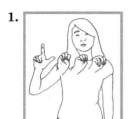
2.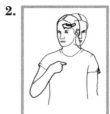
3.
4.
5.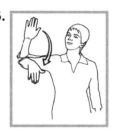

2 *Where do you live?* Write the gloss for each sentence. Most states and provinces use a fingerspelled abbreviation, while others have signs. Use the "Places" list as needed. Examples are provided.

Examples

1. English: I was born in Maine.
   Gloss: ME BORN fs-MAINE ME.

2. English: I live in California.
   Gloss: ME LIVE CALIFORNIA ME.

1. English: Are you from Tennessee?

2. English: Where were you born?

3. English: They live in British Columbia.

4. English: I live in New Jersey.

5. English: We are from Ohio.

6. English: He grew up in Nevada.

Places

United States

Alabama....fs-ALA	Montana....MONTANA
Alaska....ALASKA	Nebraska....fs-NEB
Arizona....ARIZONA	Nevada....fs-NEV
Arkansas....fs-ARK	New Hampshire....fs-NH
California....CALIFORNIA	New Jersey....fs-NJ
Colorado....COLOR+fs-ADO	New Mexico....fs-NM
Connecticut....fs-CONN	New York....NEW-YORK
Delaware....fs-DEL	North Carolina....fs-NC
Florida....fs-FLA	North Dakota....fs-ND
Georgia....fs-GA	Ohio....fs-OHIO
Hawaii....HAWAII	Oklahoma....fs-OKLA
Idaho....fs-IDAHO	Oregon....OREGON
Illinois....fs-ILL	Pennsylvania....fs-PA
Indiana....fs-IND	Rhode Island....fs-RI
Iowa....fs-IOWA	South Carolina....fs-SC
Kansas...fs-KAN	South Dakota....fs-SD
Kentucky....fs-KY	Tennessee....fs-TENN
Louisiana....fs-LA	Texas.....TEXAS
Maine....fs-MAINE	Utah.....fs-UTAH
Maryland....fs-MD	Vermont....fs-VT
Massachusetts....fs-MASS	Virginia.....fs-VA
Michigan....fs-MICH	Washington.....WASHINGTON
Minnesota....fs-MINN	West Virginia....WEST+fs-VA
Mississippi....fs-MISS	Wisconsin....fs-WISC
Missouri....fs-MO	Wyoming......fs-WYO

Canada

Alberta....ALBERTA	Ontario....ONTARIO
British Columbia....fs-BC	Prince Edward Island....fs-PEI
Manitoba....MANITOBA	Quebec....QUEBEC
New Brunswick...fs-NB	Saskatchewan....fs-SASK
Northwest Territories....fs-NWT	Yukon...fs-YUKON
Nova Scotia...fs-NS	

3 *WH-Q and RH-Q.* Two different non-manual signals accompany the sign *why*, depending on how the sign appears in a sentence. When asking a specific question, *why* appears at the end of a sentence along with the WH-Face. However, *why* is also used as a conjunction similar to the word "because" in English, and connects two separate clauses in a signed sentence. This type of *why* is accompanied with the brows up NMS and is glossed as *rh*. Look at the example provided and gloss the following sentences.

wh
―――
WHY

rh
―――
WHY

Example

ASL Sign:	
ASL Gloss:	<u>rh nod head</u> ME LEARN fs-ASL WHY ME ENJOY ME.
English:	I am learning ASL because I enjoy it.

1.
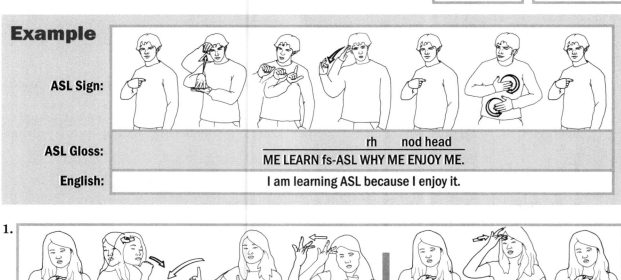

2.

3.
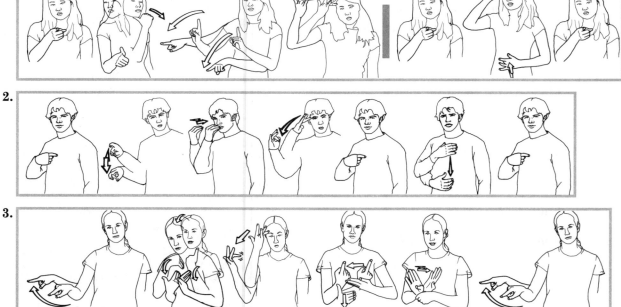

4.

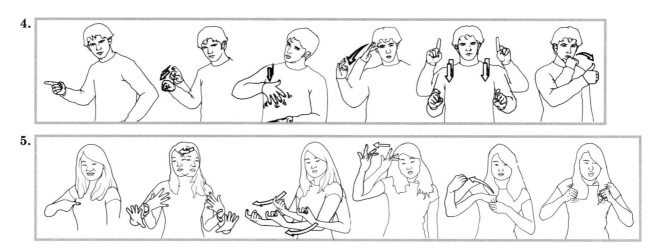

5.

4 *Glossing numbers.* To gloss numbers either alone or in a sentence, write the number rather than spelling it. Look at the examples below and then complete the gloss for each of the following numbers.

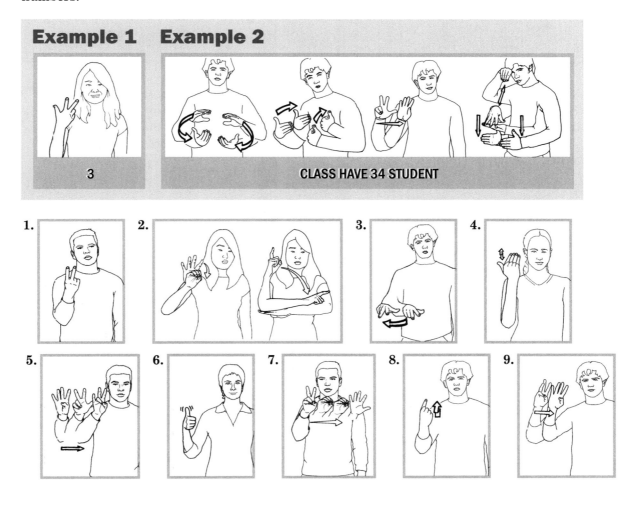

Example 1   **Example 2**

3

CLASS HAVE 34 STUDENT

1.   2.   3.   4.

5.   6.   7.   8.   9.

5 *More numbers.* Gloss the following items correctly.

1.

2.

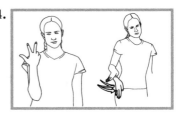

3.

4.

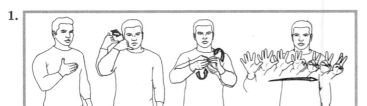

5.

6.

6 *Possessives.* Most possessive signs have specific glosses, such as *my*, *your*, *our*, and *their*. However, glossing signs like *hers*, *his*, and *its* requires the addition of POSS-IX unless the gender of the person is known. If it is, then gloss a sign as POSS-*his* or POSS-*hers*. Write the following items in both gloss and English formats.

POSS-IX

1.

2.

3.

4.

5.

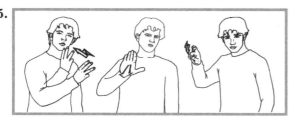

Unit 4

1   *Review.* Gloss the following items correctly.

1.
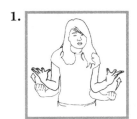

2.

3.
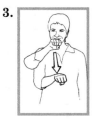

4.

5.

2   *Shoulder-Shifting.* The word "and" is often used in English to compare or contrast information, as in the sentence "I have two brothers and one sister." ASL uses a slight shoulder shift to compare or contrast information rather than signing "and". To gloss shoulder-shifting, add the term (dir-) each time the shoulders move, such as (dir-1) and (dir-2). See below for an example.

Example

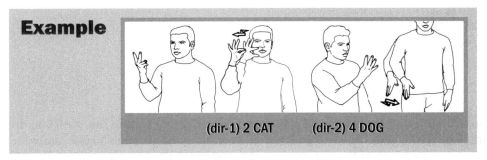

(dir-1) 2 CAT   (dir-2) 4 DOG

1.

2.

3.
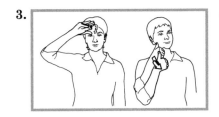

4.
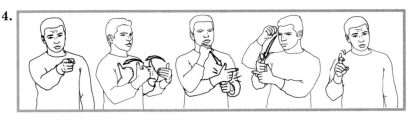

5.
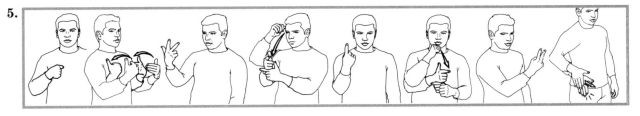

3   *Age signs.* All age-related signs are glossed with the prefix AGE-, with the exact number of years following. A common mistake is glossing AGE-10 as 10 YEARS OLD. Look at the example and then write the correct gloss for each item.

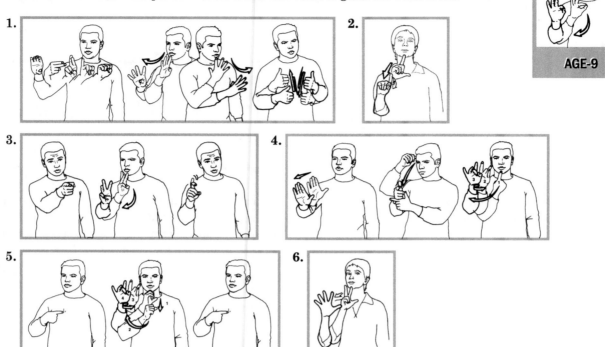

AGE-9

4   *Listing & Ordering.* The Listing & Ordering Technique is an effective way to list multiple details on the non-dominant hand. To gloss these signs, notice how many fingers are listed and which one is being pointed to or touched. If the first finger of three is referred to, then gloss that sign as 1-of-3. Avoid writing terms like first of three, second of four, or other descriptions. Gloss the following items.

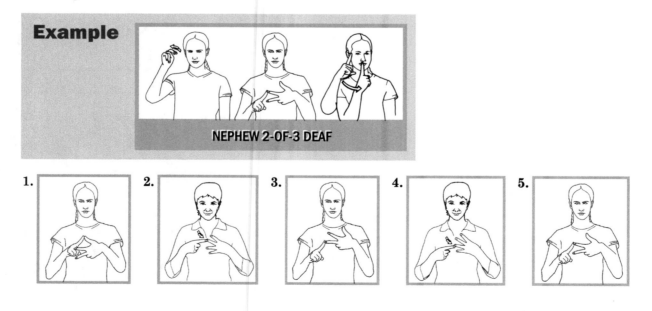

Example

NEPHEW 2-OF-3 DEAF

5 *How many are there?* The wide variety of ASL pronouns are most often glossed by one of these three labels: US-, YOU-, and THOSE-. The specific number of people referred to by the pronoun is added after the hyphen. Note that unlike glossing numbers, you must spell the number of people referred to by the pronoun. Pay attention to the hand orientation for clues to distinguish US- and THOSE-. Look at the examples below, then gloss the following signs.

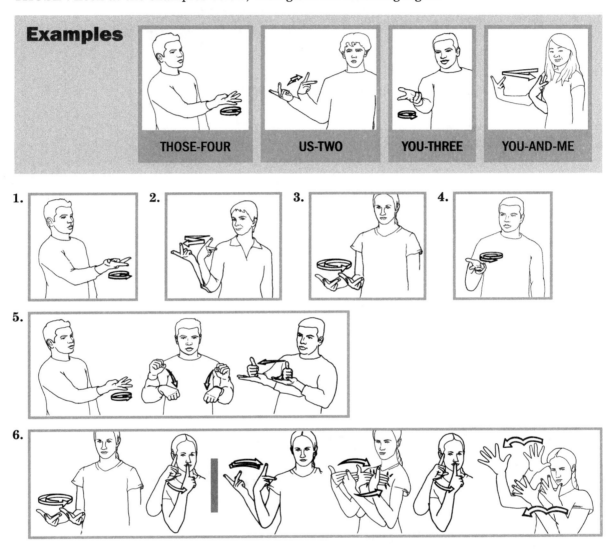

6   *Catching mistakes.* Each item contains one or more glossing mistakes. Identify the mistake and rewrite the corrected gloss in the space provided.

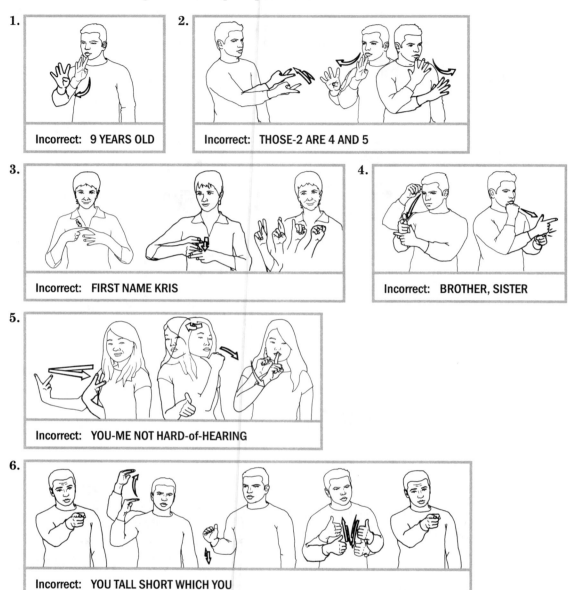

1.   Incorrect: 9 YEARS OLD

2.   Incorrect: THOSE-2 ARE 4 AND 5

3.   Incorrect: FIRST NAME KRIS

4.   Incorrect: BROTHER, SISTER

5.   Incorrect: YOU-ME NOT HARD-of-HEARING

6.   Incorrect: YOU TALL SHORT WHICH YOU

Unit 5

1 *Review.* Gloss each item correctly.

1.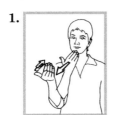
2.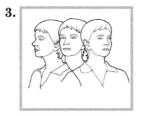
3.
4.
5.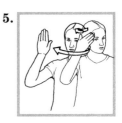

2 *Agent Markers.* The Agent Marker modifies a sign's meaning, adding the concept one who does ___. For example, LEARN + AGENT-MARKER is STUDENT. When glossing signs that include the Agent Marker, gloss the overall meaning created by both signs. You do not need to add a gloss for the Agent Marker unless it is not attached to a sign.

Agent Marker

1.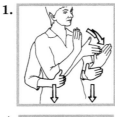
2.
3.
4.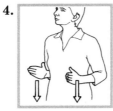
5.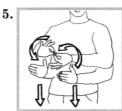

3 *Single-sign classifiers.* Classifiers that are not combined with others can be glossed by following CL: with a specific classifier gloss. Keep in mind that not all signs are classifiers, so be sure to know the correct classifier label for each. Look at the example below before glossing the following items.

Example

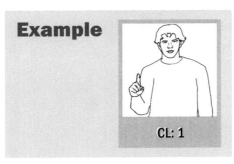

CL: 1

1.
2.
3.
4.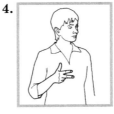
5.

4 *Sentence classifiers.* Glossing classifiers that appear with other signs uses the CL: format shown in #3 on page 145. However, a description of the classifier's activity is needed to complete the gloss. The description must be brief and contain only the most important details, be written in lower-case letters, and surrounded by quotation marks. Look at the example below before glossing the following items.

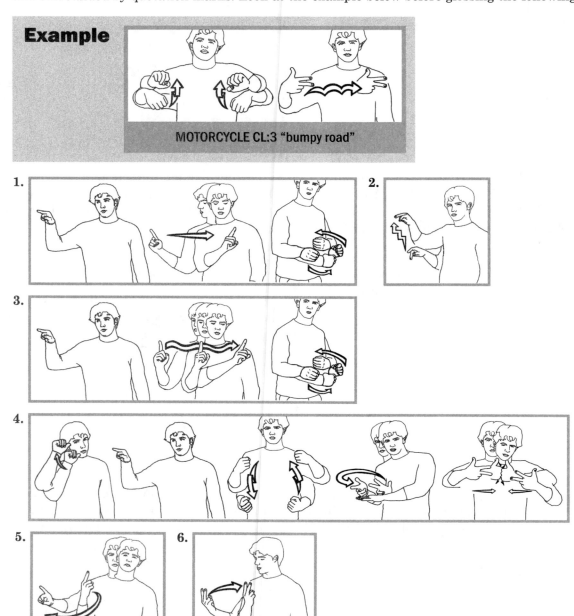

Example

MOTORCYCLE CL:3 "bumpy road"

5 *Double-sign classifiers.* Often, two classifiers are signed simultaneously. Glossing double-sign classifiers is similar to glossing sentence classifiers, with the addition of the second hand. Look at the example below to see how double-sign classifiers are glossed.

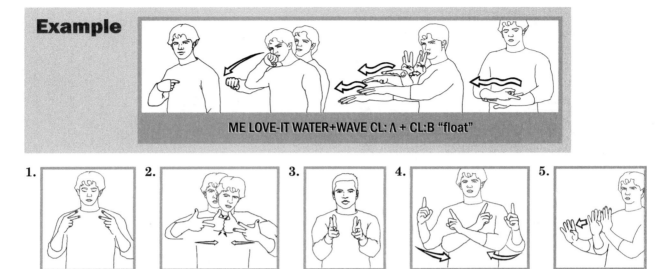

6 *Time.* Glossing time signs follows the same method as glossing age signs. The label TIME- precedes numbers showing the hour and minute. If glossing a time sign that does not include minutes, only write the number referring to the hour. If the time has both an hour and minute amount, use this format: TIME-6:15. Follow the example to gloss each sign.

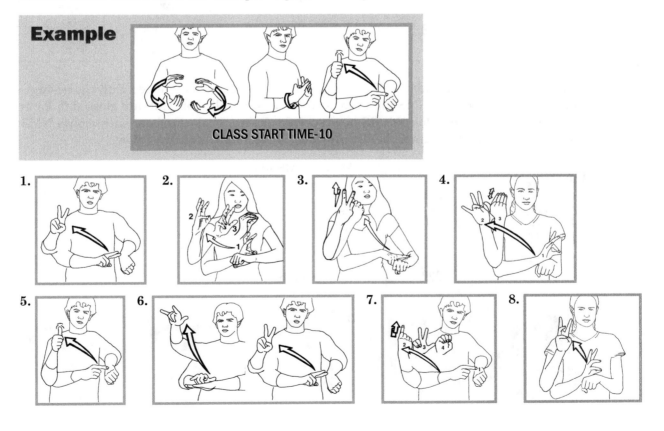

Unit 6

1 *Review.* Gloss each item correctly.

1.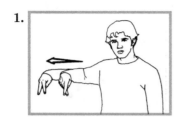
2.
3.

4.
5.

2 *Non-manual signals.* Gloss each sign and non-manual signal.

1.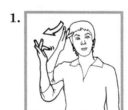
2.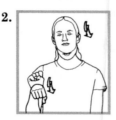
3.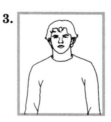
4.
5.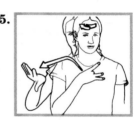

3 *Non-manual signals: The mouth.* While most non-manual signals are made with the eyebrows and head, other important NMS are formed on the lips. Recall that NMS are glossed in lower-case letters above a sign. Mouth NMS have specific glosses. Look closely at each mouth NMS and select a gloss that best fits from the list provided. An example is shown below.

Example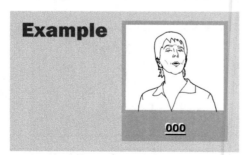

000

Mouth NMS glosses

cha	mmm
fish	oh
tongue	shh
ah	
pow	
clench teeth	

1.
2.
3.
4.
5.

4 *Classifiers.* Gloss each classifier by selecting the best description from the list provided.

1. 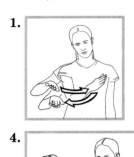   2. 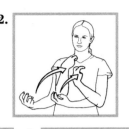   3.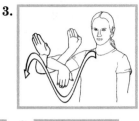

Classifier Glosses

CL: B "ears"

CL: B "winding road"

CL: Bent V "jump on me"

4.    5. 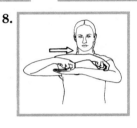   6.

CL: Bent V "seated position"

CL: Base B "flat object"

CL: Bent V "sit next to"

CL: 5 "crowded"

CL: Bent V "jump"

CL: Bent V + CL: B "crawl on surface"

7.   8.

CL: 5 "many people"

CL: B "hilly road"

5 *Tenses.* Many signs incorporate the past or future tenses into their general meaning. Follow the pattern of tense+meaning, as in LAST-WEEK, rather than WEEK-LAST when glossing tense signs. Use hypens when needed to fully gloss each sign. Gloss the following items.

1.    2.    3.    4.

5. 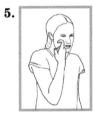   6.    7.

8.

6   *The Rule of 9.* **A unique feature of ASL is the ability to simultaneously describe a time-related concept and its duration. This feature is limited to a certain group of signs and can never exceed a duration longer than nine days, weeks, months, or other time signs. Glossing Rule of 9 signs follows the same pattern as glossing tense signs. Use the numeral rather than spelling out the number. Refrain from using suffixes to pluralize the gloss. See below for an example.**

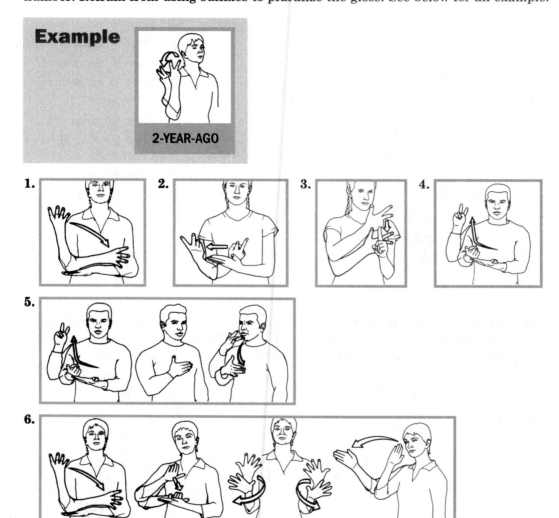

Example

2-YEAR-AGO

Unit 7

1   *Review.* Gloss each item correctly.

1.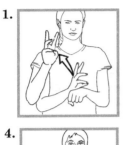
2.
3.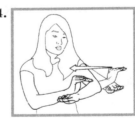

4.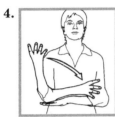
5.

2   *Glossing recurring events.* The English language has two ways to describe the same recurring event, such as "every Wednesday" and "on Wednesdays." While English uses two different labels for the same concept, ASL uses one. All recurring signs are glossed with the EVERY- label, with the exact term following. Gloss the following items correctly.

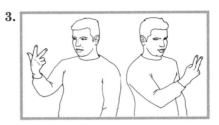

EVERY-MORNING

1.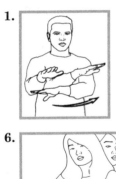
2.
3.
4.
5.

6.

3 *CL: C.* Gloss the following examples of CL: C.

1.  **2.** 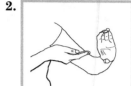 **3.** 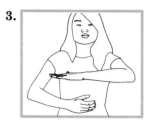 **4.**

4 *Spatial organization.* Spatial organization uses the Shoulder-Shift to distinguish concepts or details from each other. Glossing spatial organization follows the same rules of Shoulder-Shifting but also includes a GROUP: label. Look at the example below before glossing the following items. Write an English translation of each when done.

Example

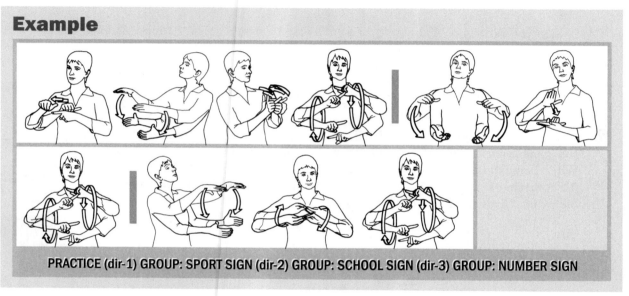

PRACTICE (dir-1) GROUP: SPORT SIGN (dir-2) GROUP: SCHOOL SIGN (dir-3) GROUP: NUMBER SIGN

1.

2.

3.

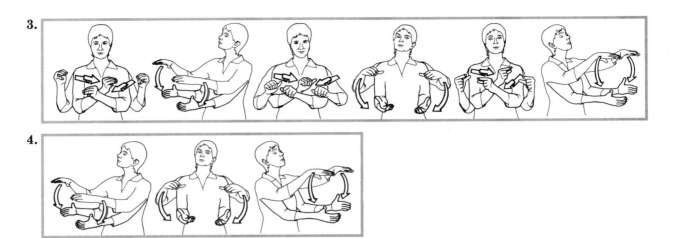

4.

5   *Noun-verb pairs.* Many ASL verbs and nouns are closely related to each other, differing only in their movement. Generally, nouns have a double back-and-forth movement while verbs tend to have one solid movement or a wider back-and-forth movement than nouns. Use these criteria to label each sign a noun or verb before writing its gloss.

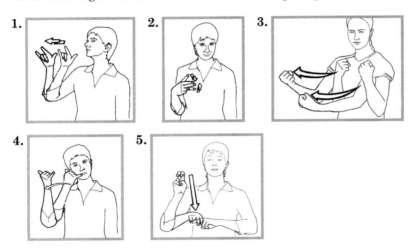

6 *Descriptions.* A variety of classifiers are often paired with clothing, particularly CL: 4 and CL: G to describe stripes and CL: F to describe dots. In the example, notice how the classifier gloss includes a brief, specific description. Gloss the following phrases correctly. How would you gloss numbers 4 and 5?

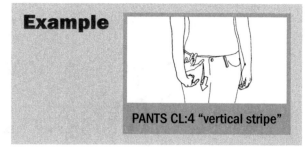

Example

PANTS CL:4 "vertical stripe"

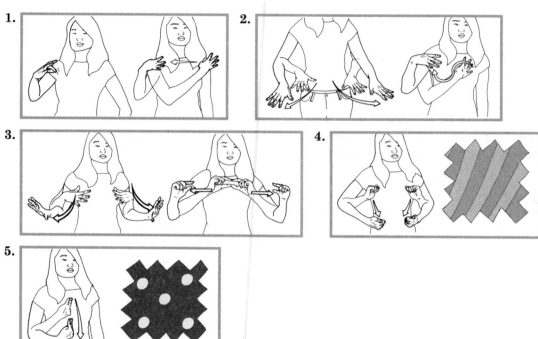

Unit 8

1 *Review.* Gloss each item correctly.

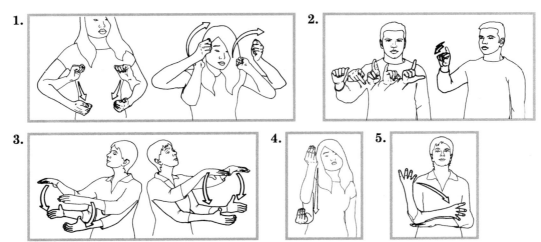

2 *Height & weight.* ASL uses a combination of signs, numbers, and fingerspelling to describe height and weight, depending on what is described:

- The *weigh* sign is used both for *weight* and *pounds.*
- A person's height is shown only with numbers.
- The height of other objects uses *measure* and the fingerspelled term *feet.*

| To weigh, pound | To measure | Height: 6'4" |

Gloss the following items and include an English translation.

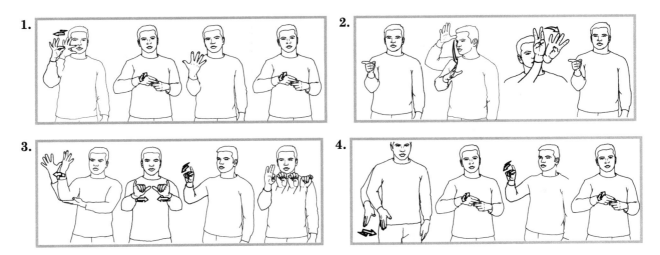

3 *Hairstyles and classifiers.* Many descriptive signs are classifiers. Part of the gloss for each sign has been provided for you. Complete the rest of the gloss.

1.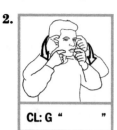

CL: 4 "   "

2.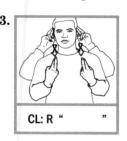

CL: G "   "

3.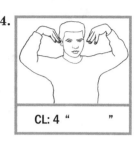

CL: R "   "

4.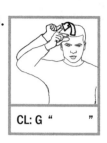

CL: 4 "   "

5.

CL: G "   "

4 *Descriptions.* Gloss the following phrases and sentences, including non-manual signals as needed.

1.

2.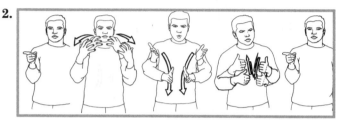

3.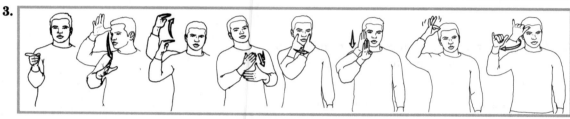

4.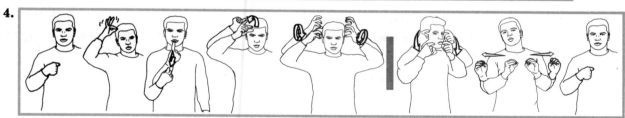

5.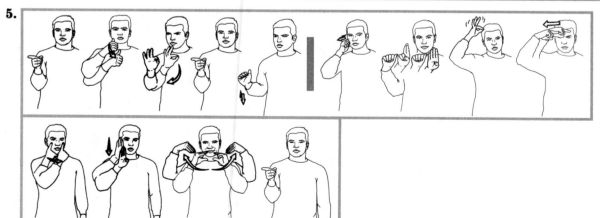

5 *Glossing rules.* Gloss the following signs and phrases correctly.

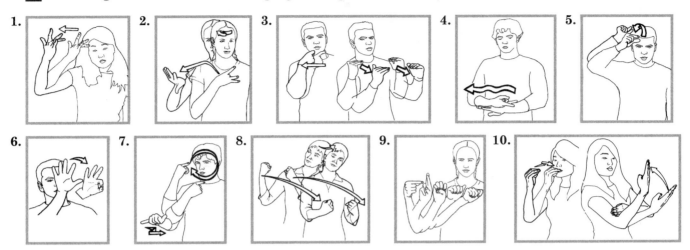

6 *Glossing errors.* Each gloss below contains one or more errors. Identify the errors and write the correct gloss.

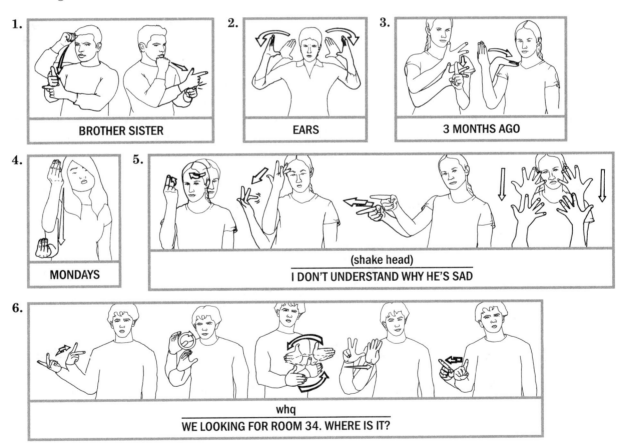

1 *Review.* Gloss each item correctly.

1.  2. 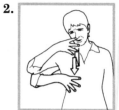 3.  4. 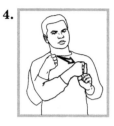 5.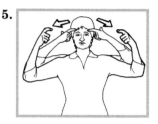

2 *Around the house.* Gloss each sign correctly.

1.  2.  3.  4.  5.

3 *Non-manual signals.* You know how to gloss a variety of non-manual signals often used in ASL conversation, including head and mouth movements, and the eyebrows. Another set of NMS is important when describing objects or proximity, as in *right there* or *huge*. When glossing a sign's NMS and you are unsure of the specific label, describe the NMS as best you can. Look at the examples below before glossing the following items.

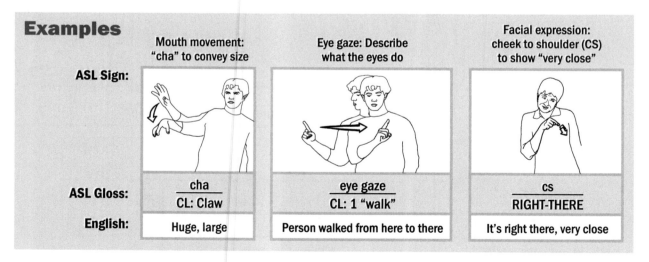

Examples

	Mouth movement: "cha" to convey size	Eye gaze: Describe what the eyes do	Facial expression: cheek to shoulder (CS) to show "very close"
ASL Sign:			
ASL Gloss:	cha CL: Claw	eye gaze CL: 1 "walk"	cs RIGHT-THERE
English:	Huge, large	Person walked from here to there	It's right there, very close

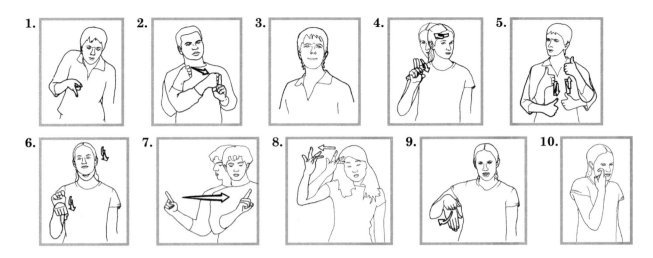

4 *CL: Claw.* When not paired with the NMS *cha*, CL: Claw refers to the physical location of an object. With *cha*, CL: Claw conveys a large object's location. Decide whether to include *cha* based on what is being described in the following sentences.

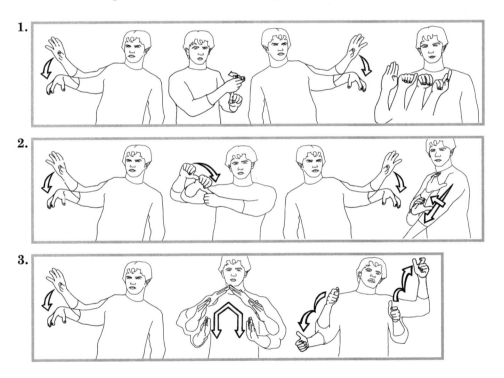

5   *Money.* Glossing monetary signs require the addition of a CENTS- prefix or -DOLLAR suffix, depending on the amount signed. Note that -DOLLAR is used with amounts up to nine dollars. Higher amounts use the DOLLAR gloss following a number sign.

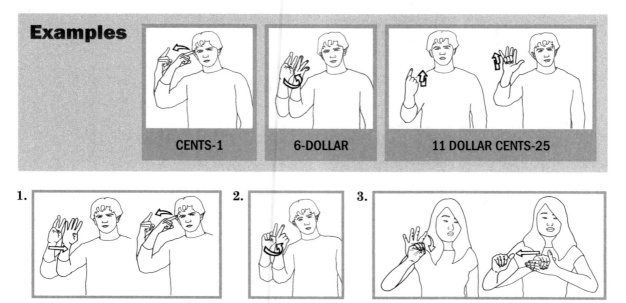

Examples

| CENTS-1 | 6-DOLLAR | 11 DOLLAR CENTS-25 |

1.   2.   3.

6   *Transportation.* Several transportation signs are, or incorporate, classifier concepts. Analyze the following signs for their classifier concepts. Gloss each and write what you think the classifier components mean.

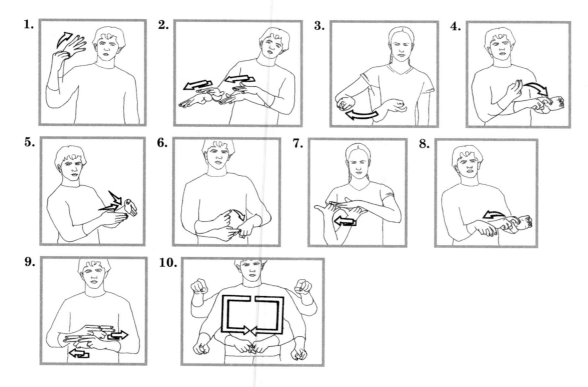

Unit 10

1 *Review.* Gloss each item correctly.

1.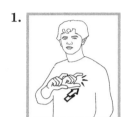
2.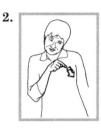
3.
4.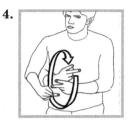

2 *Who or what?* In most cases the Agent Marker is included in the gloss for signs using this feature, so TEETH + Agent Marker is glossed as DENTIST, not TEETH+AGENT-MARKER. Gloss the following signs correctly.

1.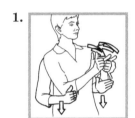
2.
3.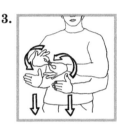
4.

3 *Using BECOME & to be.* Gloss the following sentences and include an English translation.

1.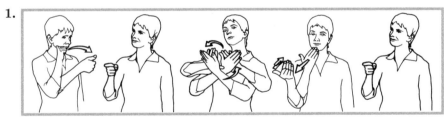

2.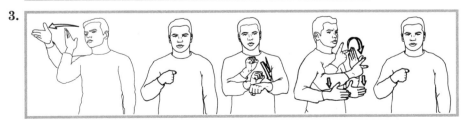

3.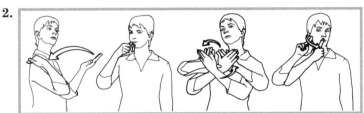

4.

4   *Glossing food.* Gloss the following signs and phrases correctly.

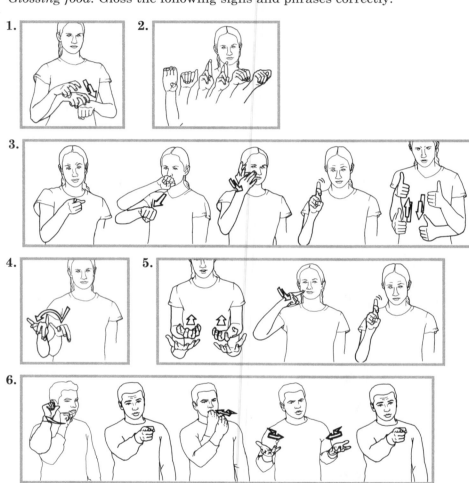

5 *Dialogue.* Gloss the dialogue including relevant non-manual signals.

6 *Classifiers.* Gloss each sign. Describe what you think the classifier describes. An example is provided.

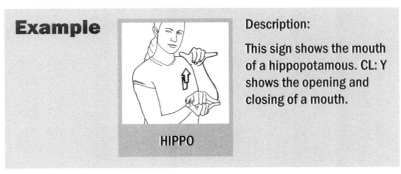

1.

2.

3.

4.

5.

Glossary

Abstract
A meaning that depends on content rather than pictorial representation: an abstract sign versus an iconic sign.

Age Spot
The lower part of the chin is called the Age Spot, the area where number signs originate to state age.

The Age Spot

Agent Marker
The Agent Marker adds the concept "someone that does" to the sign immediately preceding the Agent Marker. For example, adding the Agent Marker to *music* creates the meaning "someone who does music" or *musician*.

The Agent Marker

American Sign Language
A natural visual language used by deaf and hard of hearing individuals in the United States and Canada, commonly abbreviated as ASL. Possessing its own grammar, syntax, and linguistic structures, ASL is not related to the English language. It is one of the most commonly used foreign languages in the United States. Also known as sign language.

Americans with Disabilities Act
Commonly referred to as the ADA, the act is a broad civil rights law that prohibits discrimination against individuals with disabilities, specifically in employment, transportation, telecommunications, and public accomodation. The act also prohibits employment discrimination against a qualified individual with a disability when the disability can be reasonably accommodated. Reasonable accomodations include adapting programs, facilities, or workplaces to allow disabled individuals to fully participate. The goals of the ADA are to ensure persons with disabilities have equal opportunities as non-disabled individuals, a chance to participate in society, to live independently, and become economically self-sufficient. The act became law in 1990.

Arbitrary
Determined by preference rather than reason. Can refer to name signs. *See related entries: Abstract, Iconic, Name signs.*

Bilingual-bicultural
The belief that both American Sign Language and English are of equal value for Deaf individuals, and that to live and prosper, language and cultural skills for both the Deaf World and hearing world are vital. It is also a philosophy of educating the deaf and hard of hearing in both ASL and English to ensure deaf individuals have the language skills to communicate effectively in both languages (or the spoken language of a country) as well as understand the culture and society of both groups.

Classifier
A limited group of handshapes that convey descriptive details including appearance, behavior, movement, location, mannerisms or other physical characteristics. Each classifier has a specific range of uses depending on the topic.

CL: 1 Solo person, long cylindrical objects

Closing signal
Pointing back to yourself or another person after making a statement or asking a question. The closing signal facilitates turn-taking because it shows completion of a thought. *See related topic: Turn-taking strategies.*

Cochlear implant
A mechanical device that consists of one or more electrodes surgically implanted inside the cochlea that transforms sound vibrations into nerve impulses for transmission to the brain. Unlike a hearing aid, which amplifies sound, the implant receives and passes on electrical signals. The implant directly stimulates the auditory nerve, allowing some deaf individuals to learn to hear and interpret sounds and speech.

Coda

"Child of Deaf Adults." An acronym referring to any hearing individual who has at least one deaf parent.

Collectivism/collectivist

Refers to a number of people acting as a group or with a joint identity in which the values and beliefs of the larger whole may take precedence over absolute individual autonomy. Seeing oneself as part of a larger whole reflects collectivist beliefs. *See related topic: Individualism.*

Community

A group of people living in the same area; a group of people having common interests; a group viewed as forming a distinct segment of society; a group of people having ethnic or religious characteristics in common.

Compound sign

Two separate signs that, when combined in a continuous movement, form a unique meaning.

| Mother | Father | Compound sign: Parents |

Concept

A general idea or meaning derived or inferred from specific vocabulary or conversational context.

Conceptual topic

The intended topic of a sentence. The English sentence "I want to be a veterinarian" does not explicitly mention the conceptual topic of "work," which is implied with "to be." The ASL translation of the same sentence requires the conceptual topic to be signed: I want to work as a veterinarian. Another example is "Give it to me." The sentence is grammatically correct in English but not in ASL, which requires "it" to be identified. *See related entry: Transitional topic.*

Context

The information occurring before and after a particular word or passage that determines its meaning, or the circumstances in which an event occurs. The context of a sentence helps clarify its meaning.

Contrastive Structure

Used to compare or state more than one thing in the same sentence, similar to the English word "and." Form contrastive structure by directing your shoulders in a different direction for each comparison or detail you state. *See related entries: Shoulder-Shifting, Eye Gaze.*

She/he is 8 years old, she/he is 9 years old

Culture

The predominant attitudes and behaviors that characterize the functioning of a group, including language, behavior patterns, arts, beliefs, and institutions, transmitted from one generation to the next. The customary beliefs, social forms, and traits of a racial, religious, or social group may also form a culture.

Cultural Perspective

Those who view the Deaf as having a distinct culture and language and not needing to be "fixed" hold a cultural perspective. *See related entry: Pathological perspective.*

Deaf

Partially or completely without the sense of hearing. When capitalized, Deaf refers to the community of deaf people who use American Sign Language as their primary means of communication. *See related topic: Hearing.*

Deaf Culture

The culture of the American and Canadian Deaf communities who share the bond of relating to the world visually, having pride in American Sign Language, and considering deafness not as a deficiency but as forming a unique way of life.

Deaf World
A well-known ASL expression referring to Deaf culture.

Deixis
Using the index finger to point to a person or object. Pronounced *dike-sis*.

Descriptive
A person's name sign that depicts or mimics a particular characteristic. *See related entries: Iconic, Name sign.*

Directionality
Refers to the group of signs whose production is affected by who is the initiator or recipient of an action or sign. This group is called *directional signs*.

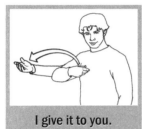

I give it to you.

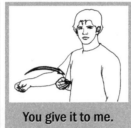

You give it to me.

Disability
A physical or mental disadvantage that inhibits or prevents access and / or achievements in a given area. Deafness, blindness, learning challenges, and physical or neurological conditions are disabilities. *See related entry: Handicapped.*

Disabled
Having a disability.

Discourse
A signed, spoken, or written expression between two or more individuals. Any type of exchange or conversation, or a formal, lengthy discussion of a subject.

Dominant hand
The hand a signer uses most often. Generally the dominant hand is the one used for writing.

Duration
A specific length of time. ASL incorporates duration into many signs. For example, the phrase three days is made by incorporating the number 3 into the sign for day. *See related entry: Rule of 9.*

Expressive
Refers to the signing component of American Sign Language, as in expressive skills. *See related entry: Receptive.*

Eye Gaze
Term used to describe situations when the signer looks towards the person or thing pointed to with deixis, the originating location of directional signs, or the originating and ending points of classifiers. Eye gaze is a key component in using the signing space clearly. See related entries: *Classifiers, Deixis, Directionality, Sign Space.*

Eye gaze with the sign you, to an individual shorter than the signer.

Facial expressions
The expression on a person's face demonstrating an emotion.

Fingerspelling space
The area to the left or right of the signer's torso where fingerspelling occurs.

Five ASL Parameters
Refers to the five components of a single ASL sign:

- Handshape
- Palm orientation
- Location
- Movement
- Non-manual signal

The Fingerspelling Space

Gender
Classifying a word as masculine or feminine. ASL has several gender-specific signs, as in male-cousin versus female-cousin. Gender is determined by a sign's location on the head, based on an imaginary horizontal line near the nose that separates the face into two areas. Masculine signs originate in the forehead area, whereas feminine signs occur in the lower portion of the face. Note that name signs are gender neutral, regardless of where they are located on the face.

Gestuno

An artificial sign system used to facilitate communication when Deaf people from around the world gather. It is not a natural sign language but is instead the most "obvious" signs for concepts from many different languages around the world. Gestuno is an Italian word meaning "unified sign language."

Grammar

The system of rules of a language. *See related topic: Syntax.*

Guide dogs

Specially trained dogs that provide service to disabled individuals. Also known as service dogs or companion animals.

Handicapped

An outdated term for a physical or mental disability. *See related topic: Disability.*

Handshape

The basic building block of a sign. One or more handshapes are used in the formation of a single sign. *See related entry: Five ASL Parameters.*

Hard of hearing

Having a partial loss of hearing that varies for each individual. *See related topic: Hearing.*

Head nod

A non-manual signal that creates the affirmative in American Sign Language. *See related topic: Non-manual signal.*

Head shake

A non-manual signal that forms the negative in American Sign Language. *See related topic: Non-manual signal.*

Hearing

To perceive sound by the ear.

- Normal hearing: Can detect all speech sounds even at a soft conversation level. Within the -10 to +15 decibel range on an audiogram.

- Minimal loss: May have difficulty hearing faint or distant speech. Rapid conversation or noisy

environments may result in missed information. Loss is between 16 to 25 decibels.

- Mild: May miss up to 50% of conversation especially if voices are soft or the environment is noisy. Loss is between 26 to 40 decibels.

- Moderate: Conversation from 3 to 5 feet away can be understood if the environment and topic is controlled. Loss is between 41 to 55 decibels.

- Moderate to severe: Without amplification (hearing aid) up to 100% of spoken information may be missed. Loss is between 56 to 70 decibels.

- Severe: Can only hear loud noises at close distances. Loss is between 71 to 90 decibels.

- Profound: For all practical purposes individuals in this range rely on vision rather than hearing to process information. A loss of 91 decibels or more is described as profound.

Hearing aid

A small electronic apparatus that amplifies sound and is worn in or behind the ear for those with at least a minimal hearing loss.

Hearing impaired

Having some loss of hearing, but not deaf. Considered by many to be insensitive due to the negative connotation of "impaired." *See related topic: Pathological perspective.*

Home signs

Term used to describe basic gestures that may be invented by hearing parents with deaf children. Part mime and part gestures, home signs are not American Sign Language.

Iconic

A meaning that depends on pictorial representation rather than content: *an iconic sign* versus *an abstract sign*. The sign sunrise is iconic. *See related entry: Abstract.*

Individualism

Belief that the individual's interests and priorities supersede those held by the larger community. Norms and social or cultural expectations are disregarded in favor of the individual's preferences. *See related topic: Collectivism.*

Initialization

Refers to signs that include the first letter of its written form in their production. An example is signing *math* with a C for *calculus*. Only a specific number of ASL signs are initialized.

Listing & Ordering Technique

A way to organize several details within the same sentence. The technique is used in place of signing "and."

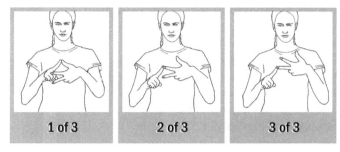

| 1 of 3 | 2 of 3 | 3 of 3 |

Literal

The exact or primary meaning of a word or idea.

Mainstreamed

Including students with special needs into regular school classrooms. For the deaf and hard of hearing, mainstreaming means attending a public school rather than a School for the Deaf.

Manual

Refers to the hand.

Manual method

An old term for sign language. Also refers to the educational philosophy of teaching deaf students via sign language.

Manually Coded English

Also known as MCE, manually coded English refers to the different forms of signing other than American Sign Language. MCEs are not languages but are signed codes that copy spoken English. *See related topics: Pidgin Signed English, Signing Exact English.*

Money Spot

The temple area near one's forehead that indicates *cents* when a number sign originates in that location.

The Money Spot

Name sign

There is no group of signs for specific names. For instance, two individuals both named Jeff would have two different name signs. Name signs are generally known and highly valued, used only within the Deaf community. For this reason it is inappropriate for a hearing person to invent a name sign for him- or herself. Hearing individuals may receive name signs after having developed friendships with Deaf people and participate in the Deaf community. Note: A name sign used only in one's ASL class is not often considered a permanent name sign. *See related entries: Arbitrary, Descriptive.*

Non-dominant hand

Refers to the hand not used for most signs. *See related entry: Dominant hand.*

Non-manual signals

Describes any non-signed aspect of American Sign Language. This includes facial expressions, the Question-Maker and WH-Face, and any lip, nose, mouth, or head movements. Also referred to as a non-manual marker.

Noun

A person, place, thing, quality, or action. Can function as the subject or object of a verb.

Noun-verb pair

Refers to the group of ASL nouns and verbs that share the same handshape but are distinguished from each other by movement.

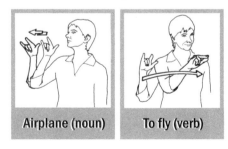

| Airplane (noun) | To fly (verb) |

Number

To constitute a group; a specific number of people or things, either abstract or concrete. The exact number of individuals can be incorporated into particular signs. For example the phrase *the three of them are walking* is made with just one sign.

Oral literature
Refers to literature not in written form. Stories, poetry, folktales, proverbs, riddles, jokes, and longer narrative works performed in American Sign Language are considered oral literature.

Oral method
The philosophy of training deaf people to speak, as well as an educational philosophy of teaching deaf students only through speech rather than a visual language.

Object-subject-verb
Commonly abbreviated OSV, it is one of the primary grammatical structures of American Sign Language. Signing the ASL translation of "I give you the book" is an example of OSV structure. Also known as topic-comment structure. *See related entry: Topic-comment structure.*

I give you the book.
(Literal: Book I-give-you)

Parameter
One of a group of identified factors that define a system or its behavior. *See related entry: Five ASL parameters.*

Pathological perspective
The perspective of deafness as an undesirable deficiency that should be eliminated or mitigated at best via speech, hearing aids, and cochlear implants. The cultural, historical, and social uniqueness of the Deaf community is not valued. *See related entry: Cultural perspective.*

Pidgin
A simplified, basic way of communicating that is usually a mixture of two or more languages, with a basic grammar and vocabulary, but lacks nuance and depth. Pidgins tend to use the grammatical system of the more powerful language. This form of communication is generally used when one person or more is not fluent in the second language. They are not spoken as a first or native language. *See*

related entries: American Sign Language, PSE (Pidgin Signed English).

Possessives
Of, relating to, or being a noun or pronoun that indicates possession: Mine, yours, his, hers, its, ours, and theirs are possessives.

Preposition
An English word or phrase that indicates the relationship of a verb or adjective, such as at, by, with, in, near, next, and to. There is no group of ASL prepositions that exist independently. Prepositional relationships are shown by the location of handshapes and sign order. *See related entry: Conceptual topic.*

(the glass is) Under

(the glass is) On

Pronoun
A word or sign that substitutes nouns or noun phrases with deixis: He, she, it, me, we, they. See related entry: Deixis.

PSE (Pidgin Signed English)
A common abbreviation for Pidgin Signed English, in which ASL signs follow English word order. PSE is not a language. Most people who use PSE sign and speak (or mouth) English simultaneously. *See related entries: American Sign Language, Pidgin, MCE.*

Question- Maker
The non-manual signal of raised eyebrows forms questions in ASL. *See related entry: Non-manual signal.*

The Question-Maker

Receptive
Refers to the comprehension component of American Sign Language, as in receptive skills. *See related entry: Expressive.*

Rule of 9
A unique system in American Sign Language that incorporates numbers up to nine with particular concepts into a single sign. For example the phrase *three days* uses just one sign that combines *three*

with *day*. Concepts that follow the Rule of 9 include: Minutes, hours, days, weeks, months, and money.

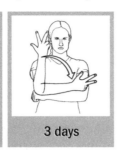

| 3 (number) | Day | 3 days |

SEE

A common abbreviation for Signing Exact English, the system of signing each English word exactly as it is pronounced or written. Since SEE is based on written English, its signs do not distinguish between words spelled the same but conceptually different. A famous example of SEE is signing *butter* and *fly* for the concept *butterfly*. *See related entry: MCE.*

Shoulder shifting

Orienting the shoulders in a different direction for contrastive structure or other grammar purposes. *See related entries: Contrastive structure and Eye gaze.*

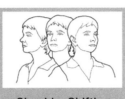

Shoulder Shifting

Sign space

The area where the majority of signed discourse occurs. *See related entry: Spatial Organization.*

The Sign Space

Spatial organization

Grouping or distinguishing information using different spatial locations. *See related entry: Sign Space.*

Spatial visualization

Describing physical characteristics and locations of objects from multiple perspectives.

Structure

The way in which words and grammar are arranged into an acceptable whole. *See related entry: Grammar, Syntax.*

Subject

The noun, noun phrase, or pronoun in a sentence that explains who does the action.

Subject-verb-object

Commonly referred to as SVO, it is the predominant grammatical structure of the English language. The sentence "I go to the store" is an example of subject (*I*), verb (*go to*), object (*the store*) structure. *See related entry: Object-subject-verb.*

Syntax

The grammatical arrangement of words into sentences. *See related entries: Grammar and Structure.*

Tactile sign language

The term used to describe the way Deaf-Blind individuals understand sign language by placing their hands on top of the signing person's hands to "see" what is signed. Other variants of tactile sign language may be fingerspelling words and sentences into a Deaf-Blind person's palm.

Temporal organization

Grouping or organizing information along a spatial time line, such as explaining activities occurring on different days of the week. *See related entry: Spatial organization.*

Tense

An indication of the time, such as past, present, or future.

Topic-comment structure

One of the major forms of ASL sentence structure whereby the main idea is stated first and subsequent information is understood as a comment on the topic. An example is the ASL sentence *I am not happy. See related entries: Object-subject-verb, subject-verb-object.*

I'm not happy.
(Literal: Happy I am not.)

Transitional topic

The intended topic of a sentence that involves change from one state of being to another. The English sentence "I want to be happy" does not explicitly mention the transitional topic of "become," which is implied with "to be." The ASL translation of the same sentence requires the transitional topic be signed: *I want to become happy*. Another example is "I will be 32 years old." The sentence is grammatically correct in English, but not in ASL, which identifies "be" as *become*. *See related entry: Conceptual topic.*

Turn-taking strategies

Refers to the ways in which two or more signers maintain discourse with each other. Knowing how to indicate you wish to interrupt another signer and doing it appropriately is an example of turn-taking strategies.

Variation

The regional differences in certain signs across the United States and Canada.

Verb

Signs that express existence, action, or occurrence. Examples are *to go to* and *run*.

Visual

Refers to the sense of sight.

Visual question mark

A sign often used with the Question-Maker to ask a question or for clarification. *See related entry: Question-Maker.*

The visual question mark

***When* signs**

Refers to any sign that indicates a specific period of time or when something happened, including: Calendar signs (day, week, month, year), time, and the past, present, or future tenses. Generally, *when* signs occur first in ASL sentences.

WH-Face

A non-manual signal paired with all the WH-signs: *Who, what, when, where, why, which*. Also used as a facial expression to show confusion and uncertainty. *See related topics: Non-manual signal, Facial expression.*

The WH-Face

Glossing Index

Term	Gloss

A

Term	Gloss
A (grade)	GRADE-A
Absent, to be	SKIP
Accident	CL:3+CL:3 "crash"
Accountant (*count* + Agent Marker)	ACCOUNTANT
Act, show	ACT
Activity center	ACTION+MIDDLE
Actor	ACTOR
Add up (see *total*)	TOTAL
Address	ADDRESS
Adult (see *older*)	ADULT
Advertise, advertising	ADVERTISE
Afraid (see *scared*)	AFRAID
Africa	AFRICA
African American (1) (see *Black*)	BLACK
African American (2)	AFRICA+AMERICAN
Afternoon	AFTERNOON
Afternoons (see *every afternoon*)	EVERY-AFTERNOON
Again, repeat	AGAIN
Agent Marker	AGENT-MARKER
Age-Spot	AGE-SPOT
Ago, past	AGO
Airplane, airport	AIRPLANE
Airport (see *airplane*)	AIRPORT
Alabama	fs-ALA
Alarm, bell	ALARM
Alarm, to set (see *to set a clock*)	SET+ALARM
Alaska	ALASKA
Alberta	ALBERTA
Algebra	ALGEBRA
All right, okay	ALRIGHT
All year	YEAR-ROUND
All, everybody	fs-ALL
Allergic, to be (see *allergies*)	ALLERGY
Allergies, to be allergic	ALLERGY
Alligator, crocodile	ALLIGATOR
Also	ALSO
Always	ALWAYS
America	AMERICA
American (America + Agent Marker)	AMERICAN
American Sign Language	fs-ASL
Angry (see *mad*)	MAD
Annoy, to bother	ANNOY

Term	Gloss
Annoyed, to be	ANNOY
Ant (see *bug*)	BUG
Antelope (see *deer*)	DEER+fs-ANTELOPE
Apartment	fs-APT
Apple	APPLE
Applicant (*apply* + Agent Marker)	APPLICANT
Apply, to	APPLY
Apricot	fs-APRICOT
April	fs-APRIL
Arab	fs-ARAB
Area (location)	AREA
Argue, to	ARGUE
Arizona	ARIZONA
Arkansas	fs-ARK
Around (time)	AROUND
Arrive, to (plane)	PLANE-LAND
Arrive, to	ARRIVE
Arrogant	BIG-HEAD
Art	ART
Artichoke	fs-ARTICHOKE
Asia	ASIA
Asian	ASIAN
Ask everybody (see *I ask everybody*)	ASK-ALL
Ask me (plural)	ASK-ME-MANY
Ask me (see *You ask me*)	ASK-ME
Ask you (see *I ask you*)	ASK-YOU
Ask, to	ASK
ASL poetry	ASL-POETRY
Asparagus	fs-ASPARAGUS
At (symbol)	AT
Athlete (*sports* + Agent Marker)	ATHLETE
Atlanta	ATLANTA
ATM (machine)	fs-ATM
Auditorium (see *stadium*)	STADIUM
August	fs-AUG
Aunt	AUNT
Auto body	fs-AUTO
Avenue	fs-AVE
Avocado	fs-AVOCADO

B

Term	Gloss
Baby	BABY
Back	BACK
Bacon	BACON
Bad at, to be	BAD-AT
Bagel	fs-BAGEL
Bald, to be	BALD

Term	Gloss
Banana	BANANA
Bangs	CL:4 "bangs"
Bank	fs-BANK
Baseball	BASEBALL
Basement	BASEMENT
Basketball	BASKETBALL
Bath, to take a	BATH
Bathroom	BATHROOM
Be together, to (see *together*)	TOGETHER
Beach	fs-BEACH
Beans	fs-BEANS
Bear	BEAR
Beard	BEARD
Beautiful (see *pretty*)	PRETTY
Become	BECOME
Bed, to go to	GET-IN-BED
Bed, to make the	MAKE+BED
Bedroom (1-2)	BED+ROOM
Beef (see *meat*)	MEAT
Before (see *used to*)	USED-TO
Begin, (see *start*)	BEGIN
Bell (see *alarm*)	ALARM
Bell pepper	fs-BELL PEPPER
Belly (see *gut*)	GUT
Berry	fs-BERRY
Best friend	BEST-FRIEND
Better, to be	BETTER
Better, to get (see *get better*)	HEAL
Between (time)	BETWEEN
Bicycle (see *ride a bike*)	BICYCLE
Big head	BIG-HEAD
Big, large	BIG
Biologist (*biology* + Agent Marker)	BIOLOGIST
Biology	BIOLOGY
Bird	BIRD
Birthday (1-3)	BIRTHDAY
Black (person)	BLACK
Black	BLACK
Blackberry	fs-BLACKBERRY
Blank face	BLANK-FACE
Blind, to be	BLIND
Block	fs-BLOCK
Blonde	BLONDE
Blouse	BLOUSE
Blow air	BLOW-AIR
Blue	BLUE
Boat	BOAT
Book	BOOK

Term	Gloss
Boots	BOOTS
Bored, to be	BORED
Born in, to be	BORN
Boss (see *coach*)	COACH
Boston	BOSTON
Boulevard	fs-BLVD
Bowling	BOWLING
Box (see *room*)	ROOM
Boxers (see *shorts*)	SHORTS
Boy	BOY
Boyfriend	BOY+FRIEND
Bra	BRA
Braid, to	BRAID-HAIR
Braids	BRAID
Bread	BREAD
Break up, to	BREAK-UP
Break, to (literal)	BREAK
Break, to take a	BREAK-TIME
Breakfast	EAT+MORNING
Bright blue	BRIGHT-BLUE
British Columbia	fs-BC
Broccoli	fs-BROCCOLI
Broke, to be (money)	CHOP-NECK
Broken hearted, to be	BROKE-HEART
Brother	BROTHER
Brown	BROWN
Brownie	fs-BROWNIE
Brunette	HAIR-BROWN
Brush hair, to	BRUSH-HAIR
Brush teeth, to	BRUSH-TEETH
Buck teeth	BUCK-TEETH
Bug, ant	BUG
Bully (*pick on* + Agent Marker)	BULLY
Bungee jump, to	BUNGEE-JUMP
Burrito	fs-BURRITO
Bus	fs-BUS
Business	BUSINESS
Busy, to be	BUSY
But	BUT
Butter	BUTTER
Buttons	BUTTON
Buy, to	BUY

C

Term	Gloss
Cabin	fs-CABIN
Café	fs-CAFÉ
Cafeteria	CAFETERIA

Term	Gloss
Cake	fs-CAKE
Calculus	CALCULUS
California	CALIFORNIA
Call a name, to	CALL-NAME
Camera (see *photography*)	CAMERA
Camp, to	CAMP
Can, may	CAN
Can't, may not	CAN'T
Canada	CANADA
Canadian (*Canada* + Agent Marker)	CANADIAN
Candy	CANDY
Cap (see *hat*)	HAT
Car, to drive	CAR
Car, to wash (see *wash the car*)	WASH-CAR
Cards (see *play cards*)	PLAY-CARDS
Carrot	fs-CARROT
Cash register	CASH-REGISTER
Cash	fs-CASH
Cashier (*cash register* + Agent Marker)	CASHIER
Casserole	fs-CASSEROLE
Cat	CAT
Caucasian (see *White*)	WHITE-PERSON
Cauliflower	fs-CAULIFLOWER
Celebrate, to	CELEBRATE
Celery	fs-CELERY
Cent	CENT
Cereal (1-2)	CEREAL
Change clothes, to	CHANGE-CLOTHES
Chat, to hang out	CHAT
Cheap	CHEAP
Check	CHECK
Cheese	CHEESE
Chef (*cook* + Agent Marker)	CHEF
Chemist (*chemistry* + Agent Marker)	CHEMIST
Chemistry	CHEMISTRY
Cherry	fs-CHERRY
Chicago	CHICAGO
Chicken (see *bird*)	CHICKEN
Chicken pox	CHICKEN+FRECKLES-ON-FACE
Child	CHILD
Children	CHILDREN
Chips	fs-CHIPS
Chocolate	CHOCOLATE
Chores, to do	fs-CHORES / DO-DUTY
Christmas	CHRISTMAS
Chubby, fat	FAT
Church	CHURCH
City, town	COMMUNITY

Term	Gloss
Clam	fs-CLAM
Class	CLASS
Classifier	CL
CL: Λ *Legs or eyes*	CL:Λ
Stairs, upstairs	WALK-UPSTAIRS
Two people look at each other	LOOK-AT-EACH-OTHER
Two people walk to me	TWO-PEOPLE-WALK-TO-ME
Walk, to (general)	WALK-LEGS
CL: 1 *An individual or cylindrical object*	CL:1
Curl (describing hairstyle)	CURL
Popular	POPULAR
Two people pass each other	WALK-PAST-EACH-OTHER
Walk away from me	WALK-AWAY
CL: 3 *Vehicles*	CL: 3
Accident	CL:3+CL:3 "crash"
Driving over a bumpy road	BUMPY-ROAD
CL: 4 *Flowing liquid or plural CL: 1*	CL:4 "flow"
Line of people	LONG-LINE
Mohawk (describing hairstyle)	CL:4 "Mohawk"
Nosebleed	CL:4 "nosebleed"
CL: 5 *Many people*	CL: 5
Crowded	CROWDED
Flock to	FLOCK-TO
Popular	POPULAR
CL: B *Flat objects*	CL:B
Door (open / close)	DOOR-OPEN / DOOR-CLOSE
Elephant ears	CL:B "elephant ears"
I walk	I-WALK
Room	ROOM
CL: Base B *Flat objects*	CL: BASE B
Dance, to	CL:Λ+BASE B "dance"
Person floating on water	CL:Λ+BASE B "float"
Ride a horse, to	CL:Λ+CL:B "ride horse"
CL: Bent V *Seated position*	CL: Bent V
Chair	CHAIR
Jump	JUMP
Sit next to	SIT-NEXT-TO
CL: C *Cylindrical objects*	CL: C
Drink, to	DRINK
Elephant body	CL:C "elephant body"
Elephant legs	CL:C + CL: C "elephant body"
Elephant proboscis	CL: C "elephant nose"
CL: Claw 5 *Spatial placeholder*	CL: Claw 5
Across from	CL: Claw 5 + CL: Claw 5 "across from"
Between	CL: Claw 5 + CL: Claw 5 "between"
Next to	CL: Claw 5 + CL: Claw 5 "next to"
CL: G *Description*	CL: G
Short hair (2)	CL: G "short hair"

Term	Gloss
Sideburns	SIDEBURNS
CL: R *Description*	CL: R
Braids	BRAIDS
Rope	ROPE
CL: S *Description*	CL: S
Pigtails (describing hairstyle)	CL: S + CL: S "pigtails"
Pony tail	PONY-TAIL
Clean, to	CLEAN
Clear, to be	CLEAR
Clinic	CLINIC
Clinician (*clinic* + Agent Marker)	CLINICIAN
Clock, to set	SET-CLOCK
Close, to be (see *near*)	NEAR
Clothes	CLOTHING
Cloudy, to be	CLOUDY
Coach, boss, dean	COACH
Coat (see *jacket*)	JACKET
Cochlear implant	COCHLEAR-IMPLANT
Coda	fs-CODA
Cold, to be	COLD
Cold, to have a	HAVE-COLD
College	COLLEGE
Color	COLOR
Colorado	COLOR+fs-ADO
Comb hair, to	COMB-HAIR
Come on	COME-HERE
Comment, to	TOPIC
Computer (1)	COMPUTER
Computer (2-3)	COMPUTER
Condominium	fs-CONDO
Confused, to be	CONFUSED
Connecticut	fs-CONN
Continue (see *go on*)	CONTINUE
Convenience store, 7-11	7-11
Cook, to	COOK
Cookie	COOKIE
Cool, to be	COOL
Cop (see *police station*)	POLICE
Corn	fs-CORN
Cornrows	CL: G "cornrows"
Corner	CORNER
Correct, to grade	CORRECT
Cost, price	COST
Cough, to	COUGH
Counselor	COUNSELOR
Count, to	COUNT
Court	fs-COURT
Cousin (female)	FEMALE-COUSIN

Term	Gloss
Cousin (male)	MALE-COUSIN
Cousin (general)	COUSIN
Crab	fs-CRAB
Crazy for, to be	CRAZY-FOR
Credit card	CREDIT-CARD
Crocodile (see *alligator*)	ALLIGATOR+fs-CROCODILE
Crowded, to be	CROWDED
Cucumber	fs-CUCUMBER
Cup, glass	CUP
Cupcake	fs-CUPCAKE
Curious	CURIOUS
Curly hair	HAIR-CURLY
Cut nails, to	CLIPPER
Cut, to	CUT
Cute	CUTE

D

Term	Gloss
Dance, to	DANCE
Dark	DARK
Date, to	DATE
Daughter	DAUGHTER
Day	DAY
Dead, to be missing	DEAD
Deaf (2)	DEAF
Deaf tend theirs	DEAF+TEND+THEIR
Deaf world	DEAF+WORLD
Deaf	DEAF
Dean (see *coach*)	COACH fs-DEAN
Debit card (see *credit card*)	CREDIT-CARD
December	fs-DEC
Deer, antelope, elk	DEER
Delaware	fs-DEL
Deodorant	DEODORANT
Depart, to (plane)	PLANE-TAKE-OFF
Depends	DEPEND
Descendants (see *pass down*)	PASS-DOWN
Desert	DESERT
Design, to	DESIGN
Designer (*design* + Agent Marker)	DESIGNER
Desk, table	TABLE
Dessert	DESSERT
Different (plural)	DIFFERENT++
Dime	10-CENT
Dining room	EAT+ROOM
Dinner, supper	EAT+NIGHT
Disabled	fs-DA
Dishes, to do the	WASH-DISH

Term	Gloss
Distant future	DISTANT-FUTURE
Dive-in	DIVE-IN
Divorce	DIVORCE
	$\underline{\quad q \quad}$
Do you have any questions?(see *Ask me*, plural)	ASK-ME
Doctor	DOCTOR
Do-do	DO-DO
Doesn't (see *not*)	NOT
Dog	DOG
Dollar Twist	DOLLAR-TWIST
Dollar	DOLLAR
Dolphin	DOLPHIN
Don't (see *not*)	NOT
Don't do that	DON'T-DO-THAT
Don't know	DON'T-KNOW
Don't like	DON'T-LIKE
Don't understand	DON'T-UNDERSTAND
Done, to be (see *finish*)	FINISH
Door, to close	DOOR-CLOSE
Door, to open	DOOR-OPEN
Dormitory	DORMITORY
Dot, period	PERIOD
Drama	ACT
Dress	DRESS
Drink, to	DRINK
Drive (address)	fs-DRIVE
Drive, to (see *car*)	DRIVE-TO
Driver (*drive* + Agent Marker)	DRIVER
Drop off, to	DROP-OFF
Due, to owe	DUE
Duplex	DUPLEX
During, in, on	DURING

E

Term	Gloss
Each weekend (see *every weekend*)	EVERY-WEEKEND
Earache (see *hurt*)	EARACHE
Early	EARLY
Earn, to	EARN
Ears (animal)	CL: B+CL:B "animal ears"
Ears (elephant)	CL:B+CL:B "animal ears"
Ears	EAR
Earth (see *geography*)	EARTH
East	EAST
Easter	EASTER
Eat, food	EAT
Economics	ECONOMICS
Economist (*economics* + Agent Marker)	ECONOMIST

Term	Gloss
Education	EDUCATION
Egg	fs-EGG
Eid	fs-EID
Elementary school	ELEMENTARY-SCHOOL
Elephant	ELEPHANT
Elevator	ELEVATOR
Elk (see *deer*)	DEER+fs-ELK
Email address (see *email*)	fs-EMAIL+ADDRESS
Email, email address	fs-EMAIL
Embarrassed, to be	EMBARRASS
Emergency	EMERGENCY
Emotional, to be	EMOTIONAL
Employee (*work* + Agent Marker)	EMPLOYEE
Engineer (*measure* + Agent Marker)	ENGINEER
Engineering	ENGINEERING
English	ENGLISH
Enjoy, to have fun	ENJOY
Enter, to (see *entrance*)	ENTER
Entrance, to enter	ENTER
Entrepreneur (*business* + Agent Marker)	BUSINESS-PERSON
Erase (board)	ERASE-BOARD
Erase (paper)	ERASE-PAPER
Errands	ERRANDS
Error (see *wrong*)	WRONG
Ethnicity	ETHNIC
Evening, night	NIGHT
Evenings (see *every night*)	EVERY-NIGHT
Every afternoon	EVERY-AFTERNOON
Every day	EVERY-DAY
Every evening (see *every night*)	EVERY-EVENING
Every Friday	EVERY-FRIDAY
Every Monday	EVERY-MONDAY
Every month, rent	EVERY-MONTH
Every morning	EVERY-MORNING
Every night	EVERY-NIGHT
Every Saturday	EVERY-SATURDAY
Every Sunday	EVERY-SUNDAY
Every Thursday	EVERY-THURSDAY
Every Tuesday	EVERY-TUESDAY
Every Wednesday	EVERY-WEDNESDAY
Every week	EVERY-WEEK
Every weekend	EVERY-WEEKEND
Every year	EVERY-YEAR
Everybody (see *all*)	ALL
Exam (see *test*)	TEST
Example (see *for example*)	EXAMPLE
Excited, to be	EXCITED
Excuse me	EXCUSE-ME

Term	Gloss
Exercise (see *practice*)	PRACTICE
Exercise, to lift weights	EXERCISE
Expensive	EXPENSIVE
Experience	EXPERIENCE
Explain it again	EXPLAIN AGAIN
Explain, to	EXPLAIN
Eye contact	EYE-CONTACT
Eyes	EYE

F

Term	Gloss
F (grade)	GRADE-F
Face	FACE
Facial expressions	FACIAL-EXPRESSION
Fall (season)	FALL
Fall asleep, to	FALL-ASLEEP
Fall in love, to	FALL-IN-LOVE
Family	FAMILY
Far, over there, not close	OVER-THERE
Far, to be	FAR
Fast, quick	FAST
Fat, to be (see *chubby*)	FAT
Father	FATHER
Favorite	FAVORITE
February	fs-FEB
Feed, to	FEED
Feel, to	FEEL
Fever	FEVER
Few days, in a	FEW-DAYS
Field	GRASS+AREA
Fifth (see *Listing & Ordering*)	5-OF-5
Fine, to be	FINE
Fingerspell, to	FINGERSPELL
Finish, to be done	FINISH
Fire station, firefighter	FIREFIGHTER
Firefighter (see *fire station*)	FIREFIGHTER
First (see *Listing & Ordering*)	1-OF__
Fish	FISH
Fish, to	FISHING-ROD
Fisherman (*fish* + Agent Marker)	FISHER
Fit, to	FIT
Five minutes	5-MINUTE
Flag	FLAG
Flirt, to	FLIRT
Flock to, to	FLOCK-TO
Floor, level (1-2)	FLOOR
Florida	fs-FLA
Florist (*flower* + Agent Marker)	FLORIST

Term	Gloss
Floss	FLOSS
Flower	FLOWER
Fly, to	FLY-TO
Focus, to pay attention	PAY-ATTENTION
Food (see *eat*)	EAT
Football	FOOTBALL
For (see *since*)	SINCE
For example	EXAMPLE
For	FOR
For-for	FOR-FOR
Forget, to	FORGET
Four days	4-DAY
Four of them, the (see *pronouns & number*)	THOSE-FOUR
Four of us, the (see *pronouns & number*)	US-FOUR
Four of you, the (see *pronouns & number*)	YOU-FOUR
Fourth (see *Listing & Ordering*)	4-OF-___
Fourth of July (see *Independence Day*)	INDEPENDENT+DAY
Freckles	FRECKLES-ON-FACE
Free	FREE
Freeway (see *highway*)	HIGHWAY
French fries	FRENCH-FRY
Freshman	FRESHMAN
Friday (1-2)	FRIDAY
Fridays (see *every Friday*)	EVERY-FRIDAY
Friend	FRIEND
Friendly, to be	FRIENDLY
From	FROM
Front	FRONT
Fruit	FRUIT
Frustrated, to be	FRUSTRATED
Funny	FUNNY
Future (see *will*)	FUTURE

G

Term	Gloss
Gallaudet	GALLAUDET
Garage	GARBAGE
Garbage, to take out (see *trash, to take out*)	DROP-OFF+GARBAGE
Garlic	fs-GARLIC
Gas station	GAS
Geography	GEOGRAPHY
Geometry	GEOMETRY
Georgia	fs-GA
Gesundheit (1-2)	GESUNDHEIT
Get along, to	GET-ALONG
Get better, to (see *heal*)	HEAL
Get better, to	IMPROVE
Get dressed, to	GET-DRESSED

Term	Gloss
Get in bed (see *go to bed*)	GET-IN-BED
Get in, to	GET-ON
Get on, to (see *get in*)	GET-ON
Get out, to	GET-OFF
Get ready (1-2)	GET+READY / PREPARE
Get something, to	GET
Get together, to	GET-TOGETHER
Get up, to stand up	GET-UP
Get worse, to	GET-WORSE
Giraffe	GIRAFFE
Girl	GIRL
Girlfriend	GIRL+FRIEND
Give to, to	GIVE-TO
Glasses	GLASSES
Go on, to continue	GO-ON
Go out, to leave	GO-OUT
Go to, to	GO-TO
Goatee	GOATEE
Golf	GOLF
Good at, to be	GOOD-AT
Good friend	GOOD-FRIEND
Good shape, to be in	GOOD-SHAPE
Good, to be	GOOD
Good-bye	GOODBYE
Government	GOVERNMENT
Grab, to	GRAB-OPPORTUNITY
Graduate, to	GRADUATE
Grandfather	GRANDFATHER
Grandmother	GRANDMOTHER
Grapefruit	fs-GRAPEFRUIT
Grapes	GRAPES
Gray	GRAY
Green	GREEN
Grits	fs-GRITS
Grocery store	FOOD+STORE
Group (organizing) (1-3)	GROUP
Group (see *tribe*)	SMALL-GROUP
Grow up, to	GROW-UP
Gut, belly	GUT
Gym, gymnasium	GYM
Gymnastics	GYMNASTICS

H

Term	Gloss
Hair	HAIR
Hairspray	HAIRSPRAY
Half hour	HALF-HOUR
Half	HALF

Term	Gloss
Halloween	HALLOWEEN
Hallway	HALLWAY
Ham	fs-HAM
Hamburger	HAMBURGER
Hand out, to	PASS-OUT
Handicapped	fs-HC
Handshape	HAND+SHAPE
Handwave	WAVE-FOR-ATTENTION
Hang out, to (see *chat*)	CHAT
Hanukkah	HANUKKAH
Happy, to be	HAPPY
Hard of hearing	HARD-OF-HEARING
Hat, cap	HAT
Have fun, to (see *enjoy*)	ENJOY
Have, to	HAVE
Hawaii	HAWAII
He, he is	IX-*he*
Head nod (see *NMS: Head nod*)	HEAD-NOD
Head shake (see *NMS: Head shake*)	HEAD-SHAKE
Headache	HEADACHE
Heal, to get better	HEAL
Health	HEALTH / HUMAN
Hear, to	HEAR
Hearing aid	HEARING-AID
Hearing	HEARING
Height	HEIGHT
Hello	HELLO
Help me	HELP-ME
Help you (see *I help*)	I-HELP-YOU
Help, to (general)	HELP
Here	HERE
Hers	POSS-*hers*
Hi	HI
High school	fs-HS
Highway, freeway	HIGHWAY
Hike, to	HIKE
Hill	HILL
Hippo	HIPPO
Hire, to be hired	HIRE
His	POSS-*his*
Hispanic	HISPANIC
History	HISTORY
Hockey	HOCKEY
Hold on	HOLD-ON
Home	HOME
Honey (see *sweetheart*)	SWEETHEART
Hospital (1)	HOSPITAL
Hospital (2)	HOSPITAL

Term	Gloss
Hot dog, sausage	HOT-DOG / SAUSAGE
Hot, to be	HOT
Hotel	HOTEL
Hour	HOUR
House	HOUSE
Houston	HOUSTON
How are you?	HOW-YOU
How many?	HOW-MANY
How much (*how many* + WH-Face)	HOW-MANY
Humble, to be	HUMBLE
Hungry, to be	HUNGRY
Hurt, to	HURT
Hybrid	fs-HYBRID

I

Term	Gloss
I am, me	ME
I ask everybody, ask everybody	ASK-EVERYBODY
I ask you, ask you	I-ASK-YOU
I don't get it (see *unclear*)	UNCLEAR
I don't mind	I-DON'T-MIND
I don't really understand (see *unclear*)	UNCLEAR
I have no money (see *blow air*)	BLOW-AIR
I have nothing (see *blow air*)	BLOW-AIR
I help you, help you	I-HELP-YOU
I walk	I-WALK
I was wondering (see *curious*)	CURIOUS
I'm fine	ME FINE
	<u>shake head</u>
I'm not, not me	ME
Ice cream	ICE-CREAM
Ice skate, to	ICE-SKATE
Idaho	fs-IDAHO
Illinois	fs-ILL
Important	IMPORTANT
In (see *during*)	DURING
	point down
In front of me	DOWN-THERE
Included, to be (see *involve*)	INVOLVE
Independence Day	INDEPENDENT+DAY
Indian	INDIAN
Indiana	fs-IND
Inside, to be	INSIDE
Interesting, to be	INTERESTING
Internet	INTERNET
Interpreter (*interpret* + Agent Marker)	INTERPRETER
Intersection	INTERSECTION
Introduce, to	INTRODUCE

Term	Gloss
Involve, to be included	INVOLVE
Iowa	fs-IOWA
Is something not clear? (see *unclear*)	UNCLEAR
Island	ISLAND
It, it is	IX
Its	POSS-*ix*

J

Jacket, coat	COAT
Jail	JAIL
Janitor (*clean* + Agent Marker)	JANITOR
January	fs-JAN
Jeans	fs-JEANS
Job (1)	WORK
Job (2)	fs-JOB
Jog, to	JOG
Journalism, newspaper	NEWSPAPER
Journalist (*newspaper* + Agent Marker)	JOURNALIST
Juice	fs-JUICE
July	fs-JULY
Jump, to (animal)	CL:BENT V "jump"
Jump, to	JUMP
June	fs-JUNE
Junior high school	fs-JR+HS
Junior	JUNIOR
Just, very recently	VERY-RECENT

K

Kansas	fs-KAN
Karate	KARATE
Keep going	KEEP-GOING
Kentucky	fs-KY
Ketchup	fs-KETCHUP / fs-CATSUP
Key	KEY
Kick back, to take it easy	KICK-BACK
Kitchen (1-3)	COOK+ROOM / KITCHEN
Know, to	KNOW
Kwanzaa	KWANZAA

L

Lab	fs-LAB
Labor Day	fs-LABOR+DAY
Lake	LAKE
Lamb	fs-LAMB
Large (see *big*)	BIG

Term	Gloss
Last month	LAST-MONTH
Last week	LAST-WEEK
Last year	LAST-YEAR
Last	LAST
Late, to be	LATE
Later	LATER
Latino/a (see *Hispanic*)	HISPANIC
Laugh, to	LAUGH
Laundry, to wash clothes	LAUNDRY
Law	LAW
Lawyer (*law* + Agent Marker)	LAWYER
Lazy, to be	LAZY
Learn, to	LEARN
Leave, to (see *to go out*)	GO-OUT
Leave, to (something)	LEAVE
Leaves, to rake	RAKE-LEAVES
Left (direction)	LEFT
Level (see *floor*)	FLOOR
Librarian (*library* + Agent Marker)	LIBRARIAN
Library	LIBRARY
License	LICENSE
Lift weights, to (see *exercise*)	EXERCISE
Light	LIGHT
Lights, to turn off	TURN-OFF-LIGHT
Lights, to turn on	TURN-ON-LIGHT
Like, to be, same as	SIMILAR
Like, to	LIKE
Line up, to	LINE-UP
Lion	LION
Listen, to	LISTEN
Little while ago, a (see *recently*)	RECENTLY
Live in, to	LIVE-IN
Living room (1-2)	LIVING+ROOM
Lobster	fs-LOBSTER
Locker	LOCKER
Long hair	LONG-HAIR
Long sleeve	LONG-SLEEVE
Long time ago	DISTANT-PAST
Long	LONG
Look at me	LOOK-AT-ME
Look at, to	LOOK-AT
Look for, to	LOOK-FOR
Look like, to	LOOK+SIMILAR
Look strong	LOOK+STRONG
Los Angeles	fs-LA
Lose weight, to	LOSE-WEIGHT
Louisiana	fs-LA
Lousy, to be	LOUSY

Term	Gloss
Love	LOVE
Love-it	LOVE-IT
Lower	LOWER
Lunch	EAT+NOON

M

Term	Gloss
Mad, to be angry	MAD
Maine	fs-MAINE
Mainstreamed	MAINSTREAM
Major in, to	MAJOR-IN
Make the bed, to (see *to make the bed*)	MAKE+BED
Makeup, to put on	MAKEUP
Mall	fs-MALL
Man	MAN
Manage, to	MANAGE
Manager (*manage* + Agent Marker)	MANAGER
Mango	fs-MANGO
Manitoba	MANITOBA
	_____cha_____
Mansion	CL:CLAW 5+HOUSE
Many mass	MANY-MASS
Many	MANY
March	fs-MARCH
Marry, to	MARRY
Martial arts (see *karate*)	KARATE
Martin Luther King, Jr. Day	fs-MLK+DAY
Maryland	fs-MD
Massachusetts	fs-MASS
Match, to	MATCH
Math	MATH
Mathematician (*math* + Agent Marker)	MATHEMATICIAN
May (see *can*)	CAN
May	fs-MAY
May not (see *can't*)	CAN'T
Mayo	fs-MAYO / fs-MAYONNAISE
Me (see *I am*)	ME
Me too, same here	ME-TOO
Mean, to be	BE-MEAN
Mean, to	MEAN
Measure, to	MEASURE
Meat, beef	MEAT / fs-BEEF
Mechanic (*wrench* + Agent Marker)	MECHANIC
Medicine	MEDICINE
Medium	MEDIUM
Meet, to	MEET
Melon	fs-MELON
Memorial Day	MEMORIAL+DAY

Term	Gloss
Mexico	MEXICO
Michigan	fs-MICH
Mickey Mouse	MICKEY-MOUSE
Middle school	MIDDLE+SCHOOL
Midnight	MIDNIGHT
Mile	fs-MILE
Military	ARMY
Milk	MILK
Milkshake	fs-MILKSHAKE
Minivan	fs-MINIVAN
Minnesota	fs-MINN
Minute	MINUTE
Mischievous	MISCHIEVOUS
Missing, to be (see *dead*)	GONE
Mississippi	fs-MISS
Missouri	fs-MO
Mix, to	MIX
Mobile home	MOBILE-HOME
Monday (1-2)	MONDAY
Mondays (see *every Monday*)	EVERY-MONDAY
Money Spot	MONEY-SPOT
Money	MONEY
Monkey	MONKEY
Montana	MONTANA / fs-MONTANA
Month ago, a (see *last week*)	LAST-MONTH
Month	MONTH
Moon	MOON
More than	ABOVE
Morning	MORNING
Mornings (see *every morning*)	EVERY-MORNING
Mosque	fs-MOSQUE
Mother	MOTHER
Motivated, to be	MOTIVATED
Motorcycle	MOTORCYCLE
Motormouth, to be a	MOTORMOUTH
Mountain	MOUNTAIN
Mouthwash	MOUTHWASH
Move to, to	MOVE-TO
Movie	MOVIE
Mow, to	MOW
Muscular (see *well built*)	MUSCULAR
Museum	MUSEUM
Music, to sing	MUSIC
Musician, singer (*music* + Agent Marker)	MUSICIAN
Mustache	MUSTACHE
Mustard	fs-MUSTARD
My	MY

Term	Gloss

N

Term	Gloss
Nachos	fs-NACHO
Nada (see *blow air* or *nothing*)	BLOW-AIR
Nail polish	NAIL-POLISH
Name	NAME
Native American	INDIAN / NATIVE-AMERICAN
Nauseous, to feel	FEEL-NAUSEOUS
Near, to be close to	NEAR
Nebraska	fs-NEB
Need, to	NEED
Negative, to be	NEGATIVE
Neighborhood	HOME+AREA
Nephew	NEPHEW
Nervous	NERVOUS
Nevada	fs-NEV
Never	NEVER
New Brunswick	fs-NB
New Hampshire	fs-NH
New Jersey	fs-NJ
New Mexico	fs-NM
New Orleans	NEW-ORLEANS
New Year's	NEW+YEAR
New York City (see *New York*)	fs-NYC / NEW-YORK
New York	NEW-YORK
New	NEW
Newfoundland	fs-NFLD
Newspaper (see *journalism*)	NEWSPAPER / JOURNALISM
Next Tuesday	NEXT-WEEK TUESDAY
Next week	NEXT-WEEK
Next weekend	NEXT-WEEK WEEKEND
Next year	NEXT-YEAR
Nice to meet you	NICE MEET YOU
Nice	NICE
Nickel	CENT-5
Niece	NIECE
Night (see *evening*)	NIGHT
Nights (see *every night*)	EVERY-NIGHT
Non-Manual Signals	
Cha	<u>cha</u>
Diff-diff-diff	<u>diff-diff-diff</u>
Fish	<u>fish</u>
Head nod	<u>nod head</u>
Head shake	<u>head shake</u>
Po	<u>po</u>
No	NO
None	NONE
Noon	NOON

Term	Gloss
North Carolina	fs-NC
North Dakota	fs-ND
North	NORTH
Northwest Territories	fs-NWT
Nose	NOSE
Nosebleed	NOSEBLEED
Nosy, to be	NOSY
Not a dime (see *blow air*)	BLOW-AIR
Not crazy for, to be	NOT-CRAZY-FOR
Not me (see *I'm not*)	NOT-ME
Not much (see *nothing*)	NOTHING
Not scared at all	NOT-SCARED
	<u> tongue </u>
Not yet, haven't	NOT-YET
Not, don't, doesn't	NOT
Nothing, not much	NOTHING
Notice, to (see *spot*)	EYE-SPOT
Nova Scotia	fs-NS
November	fs-NOV
Now (see *today*)	TODAY
Number	NUMBER
Nunavut	fs-NVT
Nurse	NURSE

O

Term	Gloss
Ocean	OCEAN / WATER+WAVE
October	fs-OCT
Office	OFFICE
Ohio	fs-OHIO
Oh-I-see	OH-I-SEE
Okay (see *all right*)	ALRIGHT
Okay, to be	(see *so-so*)
Oklahoma	fs-OKLA
Old, to be	OLD
Older, tall, adult	TALL
On (see *during*)	DURING
	<u> *point down* </u>
On the ground (see *in front of me*)	DOWN-THERE
One cent	CENT
One in a crowd	ONE-IN-MAINSTREAM
One week	WEEK
Only	ONLY
Ontario	ONTARIO
Oops	OOPS
Optometrist	EYE+DOCTOR
Oral education	ORAL-EDUCATION
Orange (fruit) (see *orange*)	ORANGE

Term	Gloss
Orange	ORANGE
Oregon	OREGON
Ours	OURS
Outgoing, to be	ASSERTIVE
Outside	OUTSIDE
Over there (see *that way*)	OVER-THERE
Overalls	OVERALLS
Overcoat	THICK+COAT
Oversleep, to	OVERSLEEP
Owe, to (see *due*)	OWE NUMBER
Oyster	fs-OYSTER

P

Term	Gloss
Page	PAGE
Pager	PAGER
Pajamas	fs-PJ
Pancake	fs-PANCAKE
Panties	PANTIES
Pants (1-2)	PANTS
Papaya	fs-PAPAYA
Paper	PAPER
Parents	PARENTS
Park	fs-PARK
Party	PARTY
Pass down, descendants	PASS-DOWN
Passover	PASSOVER
Past (see *ago*)	AGO
Pasta	fs-PASTA
Pastrami	fs-PASTRAMI
Patterned	DECORATED-SHIRT
Pay attention, to (see *focus*)	PAY-ATTENTION
Peach	PEACH
Pear	fs-PEAR
Peas	fs-PEAS
Pen, pencil	WRITING-INSTRUMENT
Pencil (see *pen*)	WRITING-INSTRUMENT / fs-PEN
Pennsylvania	fs-PA
Penny	CENT
People	PEOPLE
Pepperoni	fs-PEPPERONI
Perfume	PERFUME
Period (see *dot*)	PERIOD
Person (standing)	CL:
Personality	PERSONALITY
Pharmacist (*medicine* + Agent Marker)	PHARMACIST
Pharmacy, drug store	MEDICINE+STORE
Philadelphia	PHILADELPHIA

Term	Gloss
Photographer (*camera* + Agent Marker)	PHOTOGRAPHER
Photography, camera	PHOTOGRAPHY
Physical education	fs-PE / GYM
Physical therapist (*physical therapy* + Agent Marker)	PHYSICAL+THERAPIST
Physical therapy	PHYSICAL+THERAPY
Physicist (*physics* + Agent Marker)	PHYSICIST
Physics	PHYSICS
Physiologist (*physiology* + Agent Marker)	PHYSIOLOGIST
Physiology	PHYSIOLOGY
Pick on, to	PICK-ON
Pie	fs-PIE
Pilot (*airplane* + Agent Marker)	PILOT
Pineapple	PINEAPPLE
Pink	PINK
Pizza	PIZZA
Plaid	PLAID
Plan, to	PLAN
Plant	PLANT
Play cards, to	PLAY-CARDS
Play sports, sports	PLAY-SPORTS
Play, to	PLAY
Please	PLEASE
Plum	fs-PLUM
Poetry	POETRY
Police officer (see *police station*)	POLICE
Police station, police officer, cop (1)	POLICE
Police station, police officer, cop (2)	POLICE
Polite, to be	POLITE
Polka dot	POLKA-DOT
Pony tail	PONY-TAIL
Pool	fs-POOL
Popular	POPULAR
Pork chops	fs-PORKCHOP
Pork	fs-PORK
Positive, to be	POSITIVE
	po
Post office	fs-PO
Potato	POTATO
Pound (see *weigh*)	WEIGH
	pow
Pow	POW
Practice, to	PRACTICE
Pregnant, to be	PREGNANT
Pretty, beautiful	PRETTY
Price (see *cost*)	COST
Prince Edward Island	fs-PEI
Principal	PRINCIPAL
Prisoner (*jail* + Agent Marker)	PRISONER

Term	Gloss
Program	PROGRAM
Programmer (*program* + Agent Marker)	PROGRAMMER
Psychologist	PSYCHOLOGIST
Psychology	PSYCHOLOGY
Purple	PURPLE

Q

Quarter	CENT-25
Quebec	QUEBEC
Question Mark	HUH
Question-Maker (see *NMS: Question-Maker*)	_q_
Quick (see *fast*)	FAST
Quiet, to be	QUIET
Quiz (see *test*)	TEST / fs-QUIZ

R

Radish	fs-RADISH
Rain, to	RAIN
Raisins	fs-RAISINS
Rake leaves, to (see *to rake leaves*)	RAKE-LEAVES
Ramadan	fs-RAMADAN
Raspberry	fs-RASPBERRY
Read, to	READ
Ready, to be	READY
Ready, to get (see *get ready*)	GET+READY / PLAN
Recently, a little while ago	RECENTLY
Red	RED
Redhead	HAIR+RED
Relationship	RELATIONSHIP
Relatives	RELATIVES
Relax, to (see *rest*)	REST
Remember, to	REMEMBER
Rent (see *every month*)	RENT
Repeat (see *again*)	AGAIN
Rest, to relax	REST
Restaurant	RESTAURANT
Rhode Island	fs-RI
Ribs	fs-RIBS
Rice	fs-RICE
Ride a bike, to	BICYCLE
Ride a horse, to	RIDE-HORSE
Ride for a while, to	RIDE-AWHILE
Ride in, to	RIDE-IN
Ride on, to (see *ride in*)	RIDE-IN
Right (direction)	RIGHT
Right there, very close	_cs_

Term	Gloss
River	RIVER
Road	fs-ROAD / STREET
Roast beef	fs-ROAST BEEF
Rollerblade, to	ROLLERBLADE
Room, box	ROOM
Rude, to be	RUDE

S

Term	Gloss
Sad, to be	SAD
Salad	SALAD
Salami	fs-SALAMI
Sale, to be on	fs-SALE
Sales person (*store* + Agent Marker)	SALESPERSON
Salt Lake City	fs-SLC
Same as (see *like, to be*)	SIMILAR
Same here (see *me too*)	ME-TOO
Same old, the usual	SAME-OLD
San Francisco	fs-SF
Sandals	SANDALS
Sandwich	SANDWICH
Saskatchewan	fs-SASK
Saturday (1-2)	SATURDAY
Saturdays (see *every Saturday*)	EVERY-SATURDAY
Sausage (see *hot dog*)	HOT-DOG / SAUSAGE
Scared, to be (see *afraid*)	AFRAID
Schedule	SCHEDULE
School for the deaf	SCOOL-FOR-DEAF
School	SCHOOL
Science	SCIENCE
Scientist (*science* + Agent Marker)	SCIENTIST
Scissors	SCISSORS
Scooped	SCOOP-NECK
Scuba dive, to	fs-SCUBA
Season	fs-SEASON
Seattle	SEATTLE
Second (see *Listing & Ordering*)	2-OF-__
Second (time)	fs-SEC
Secretary	SECRETARY
See you (see *see*)	SEE-YOU
See you later	SEE-YOU LATER
See you tomorrow	SEE-YOU TOMORROW
See, to , to see you	SEE
Senior	SENIOR
September	fs-September
Serve, to	SERVE
Shampoo	SHAMPOO
Shark	SHARK

Term	Gloss
Shave (1-2)	SHAVE-FACE
Shave head, to	SHAVE-HEAD
Shave legs, to	SHAVE-LEG
Shave underarms, to	SHAVE-UNDERARM
She, she is	IX-*she*
Shirt	SHIRT
Shoes	SHOES
Short hair (1-3)	SHORT-HAIR
Short sleeve	SHORT-SLEEVE
Short, to be (see *child*)	SHORT
Short, to be (see *younger*)	SHORT
Shorts, boxers	SHORTS
Shoulder tap	SHOULDER-TAP
Shoulder-shifting	SHOULDER-SHIFT
Shower, to	SHOWER
Shrimp	fs-SHRIMP
Shy, to be	SHY
Sick, to be	SICK
Sideburns	SIDEBURNS
Sign language (see *sign*)	SIGN-LANGUAGE
Sign, sign language	SIGN-LANGUAGE
Since, for	SINCE
Sing, to (see *music*)	SING
Singer (see *musician*)	SINGER
Single, to be	SINGLE
Sister	SISTER
Sit down, to	SIT-DOWN
Sit next to, to	SIT-NEXT-TO
Six dollars thirty-four cents	6.34
Six dollars	6-DOLLAR
Sixty-four dollars	64-DOLLAR
Skateboard, to	SKATEBOARD
Ski, to	SKI
Skier (*ski* + Agent Marker)	SKIER
Skydive, to	SKYDIVE
Sleep, to	SLEEP
Sleepy, to be	SLEEPY
Slip-mind	SLIP-MIND
Slow down, to (see *slow*)	SLOW
Slow, to slow down	SLOW
Small, to be	SMALL
Smart	SMART
Smile	SMILE
Snack (see *eat*)	FOOD / fs-SNACK
Snack machine	FOOD+MACHINE
Snake	SNAKE
Sneeze, to	SNEEZE
Snow, to	SNOW

Term	Gloss
Snowboard, to	SNOWBOARD
Soap	SOAP
Soccer	SOCCER
Sociology	SOCIOLOGY
Socks	SOCKS
Soda machine	DRINK+MACHINE
Soda	SODA
Softball	SOFTBALL
Soldier (*military* + Agent Marker)	SOLDIER
Sometimes	SOMETIMES
Son	SON
Soon (1-3)	SOON
Sophomore	SOPHOMORE
Sore throat	SORE-THROAT
So-so	SO-SO
Soup	SOUP
South Carolina	fs-SC
South Dakota	fs-SD
South	SOUTH
Spaghetti	SPAGHETTI
Speech	PRESENTATION
Spinach	fs-SPINACH
Sports (see *play sports*)	PLAY-SPORTS
Spot, to see, to notice	EYE-SPOT
Sprain, to	SPRAIN
Spring	SPRING
St. Patrick's Day	ST-PATRICK+DAY
Stadium, auditorium	STADIUM
Star	STAR
Start, to begin	START
Stay, to	STAY
Step-	STEP
Stomachache (see *hurt*)	STOMACHACHE
Stop light	STOP-LIGHT
Stop sign	STOP-SIGN
Store	STORE
Story, to tell	STORY
Strawberry	STRAWBERRY
Street (address)	fs-STREET
Street (general)	STREET
String beans	fs-STRING BEAN
Striped (horizontal) (see *striped*)	STRIPE-HORIZONTAL
Striped (vertical) (see *striped*)	STRIPE-VERTICAL
Striped (wavy) (see *striped*)	STRIPE-WAVY
Striped (wide)	STRIPE-WIDE
Striped	STRIPE
Strong, to be	STRONG
Student center	STUDENT+CENTER

Term	Gloss
Student (*learn* + Agent Marker)	STUDENT
Studio	fs-STUDIO
Study, to	STUDY
Stupid	STUPID
Subway	SUBWAY
Suit	fs-SUIT
Summer	SUMMER
Sun screen	fs-SUNSCREEN
Sun	SUN
Sunday	SUNDAY
Sundays (see *every Sunday*)	EVERY-SUNDAY
Sunglasses	fs-SUN+GLASSES
Sunny, to be	SUNNY
Supper (see *dinner*)	EAT+NIGHT
Sure	SURE
Surf, to	SURF
Sushi	fs-SUSHI
SUV	fs-SUV
Sweater	SWEATER
Sweatshirt	SWEATSHIRT
Sweep, to	SWEEP
Sweet	SWEET
Sweetheart, honey	SWEETHEART
Swim, to	SWIM
Switch, to	TRANSFER

T

Term	Gloss
Table (see *desk*)	DESK
Table, to set the	TABLE-PUT-ON
Taco	fs-TACO
Take care, to	TAKE-CARE
Take it easy, to (see *kick back*)	KICK-BACK
Take off (person)	GET-GOING
Take, to (abstract)	TAKE-UP
Take, to (literal)	TAKE
Take, to	TAKE
Talk, to	TALK
Tall, to be (see *adult*)	TALL
Tall, to be (see *older*)	TALL
Tangerine	fs-TANGERINE
Tank top	TANK-TOP
Tax	fs-TAX
Taxi	fs-TAXI
Teach	TEACH
Teacher (*teach* + Agent Marker)	TEACHER
Teacher's assistant	TEACHER+ASSISTANT
Team	TEAM

Term	Gloss
Tech center	TECHNOLOGY+CENTER
Tech, technology	TECHNOLOGY
Technician (*tech* + Agent Marker)	TECHNICIAN
Teenager	TEENAGER
Telephone	TELEPHONE
Television	fs-TV
Temple	TEMPLE
Ten months, in	FUTURE-TEN-MONTH
Tend to, usually	TEND-TO
Tennessee	fs-TENN
Tennis	TENNIS
Terrified (see *scared*)	VERY-SCARED
Test, exam (1-2)	TEST
Texas	TEXAS
Thank you	THANK-YOU
Thanksgiving	THANKSGIVING
That way, over there	OVER-THERE
Theater	THEATRE
Theirs	POSS-*theirs*
Therapist (*therapy* + Agent Marker)	THERAPIST
Therapy	THERAPY
These four (see *pronouns & number*)	THOSE-FOUR
These three (see *pronouns & number*)	THOSE-THREE
These two (see *pronouns & number*)	THOSE-TWO
They (see *they are*)	IX-THEY
They are, they	IX-THEY
Thin, to be	THIN
Think, to	THINK
Third (see *Listing & Ordering*)	3-OF-__
Those four (see *pronouns & number*)	THOSE-FOUR
Those three (see *pronouns & number*)	THOSE-THREE
Those two (see *pronouns & number*)	THOSE-TWO
Three months	3-MONTH
Three of them, the (see *pronouns & number*)	THOSE-THREE
Three of us, the (see *pronouns & number*)	US-THREE
Three of you, the (see *pronouns & number*)	YOU-THREE
Thursday (1-3)	THURSDAY
Thursdays (see *every Thursday*)	EVERY-THURSDAY
Tie	TIE
Tiger	TIGER
Time Spot	TIME-SPOT
Time	TIME
Tip	fs-TIP
Tired, to be	TIRED
Title (see *topic*)	TITLE
To be (see *conjugating verbs: To be*)	fs-TO BE
To go (see *conjugating verbs: To go*)	fs-TO GO / GO-TO
Toast	TOAST

Term	Gloss
Today, now	NOW
Tofu	fs-TOFU
Together, to be together	TOGETHER
Tomato	TOMATO
Tomorrow	TOMORROW
Tonsils	TONSILS
Too big, to be	TOO-BIG
Too small, to be	TOO-SMALL
Toothbrush	TOOTHBRUSH
Toothpaste	TOOTHPASTE
Topic, title	TITLE
Tortilla	fs-TORTILLA
Total, to add up	ALL-TOGETHER
Town (see *city*)	CITY
Townhouse	fs-TH
Traffic	TRAFFIC
Train	TRAIN
Trainer (*practice* + Agent Marker)	TRAINER
Transfer, to (see *switch*)	TRANSFER
Trash, to take out	DROP-OFF+GARBAGE
Tree	TREE
Tribe, group	SMALL-GROUP
Trigonometry	TRIGONOMETRY
Troublemaker (*mischievous* + Agent Marker)	MISCHIEVOUS
Truck	fs-TRUCK
TTY	fs-TTY
Tuesday (1-2)	TUESDAY
Tuesdays (see *every Tuesday*)	EVERY-TUESDAY
Turkey	TURKEY
Turn off voice, to	TURN-OFF-VOICE
Turtle	TURTLE
Turtleneck	TURTLENECK
Twelve weeks ago	12-WEEK-AGO
Twins	TWINS
Two days ago	TWO-DAY-AGO
Two of them (see *pronouns & number*)	THOSE-TWO
Two of us, the (see *you and me*)	US-TWO
Two of you, the (see *pronouns & number*)	YOU-TWO
Two weeks ago	TWO-WEEK-AGO
Two weeks	TWO-WEEK
Two years ago	TWO-YEAR-AGO

U

Term	Gloss
Ugly, to be	UGLY
Uh (see *um*)	UM
Um, uh, well (1)	UM
Um, uh, well (2)	UM

Term	Gloss
Umpire	fs-UMPIRE
Uncle	UNCLE
Unclear, to be	UNCLEAR
Understand, to	UNDERSTAND
Underwear	UNDERWEAR
United States	fs-US
University	UNIVERSITY
Us four (see *pronouns & number*)	US-FOUR
Us three (see *pronouns & number*)	US-THREE
Us two (see *you and me*)	US-TWO
Use, to	USE
Used to, before	USED-TO
Usual, the (see *same old*)	SAME-OLD
Usually (see *tend to*)	TEND-TO
Utah	fs-UTAH

V

Term	Gloss
Vacation	VACATION
Valentine's Day	VALENTINE+DAY
Van	fs-VAN
Vary, to	VARY
Vegetable	VEGETABLE
Vegetarian (*vegetable* + Agent Marker)	VEGETARIAN
Verbal-fight	VERBAL-FIGHT
Vermont	fs-VT
Very recently (see *just*)	VERY-RECENTLY
Very scared	VERY-SCARED
Veterans Day	fs-VETERAN+DAY
Vice president	VICE-PRESIDENT
Videophone	VIDEOPHONE
Virginia	fs-VA
Visit, to	VISIT
Visitor (*visit* + Agent Marker)	VISITOR
V-neck	V-NECK-SHIRT
Volleyball (1-2)	VOLLEYBALL
Vomit, to	VOMIT
Vote, to	VOTE
Voter (*vote* + Agent Marker)	VOTER

W

Term	Gloss
Waffle	fs-WAFFLE
Waiter (*serve* + Agent Marker)	WAITER
Wake up, to	WAKE-UP
Walk to (general)	WALK-TO
Want, to	WANT
Warm, to be	WARM

Term	Gloss
Warning, watch out	WARNING
Wash clothes, to (see *laundry*)	LAUNDRY
Wash the car, to	WASH-CAR
Washington	WASHINGTON
Washington, DC	WASHINGTON+fs-DC
Watch out (see *warning*)	WARNING
Watch	WATCH
Watch, to	TO-WATCH
Water fountain (see *water*)	WATER
Water polo	WATERPOLO
Water, water fountain	WATER
Wave-no	WAVE-NO
Waves	WAVES
We (see *we are*)	WE
We are, we	WE
Weak, to be	WEAK
Wear clothes, to (see *clothes*)	CLOTHES
Wear objects, to (see *use*)	USE
Weather (1-2)	WEATHER
Web page	fs-WWW
Wednesday (1-2)	WEDNESDAY
Wednesdays (see *every Wednesday*)	EVERY-WEDNESDAY
Week ago, a (see *last week*)	LAST-WEEK
Week	WEEK
Weekend	WEEKEND
Weekly (see *every week*)	EVERY-WEEK
Weigh, weight, pound	WEIGH
Weight (see *weigh*)	WEIGH
Weight, to lose (see *lose weight*)	LOSE-WEIGHT
Weights, to lift (see *exercise*)	EXERCISE
Well (see *um*)	UM
Well built, muscular	MUSCULAR
Well, to be	(see *good*)
West Virginia	WEST+fs-VA
West	WEST
Whale	WHALE
What are you doing?	(see *do-do*)
What did you do? (see *do-do*)	DO-DO
What do you do? (see *do-do*)	DO-DO
What does it mean?	MEAN WHAT
What for? (see *for-for*)	FOR-FOR
What is your name?	YOU NAME WHAT YOU __whq__
What kind? (*kind* + WH-Face)	_____whq_____ KIND
What time is it?	(*time* + WH-Face) _____whq_____
What year are you?	YEAR-IN-SCHOOL

Term	Gloss
What	WHAT
What's for homework?	HOME+WORK WHAT
What's up?	WHAT'S-UP
When	WHEN
Where	WHERE
WH-Face (see NMS: WH-Face)	__whq__
Which	WHICH
White (person)	WHITE-PERSON
White	WHITE
Who (1-3)	WHO
Why did you do that? (see *for-for*)	FOR-FOR
Why, because (1-3)	WHY
Will, future	WILL
Winding road	CL: B "winding road"
Windy, to be	WINDY
Winter	WINTER
Wisconsin	fs-WISC
With	WITH
Woman	WOMAN
Woodshop	WOOD
Work hard, to	WORK-HARD
Work, job	WORK
Worry, to	WORRY
Worse, to get (see *get worse*)	GET-WORSE
Wow	WOW
Wrench	WRENCH
Wrestling	WRESTLE
Write, to	WRITE
Writer (*write* + Agent Marker)	WRITER
Wrong, to be, error	WRONG
Wyoming	fs-WYO

X

Y

Term	Gloss
Yard work, to do	WORK+fs-YARD
Year ago, a (see *last year*)	LAST-YEAR
Year	YEAR
Yearbook	YEAR+BOOK
Yearly (see *every year*)	EVERY-YEAR
Years old (see *Age-Spot*)	AGE-SPOT
Yellow	YELLOW
Yes	YES
Yesterday	YESTERDAY
Yogurt	fs-YOGURT
You (plural) (see *you are*, plural)	YOU-PLURAL
You (see *you are*)	YOU

Term	Gloss
You and I (see *you and me*)	YOU-AND-ME
You and me, you and I	YOU-AND-ME
You are (plural)	YOU
You are, you	YOU
You ask me, ask me	ASK-ME
You four (see *pronouns & number*)	YOU-FOUR
You three (see *pronouns & number*)	YOU-THREE
You two (see *pronouns & number*)	YOU-TWO
You're welcome (1) (see *thank you*)	THANK-YOU
You're welcome (2)	NOD-HEAD
Young, to be	YOUNG
Younger, short	SHORT
Your, yours	YOUR
Yours (plural)	YOURS-PLURAL
Yours (see *your*)	YOUR
Yukon	fs-YUKON

Z

Term	Gloss
Zilch (see *blow air*)	BLOW-AIR
Zip (see *blow air*)	BLOW-AIR
Zoo	fs-ZOO